Standing with you
For Kids and Country,

Rebecca Friedrichs

ADVANCE PRAISE FOR
STANDING UP TO GOLIATH

"*Standing Up to Goliath* is a brave and enormously important book. A blow-by-blow account of arguably the most meaningful battle of our times—the ongoing fight for the nation's children against the all-powerful teachers' unions—it is simultaneously a deeply affecting personal memoir. Rebecca Friedrichs did not sign up to be a hero, but circumstances, and her own indomitable will, made her one. It should be mandatory reading for parents, and anyone else concerned with America's future."
—Harry Stein, Contributing Editor, *City Journal*

"Friedrichs masterfully weaves the personal and the political. A must read! Warning: Not easy to put down!"
—Larry Sand, President, California Teachers' Empowerment Network

STANDING UP TO GOLIATH

BATTLING STATE AND NATIONAL TEACHERS' UNIONS
— FOR THE —
HEART AND SOUL OF OUR KIDS AND COUNTRY

REBECCA FRIEDRICHS

Post Hill
PRESS

A POST HILL PRESS BOOK
ISBN: 978-1-64293-053-5
ISBN (eBook): 978-1-64293-054-2

Standing Up to Goliath:
Battling State and National Teachers' Unions for the Heart and Soul of Our
Kids and Country
© 2018 by Rebecca Friedrichs
All Rights Reserved

Cover design by Cody Corcoran

Post Hill Press
New York • Nashville
posthillpress.com

Published in the United States of America

DEDICATION

To Aunt Julane and Ruth Finnegan, two great teachers who inspired children for decades while exemplifying The Golden Rule. To the brave parents, educators, and students who allowed me to share their stories, and to every educator, school employee, parent, or student who's been hurt by state and national bully unions. Finally, this is dedicated with great respect to the loving teacher the unions labeled "Rotten Apple."

TABLE OF CONTENTS

CHAPTER 1

DEADLOCKED

"BWAHAHAHAHA. You lost!…LONG LIVE LABOR."

She sat across the ballroom from me. I was drawn to her because she dared to ask the question that haunted me for years. They denounced and berated her from the stage for having committed that most unpardonable sin—her independent thinking could not be tolerated.

I tried to make eye contact with her, but her eyes were downcast, and our line of vision lost when they closed in on her. I willed myself to save her, but dread paralyzed me. She was shrinking from my sight—growing smaller, frailer, and more defenseless by the moment.

With their air of superiority, those on stage hurled their self-righteous accusations at the woman isolating her as if she were a criminal, and those positioned within the crowd stood with arms folded; faces smug ensuring that each of us experienced heightened anxiety.

She was our example, ensuring no one else dare follow her lead. They harangued her, while lecturing all of us—that if we didn't agree with their politics, we were not tolerant; in fact, their words made us feel like we were backward, evil, and cruel if we did not agree with them. They made it crystal clear to everyone in the room that their stance on all political matters is the only moral stance and anyone who disagrees with their political agenda is a bigot.

Then they educated us on the only "right" way to think.

The looks around my table told me the verbal beating of the woman served its purpose. I saw faces dropped, mouths agape, eyes downcast, and shoulders slouched in motions of total defeat. I knew the people at my table personally, and I knew most of them agreed with the woman. I was positive some were glad she'd asked the question because they were also sick and tired of being forced to fund an extreme social, sexual and political agenda that attacked their beliefs, undermined their values, and compelled them to look the other way while parents were disempowered, and children were harmed.

An awkward silence followed the emotional bludgeoning of the woman. She sat in her chair, utterly dejected, while all three hundred of us sat stunned. I cannot remember how long the silence hung over the room, but it was long, and it was intense. It's hard to describe exactly the visceral reaction I experienced that day, but it hurt—physically—down deep in the gut. My throat felt tight like someone large was standing over me pressing on it hard, and my body froze as if that same person were pushing me down into my chair with a force so heavy I could not will myself to stand up.

We were representatives of those standing for intellectual excellence, safety, honesty, and kindness, and they were supposed to be our leaders. We thought we'd be able to voice concerns and participate in respectful deliberation. Instead, the ridicule was so severe as the ugly words spewed from their mouths, that every single one of us just sat there like little children tormented by bullies on a playground. Dumbfounded, we sat silently and took the beating.

I can't shake the feeling I've had ever since that California Teachers' Association (CTA) leadership conference in 2008. Three hundred other teachers and I sat immobile and terrified and watched as a gang of union bullies belittled a fellow California teacher. Her offense? She asked if teachers could have a voice in the way our union dues are spent. She and her colleagues were troubled by the way state and national teachers' unions spend our money on controversial, one-sided politics that have nothing to do with our jobs and often bring harm to the very children we're hired to serve.

I don't know about the other three hundred teachers in the ballroom that day, but my total lack of courage was a complete betrayal of my birthright, and I never intend to repeat the tragedy. My father taught me by daily example to stand up for the weak, yet I failed to come to the aid of a sweet teacher who was withered to a place beyond weakness—she was emotionally abused and shattered.

I can't express deeply enough how much I wish I knew the name of that brave woman who stood up that day because I would love to take her to dinner, bring her some flowers, give her a big hug, and tell her I'm sorry. I'm profoundly ashamed to admit that I didn't stand up to defend her. I've never been so sorry I didn't come to someone's defense. She must be carrying a scar from that horrible day because even though she was sticking up for teachers and kids everywhere, three hundred teachers left her sitting all alone while hateful tyrants persecuted her and singled her out as a fanatic when she was the only one in the room demonstrating sanity.

Throughout my twenty-eight years as a teacher forced to fund unions, and two decades as a parent with children in union-controlled public schools, I have witnessed union forces bully and intimidate teachers, parents, and children. Among other things, I've watched as union leaders have drowned out debate at school board meetings, pushed for sexually explicit sex education lessons, groomed students and teachers to become social justice warriors, and used indefensible intimidation tactics to bring down anyone who refused to cower to the control of state and national unions.

Teachers and students deserve better, so a US Supreme Court case, *Friedrichs v CTA*, was brought to help combat this bullying.

I'm Rebecca Friedrichs—an elementary school teacher from Southern California. I guess you could say the *Friedrichs* case was me. Actually, nine other California teachers and I brought the case against the California Teachers' Association (CTA) and the National Education Association (NEA), because we believe teachers and all public-sector employees should be free to choose for ourselves, without fear or coercion, whether or not to fund unions.

I knew having my name on the case would leave me vulnerable to harassment, perhaps even physical violence, and union leaders would likely use their polarizing tactics on me, but I'd been bullied and voiceless for almost three decades, so I couldn't wait to share my story and work to liberate my colleagues and America's kids.

Whether unions will actually bring physical harm to those who oppose them or not, many people believe they will. The culture of fear is so heightened, and the outright intimidation of educators so constant and palpable that almost every unionized worker who supported my case would thank me only in secret.

Over and over school employees, teachers, and administrators pulled me into darkened rooms desperate to let me know they agreed with my stance but were terrified of the consequences associated with talking to me. They would typically look up at the ceiling and ask, "Is there a camera or microphone in this room?" before thanking me, hugging me, or telling me they were praying for the success of our case. The minute we'd walk out of the room, they'd act like I wasn't even there.

The most common question I was asked throughout our case was, "Are you afraid for your life?" The second was, "Are you afraid for your job?"

The fear of retaliation is real.

I was anything but afraid after our case was heard because even our opponents knew we won the arguments. If you'd sat in the United States Supreme Court on January 11, 2016, you didn't have to be an expert to figure out Justice Scalia (considered the swing vote) had been convinced by our principled arguments and was one of five Justices who seemed prepared to vote in our favor.

Exactly one month later, my husband Charles and I spent the evening celebrating with a couple hundred friends all filled with hope and anticipation for a brighter future for America's school kids, their families and teachers. Friends sought us out from every direction: hugging us, high fiving, kissing me, and patting Charles on the back.

A few friends jokingly asked for my autograph, and others asked us to share details from inside the Courtroom, but one question that seemed to be nagging at everyone was, "When will the decision come down?"

Saturday morning, February 13, Charles and I were preoccupied with conversations from the night before. We were giddy with excitement and pinching ourselves over the reality that we were poised to receive a ruling in our favor.

As we got ready to celebrate Valentine's Day, news played in the background. The commentators droned on and on about the presidential primaries, but suddenly "Breaking News" interrupted the news monotony and sent our world into a tailspin.

"Supreme Court Justice Antonin Scalia has died at age seventy-nine."

Stunned and unable to move, we listened as the news anchor highlighted the three cases that would be most impacted by Scalia's death. Ours was the first.

"The *Friedrichs* case challenging forced union fees will likely end in a 4–4 tied decision providing the unions with a huge and unexpected victory."

In less than one minute, our world spun from right side up to upside down. We stood in shock in front of our bedroom TV, mouths agape yet unable to utter a word. Just standing was a challenge.

Charles knew every ounce of my passion had been thrown into our case for years, and he was behind me completely because he'd been forced to fund teachers' unions throughout his lifelong career as a university professor and watched as they pushed their political agenda into our colleges too. Wracked with anguish, our only comfort was prayer. God made our men to be strong when we need them; my Charles did not disappoint. He asked God to give us peace and the ability to trust Him in this storm. I asked for faith.

I emailed our lawyers immediately. Stunned with grief, words escaped me, so my message was brief. "Justice Scalia died."

Media thrives on calamity, and our case had just imploded. Within minutes we had requests for statements and interviews from television news stations, print media, and online news outlets, but my lawyers and I knew instinctively it wasn't time to make statements about us. An American family had just lost its patriarch. It was our place to grieve for them, and grieve for the country, so we worked together on a statement, sent it out to media, and doubled over in private grief.

We received hundreds of emails and calls from supporters; everyone was devastated. In our worst nightmares none of us dreamed an untimely death would undermine our decades-long fight for freedom and justice for America's kids and teachers. This message from our dear friend Chalone Warman, a grandmother and retired English teacher, says it all:

> *"I wish I could think of something positive to say, but I am completely bereft. I cried today, the first time since my dad died."*

Our grief was met with glee from union leaders and supporters. Within hours they were celebrating all over social and news media. Several union supporters posted negative comments on our Facebook page. In response to our statement, "We are deeply saddened by the news of Justice Scalia's passing. We have lost a legal giant and our thoughts and prayers are with his family," one union supporter, "Tim," crowed:

"BWAHAHAHAHA. You lost!…LONG LIVE LABOR."

There are three vital ingredients for a successful education, and none of them include the policies or politics pushed into schools today by unions. The imperative key for educational success is what my friend Kurt James calls The *Education Triangle*. The three corners of the triangle have equal weight and importance. The first and top corner is the child, the second corner is the parent(s), and the third corner is the teacher(s). If those three corners are working together as a respectful, kind, and communicative team with high expectations and accountability for all, the child will be educated well every time. Incredibly, union forces actively work against the triangle because as you will see, one of the unions' main tactics and sources of strength is to divide and isolate, so the relationships between many parents, teachers, and kids have been damaged.

It's time we all knew how state and national unions damage those relationships in America's schools: things like union leaders shouting down parents at school board meetings, terrified children with no hope of escaping the grip of abusive teachers protected by unions, exceptional teachers harassed for independent thoughts, men in black suits threatening lone female teachers in their classrooms, and sex education lessons leading mortified eleven-year-olds and their disgusted teachers to participate in "condom relay races" using fully erect adult male penis models.

The unions branded us "pawns of wealthy special interests," "education deformers," and "the spawn of Satan," among other hurtful and deceptive terms, but we didn't allow slander to undermine the truth. We held our heads high because we entered the teaching profession to serve the needs of children and their families, not to cower before abusive government unions and unprincipled leaders.

It was Justice Scalia's questioning that got our opposition to concede to our central argument: all collective bargaining in the public sector is political—all the time, so no one should be forced to fund it. We were poised to win with a 5–4 decision in June 2016. But our tie-breaking vote and the hope of millions of families and teachers across America died with Justice Scalia.

You can see why our case was so important. Our victory was going to give teachers and parents the right to vote with our feet, and the power to fight for the best interests of children on a level playing field, so we grieved heavily, and many of our supporters were in deep depression.

I've been in this battle for decades, so I can relate to the temptation toward hopelessness, but I can tell you from personal experience, it's a pit that holds us down allowing unscrupulous individuals to exploit us for their own self-interests.

If we want freedom for our kids, families, and teachers, we're going to have to fight for it. Things have gotten so bad in our schools that finally leaders from all parties agree on one thing and use the same talking points to express it. They admit, "Education is the civil rights issue of our day."

If leaders on all sides agree with this statement, why is it taking so long to fix our educational system? The answer to that question lies in the pages of this book. You're about to meet parents like Kelley who was jailed—*Jailed!*—for the crime of rescuing her two girls from a dangerous and low-performing school. School administrators like Eileen, who courageously stood up to protect the teachers and students in her care from an abusive teacher, and was not only demoted for doing so, but has been unemployed for several years as a result. Outstanding teachers like Aaron who was prohibited by federally mandated, union negotiated, "racial equity" guidelines from disciplining his students—including one who punched him—and was falsely accused of abusing children.

My Charles has an aunt—Aunt Julane. She's one hundred one years old, and for nearly half that time, forty-six years, she was a teacher. She spent most of those years in a one-room schoolhouse in Minnesota. One day Charles asked her to share her secret to a happy life. Without skipping a beat, she said, "Be kind."

Kindness is what America's teachers taught children for two hundred years. You can see it in their emphasis on "The Golden Rule." You can see it in the old *McGuffey's Eclectic Readers*, which teachers used until the 1960's, that highlighted not only Dickens and Thoreau, but Scripture from the Holy Bible, poetry, stories of American heroism, upright character, wholesome values, and beauty in various forms.

Imagine the negative impact our school system and culture have suffered since the removal of those values. Our focus on teaching children "Do unto others" and "Love your neighbor as yourself," has been degraded by union-led cruelty, a self-serving grievance mentality, attacks on American values, and a culture of fear forcing American families, teachers, and kids into schools that have become social, sexual, and political war zones.

This is not an overstatement; in fact, union leaders not only admit it, but boast about it. Witness Bob Chanin, longtime National Education Association (NEA) counsel, speaking to the top union leadership at the Representative Assembly:

> *When I first came to NEA in the early sixties, it had few enemies and was almost never criticized, attacked, or even mentioned in the media. This was because no one really gave a damn about what NEA did or what NEA said. It was the proverbial sleeping giant. A conservative, apolitical, do nothing organization. But then NEA began to change. It embraced collective bargaining. It supported teacher strikes. It established a political action committee. It spoke out for affirmative action, and it defended gay and lesbian rights. What NEA said and did began to matter. And the more we said and did, the more we pissed people off, and in turn, the more enemies we made.[1]*

There you have it. The problem is clear. Government unions have politicized and polarized our teachers—on purpose—by silencing the voices and values of teachers and parents and pissing people off. I learned that damaging undertow my very first month as a student teacher. We can debate, deliberate, and assign "experts" to the issues and rob another fifty years' worth of students of their best hope at success, or we can start listening to the real experts—parents and teachers—and win our schools and country back.

"Pissed off" or "Be kind"? The choice—and responsibility—is ours.

CHAPTER 2

———◦—❦———❧—◦———

THE MASTER AND THE WITCH

"My heart always broke for the wiggly little boys who had no more control over their moving bodies than their teacher had over her temper."

In the spring of 1988, I was finishing my teaching credential serving as a student teacher in a first grade classroom in a lower-middle income neighborhood in Orange County, California. I'd been dreaming of being a teacher since I was twelve. I was assigned to the most remarkable teacher I've ever encountered—truly a Master. Not only did every one of her students leave the first grade reading at or above grade level, they all loved her. Her classroom was a refuge, a place where dreams and imaginations could thrive.

The Master was a veteran educator likely in her late fifties. The first time I entered her classroom, the environment drew me in. Pint-sized kids sat in miniature chairs folding their tiny hands atop miniature desks that were arranged in a horseshoe pattern in the middle of the room. The children were showing off their best manners and listening skills, so I would be duly impressed. A sea of little boy and girl heads covered in various shades of black, brown, blond, and red bobbed up and down to see the new teacher. All of them wore bright smiles and looks of anticipation because the Master had just announced my arrival.

She informed them (and me) that I was a Master-in-training—not inferior in any way—just younger and in need of their help because I didn't have a class of my own yet. I introduced myself and shared an interesting fact in hopes of making a connection with them. "I have four siblings—an older sister, an older brother, a younger sister and younger brother, so no matter what you're going through with your siblings, I completely understand." Some of them laughed, but most of them looked relieved to know I could relate to their troubles.

The kids shared some adorable facts about themselves, and I thought I was doing a pretty good job of learning the role of teacher until one little boy, Alex, looked at me as matter-of-fact as could be and said, "Hey, you're a teenager!" I felt my face heating up into red embarrassment, and informed him I was twenty-two, but when we released the kids for recess I heard Alex shouting to his playground buddies from the top of his lungs, "Hey, guys, our new teacher is a teenager!" I knew immediately I was going to have to learn the art of loving authority fast. Thankfully, though I didn't realize it that first day, an expert who had mastered every angle of the teacher–student relationship was schooling me.

Bookshelves flanked each side of one of the blackboards creating a rectangular cove learning area on the floor where our thirty-two students gathered for lessons. The Master would sit in her rocking chair in front of the children, and they would sit on the carpet in five rows. One day in the middle of her instruction she paused and looked down over her reading glasses at Jose. He'd become fascinated by the Master's panty hose and in a day dream state perfected by most little boys was running his fingers up and down the front of her calf examining the texture of the nylon.

She was always so gracious with kids when they did these sorts of things. Without embarrassing Jose or using his name, she asked the class to remind her of their listening rule for cove learning. "Crisscross applesauce, hands in your lap," the kids "reminded" her, while all of them, including Jose, sat up straight and put their hands in their laps. "Oh, I had forgotten the rule," the Master said with a puzzled look, "Thanks for reminding me," and then she went on teaching the lesson.

The Master understood children—they think differently than adults and are very easily distracted. Instead of belittling them or acting disgusted by their quirks, she found ways to redirect their behavior and save their dignity. Although Jose was able to redirect on this occasion, sitting right next to the teacher's nylon-covered legs turned out to be too great a distraction for him. I know because he started doing it to me when I took over the class, so we moved him to a different spot on the carpet, but as things typically go in a first grade classroom, a new nylon inspector took over the job and had to be redirected too.

The Master was a genius at creating a classroom environment that felt like a sanctuary. Even if we were working on loud and busy endeavors, there was a profound calmness over our room—a peace that brought serenity—a structure that made us all feel safe. The only time this tranquility ever broke for me was when a raucous sound came through the wall from the classroom next door. A certain eerie feeling came over me whenever I overheard the noises, but I'd get drawn back to supporting kids with learning and reemerge into the serene and sheltered world of the Master.

Every time the Master finished a lesson at the carpet and it was time for independent seatwork, she'd perch her black plastic-framed reading glasses onto the tip of her nose, lean in closely to the kids, and start to whisper. They knew the routine, so they'd lean in close too.

"The magic word," she'd whisper, "is 'ice cream cone.' When I say the magic word, you need to stand up, jump up and down five times, clap your hands three times, and tiptoe as quiet as a mouse to your seat. When you get there, pull out your chair, sit down, and get to work. Ready?…Ice cream cone!"

Excitedly, the kids would jump up and obey every single direction. You've never seen kids tiptoe so quietly (some would squeak in hushed mouse tones too) or get to work so enthusiastically. Whoever thinks great teachers are not also amateur psychologists never watched the Master at work, and I'm eternally grateful that she would become my standard.

The Master taught me, by example, everything I needed to know to be a great teacher. Approach all learners with grace and loving assertive discipline, make learning fun, motivate with a positive demeanor and lots of energy, set high expectations and don't accept sloth, reward positive behaviors and results, insist on parental involvement, and treat your students the way you'd want your own children treated.

I adored every one of the kids, but my favorites were the ones who needed us most. I'll never forget one little girl with olive skin, black shoulder-length bobbed hair, and thick black glasses. She captured my heart from day one. She was struggling with reading, but between the Master and me she started to gain confidence and skill.

One day she came to school in a cute flowery sundress. As I kneeled behind her chair to help her with some math problems, I noticed a bright red adult-sized hand mark on her right shoulder blade; it appeared to be a few days old. My heart fell and broke for this little child. She was no taller than my waist, but some adult had mistreated her already.

I'd been learning about educational laws and knew as a teacher I was a mandated reporter of child abuse. I discreetly alerted the Master. Up to this point, everything she had taught me was cheerful and education-focused, but on this day, she taught me how to file a child abuse report. I'm not sure whatever happened as a result of the report—teachers are required to report, but we're rarely given any information on the outcome or remedies—but I was glad the little girl remained in our class for the rest of the year. She was loved in the Master's environment, and I believe God's grace had placed her there.

Although the Master's classroom was the ideal learning environment and her students were thriving in every way, the group of kids in the classroom next door wasn't as fortunate. From my first week with the Master, I was disturbed by what I saw every time we went outside to retrieve the children from recess, and those eerie sounds coming through the wall were unsettling too.

The teacher next door could never seem to manage her class; although her students seemed to be just as lovely as the kids in our room. She would grab them, yank them into their places in line, and scream right into their little faces. My heart always broke for the wiggly little boys who had no more control over their moving bodies than their teacher had over her temper.

The movie reel that plays in my mind when I recall this memory shows an angry woman, her face twisted into a scowl, towering over children half her size. Everything about her was tight. Her hair was twisted into taut curls that sprung from her head whenever she manhandled the kids. During this unfortunate memory, I always see bobby pins flying from her head. Honestly, I think my mind added this last detail because the only witch I'd ever seen in action was *Looney Toons'* Witch Hazel, perhaps an attempt by my shocked senses to define what I was witnessing. That's how I coped. I wonder how the kids coped and what sort of picture is burned into their adult minds today.

I'm positive it was almost impossible to learn in that classroom environment. I wonder how many of those kids fell far behind in school because they weren't given a strong foundation in first grade. I have no idea what happened to those kids once they were trapped inside of the classroom with her—I can imagine from those noises through the classroom wall, but from what we were witnessing outside the room, school authorities should have been sent to rescue the children immediately.

Since the Witch's behavior was on full display, I couldn't understand why the children weren't being delivered from her. As the Master and I were grading papers one day, I found the nerve to ask her how a mandated reporter like me could file a complaint about a teacher. The Master slowly turned to me, removed her glasses and locked into my eyes preparing, it seemed, to tell me a hard truth about life. "Today's the day," she said, "you learn about teachers' unions."

She explained that the woman next door had something called tenure and because of that status the teachers' union protected her, and it was nearly impossible for a principal or school district to get rid of her. First grade is the most crucial year for learning the fundamentals of reading and math, yet these kids had to navigate the most important foundations of their educational careers in the deep and stormy waters of abuse. She further explained that the teachers' union was supporting all kinds of political and social efforts the Master and many other teachers opposed and believed were bad for our schools and country.

I was indignant. Why were teachers being forced to support policies against their own consciences? Why were teachers' voices being ignored on issues important for students? But most of all, I ached for the kids in the class next door and grieved for their parents. Would they bring their kids to school each day if they knew the teacher was manhandling them? Had the kids already pleaded with their parents to rescue them from the abuse but the parents were powerless to protect them? Why wasn't anyone challenging these backward union positions? If they were a "teachers' union," why weren't union forces "uniting" to protect the most precious treasures in a teacher's world—the children?

I decided that day I didn't want anything to do with an organization that placed the desires and jobs of abusive adults above the safety and needs of the very children they were hired to serve. I would later discover that children were *never* the first concern of the union; rather, they were merely a lucrative means to an end.

Longtime NEA counsel Bob Chanin said as much to the NEA Representative Assembly during his retirement farewell address:

> *This is not to say that the concern of NEA and its affiliates with closing achievement gaps, reducing dropout rates, improving teacher quality and the like are unimportant or inappropriate. To the contrary, these are the goals that guide the work we do, BUT they need not and must not be achieved at the expense of due process, employee rights, and collective bargaining. That simply is too high a price to pay. When all is said and done, NEA and its affiliates must never lose sight of the fact that they are unions, and what unions do first and foremost is represent their members.[2]*

In September 1988 I signed my first teaching contract. Thanks to the Master, I knew I could "opt out" of union membership. While signing the stack of papers placed in front of all newly hired teachers, the union representative told me of all the "benefits" of joining the union and urged me to join. I told her I wasn't interested in joining. She informed me that if I wanted to teach, I had to sign the paper and accept union representation.

I discovered that I did not have to become a "member" of the union and pay their "dues," but I had to accept the "representation" of the union and pay their "fees." The difference between dues and fees in those days was about fifty bucks a year (I was still forced to pay hundreds), and the difference since then has ranged from zero to about thirty percent (depending on the district) of the more than 1,000 dollars most teachers have been forced to fork over each year.

For decades, teachers "opting out" of the union have been labeled "agency fee payers," and been forced to pay "Fair Share Fees." Full union fees have been automatically deducted from our paychecks every month, and at a union appointed time of year we've been permitted to mail in a written request for a rebate of what the union gets to decide is their "overt" political spending, which has nothing to do with our jobs or collective bargaining. If we forgot to send our rebate request within the narrow time window they assigned, or if no one alerted us to the need to send in a request, we received no rebate.

As punishment for refusing to fund union overt politics, we've lost all rights of membership including the right to vote within collective bargaining, the right to serve in union leadership, and the legal protection provided in the form of liability insurance. So, we've paid full union collective bargaining fees, but were given no voice and no vote in collective bargaining. In addition to these unfair practices, the union leadership makes teachers very uncomfortable if they opt out. We're belittled, shunned, labeled "anti-union," and our colleagues are told not to trust us. Make no mistake: the unions heap these punishments on teachers to make it very unattractive to opt out of funding their political agenda.

The Master hadn't prepared me for these shocking realities, but I became an agency fee payer anyway since it was my only option. At least I could avoid giving an extra fifty bucks a year to the organization responsible for the horrors I witnessed in the room next door. I've never been able to shake off the disgust I feel knowing that my money is used to protect teachers like the Witch, and to support the convoluted "grievance" procedures that continue to tie the hands of honest administrators who really would like to place outstanding and loving teachers in every classroom.

I've learned a lot more about those grievance procedures throughout my career, and most of what I've witnessed has been counterproductive for our educational system and harmful to our students. The protection of ineffective and abusive teachers drives good teachers crazy, but we still have to pay for it.

Union leaders dismissed me or shrugged their shoulders when I shared these concerns. School administrators, beaten down by years of union domination, have said to me on many occasions "Kids are resilient. They'll be just fine." Those attitudes are totally counter to my values, and they stomp on the face of American values and teacher values also, but they're all too common in our union-dominated public schools.

Parents everywhere tell me stories of abusive and ineffective teachers on their children's campuses. They say things like, "We all know the bad ones." Parents who are involved can sometimes find ways to work around these substandard teachers. They request to have their children placed in a different classroom, or they have the resources to move their kids to a private school.

But what about the parents and kids who don't have these options? What about the precious children whose parents are not involved at all? Those children should have the greatest teachers possible to make up for the lack of support from home, yet those are the very children who end up in classrooms headed by abusive and underperforming teachers protected by the union.

And what about teachers? Though state and national unions claim to protect us, the truth is their forced representation has degraded our profession and reputation. For several decades, the Harris Poll has published a list of the most prestigious professions in America.[3] Teachers topped the list for years, but the longer unions have been allowed to meddle in education policy and claim to be the voice of teachers, the lower teachers have fallen on the list. In 1992, teachers were listed as the third most prestigious profession in the country, and union leaders were listed dead last. Ten years later, teachers were number four, and by 2016, teachers had dropped to number eleven.

One day a couple years into our lawsuit, a teacher friend approached me. She'd watched an interview I'd given in which I'd shared the story of the Witch. She'd worked on that same campus and told me she knew the identity of the Witch because she'd witnessed the abuse too. As it turned out, the teacher she mentioned was not the Witch, so I'd never seen *her* actions. What a tragedy. What I witnessed was not an isolated situation. There were at least two teachers on the same campus abusing innocent kids.

Lest you think that campus is an anomaly and desire to rise up against that particular administration, the truth is that what my teacher friend and I witnessed is common in many schools across the country. Very often administrators' hands are tied by those highly restrictive collectively bargained grievance procedures pushed by unions using our schools as government jobs programs instead of institutes designed to protect and educate children. If you want to rise up against the culprits, set your sights on the government teachers' unions and their political allies.

CHAPTER 3

THOUGHTLESS AND TOPLESS

"We don't get rid of the dirt in America's unionized schools; we just move it around and sweep it under the rug."

The protection of teachers like the Witch has seriously injured the standing of teachers across the country, but there are many other obvious reasons the relationship with state and national teachers' unions is damaging the teaching profession. Tragically, union work rules force school districts to lay off teachers based on seniority rather than performance, so when districts are forced to thin out the workforce, teachers with the least seniority are let go, even if they're the best teachers in the district. It's called "Last in, first out," or LIFO.

A California teacher, Bhavini Bhakta, shared her story in the *LA Times* in 2012[4] because even though she was awarded "Teacher of the Year," she was laid off four times before finding a steady teaching job. Thanks to union-imposed rules, her district didn't even have the authority to choose her above other teachers with the same level of seniority—instead a tie-breaker straw pull was conducted, and the Teacher of the Year (and her students) pulled the short straw. Even though her principal fought for her job, Bhavini was laid off without apology.

Every teacher knows these nightmares are true because it's the reality in our public schools today. I distinctly remember having conversations with experienced teachers during my first few years of teaching during which they told me the only way I would achieve job security and higher pay was to obtain tenure and remain in the same district for my entire career. Why? When teachers move districts, we not only lose seniority, but we also drop down on the pay scale—often down to the five-year mark no matter how long we've been teaching or how superior our skills. I cannot think of any other career in which professionals are automatically penalized for making a move.

Another exceptional teacher, Nathan Strenge, lost his job to LIFO. Like Bhavini, Nathan was the top teacher in his field—advanced high school math. Although he carried a full teaching load in a public school district in Minnesota and provided stellar instruction in AP Statistics, Algebra II, and Pre-Calculus and was the only teacher accredited to teach AP Statistics, he was laid off at the end of his second school year. His principal went on a mission to save Nathan's job because Nathan had higher evaluations than his colleagues, his position would be almost impossible to fill, Nathan deserved to be rehired, and the children deserved to have an outstanding teacher. No matter how hard this principal fought to retain Nathan, union work rules destroyed the efforts.

Nathan, a full union member, talked to his union president; after all, massive dues were being automatically deducted from his paycheck each month, but the union leader told him they were powerless to help until he'd established tenure. They took his substantial dues but did nothing to save Nathan's job.

"Union work rules in our schools have nothing to do with me being highly qualified," Nathan told me. "There was no thoughtful process on who should be retained and who should be laid off—that conversation is never had. I was let go blindly. This provides huge disincentives for new teachers—especially those who are highly qualified and gifted in their subjects. Great teachers have other options, so why should they stay in the union-dominated schools and be abused?"

It's ironic to teachers like Nathan and me that the unions continually spread hype that we have a teacher shortage in America's schools—especially in the STEM (Science, Technology, Engineering, and Math) areas, yet when bright and highly capable individuals like Nathan provide remarkable STEM teaching they're unprotected from being laid off due to union work rules. Even more incredible is that the unions use this to their advantage by complaining about the lack of STEM teachers and shake taxpayers for more money for education.

This is infuriating to great teachers. Here's the other rub: many of these terrific teachers find refuge in charter or private schools, but our unions spend so many millions fighting against school choice that our charter and private schools are often barely surviving, and grossly underfunded. As a result, many of our finest teachers are making the lowest salaries, and many of our most needy public schools are losing our best teachers. Nathan and many other teachers I know really want to work with struggling students in challenging situations, but the unions who claim to be protecting the teachers and kids have chased them out.

This is a nightmare of pandemic proportions, yet we have politicians, educators, community leaders, and school leaders who condone these practices because they're either too afraid to stand up to the unions, blindly believe union arguments, or are personally benefitting from the arrangement.

The union I'm forced to fund was certified in my district when I was a small child, and many teachers weren't even born when their unions were organized, so we've never been given the chance to vote on whether or not we want this sort of representation. Most teachers trapped in unions today inherited their forced union status from teachers who've long since retired.

In an attempt to gain a voice for my colleagues and myself, I eventually became a full union member. I even served as a union leader on my local union board for three years. Around 2009–2010, during the extreme downturn in the economy, we were told our district would have to lay off several bright new teachers—the ones lowest on the seniority-hiring list. I had witnessed the terrific results these teachers were producing with children, and I had even mentored three of them personally. They were beloved on our campuses; the parents and children loved them, and they were wonderful team players within their school faculties and staff groups. They even brought up district writing scores to remarkable levels.

As the local union representative, I took an informal survey of teachers on my campus asking them how they felt about taking a small cut in pay to save the jobs of our talented colleagues and keep class sizes down. Many of the teachers with whom I spoke were very supportive of the idea, so at the next union leadership meeting, I reported my findings and suggested we consider going into collective bargaining negotiations with an offer to take about a three percent pay cut. I reminded our union board that many parents in our district had lost their jobs or had wages and hours cut and were forced to live with family members, so our offer of a cut would be good for community relations.

Unfortunately, union values rarely match teacher values, so the union leadership responded immediately with, "No, Rebecca, the teachers will never go for it." They wouldn't even have the conversation with me. Had they missed the fact that I had already surveyed teachers on my campus and was offering the suggestion as their representative because many *wanted* to go for it?

Over the next several months, I urged our union leadership to reconsider their opinion. Every time, I was dismissed, told teachers wouldn't go for it, and administrators couldn't be trusted.

Woefully, state and national unions control teachers in a culture of fear using four psychological manipulations: fear, intimidation, isolation and ignorance. They create a constant undercurrent of mistrust between teachers and administrators. Since the first day I walked onto a public school campus as a teacher, I've faced a constant barrage of negative information, ideas, and comments about administrators, and most teachers I know within other unionized districts tell me they've experienced the exact same thing.

I know administrators who work their tails off to provide outstanding school environments, but state and national union leaders who work tirelessly to divide teachers and school leadership continually undermine them. This division between faculty and administration has produced a very real sense of paranoia in the hearts and minds of teachers, so many really believe that if teachers offer a pay cut during hard times, school leaders will deny them recovered wages once the financial situation improves. Instead of coming together in good faith and taking positive action for the good of the kids and community, this paranoia short circuits our efforts and makes it almost impossible to make decisions that are equitable and positive for taxpayers, workers, and families alike.

After being ignored for months, I offered to write an anonymous survey and asked if the union would be willing to send it to all the teachers. If fifty-one percent of the teachers said they wanted to save the jobs, I told them, then we could work to represent their true desires. If fifty-one percent or more said they were unwilling to take the cut in pay, I promised to back off and never bring up the issue again. Not surprisingly, they turned me down flat.

Now you might be wondering why I didn't simply send out that survey on my own. Well, the teachers' unions have monopoly control over teachers' email addresses and physical mailboxes at school. In other words, they can place flyers in our boxes, and they can approve or disapprove of emails we send and receive, but if we cross their line and send out messages they don't like, we suffer reprimand from our superiors, warnings placed into our employee files, and we will be punished if we continue to use district email to communicate our true desires.

A friend of mine learned this the hard way when she shared a message from the Association of American Educators (AAE), a non-union alternative association for teachers that offers connections with like-minded educators as well liability insurance. After she sent out her email, union leaders complained, and her principal wrote her up for it. He told her he felt awful for having to place a negative warning in her file (especially since she had a stellar record), but union rules and leadership required him to do so.

No matter what I said to express the desires of my colleagues to save the jobs of our friends, the union ignored me. One day, out of complete exasperation, a top union leader said to me, "Rebecca, don't worry about those teachers, the union is going to take care of them. We're going to offer them a seminar on how to get unemployment benefits."

My jaw dropped. I was appalled and said, "These teachers pay you one-thousand dollars a year for your representation, and you're going to 'represent' them out of a job? They don't want to be unemployed, they want to teach!"

Just like when I learned the unions protected abusive teachers at the expense of vulnerable children, I grew sick to my stomach. These union leaders were teachers too. Would they want others treating them this way if *their* jobs were on the line?

Right then, my years of confusing union experiences started coming together in my head and my heart, and I realized no matter how hard I fought, I wasn't going to be able to get the union to consider commonsense approaches because they didn't care about teachers or kids; they just cared about their narrow-minded work rules, power, control, and getting their hands on teacher money.

I thought back to earlier that year when we had a district-wide union meeting led by our local CTA UniServ director (the liaison provided by the state union to work between teachers and the school district). We were gathered in an auditorium, and the UniServ director was educating us on all of the financial woes in our country and the cuts that had been imposed on our district. Because of union divisiveness, many teachers thought the district's claims of severe cuts were untrue; even though news accounts made it clear the country was in deep trouble. But once the teachers saw and understood the truth of the financial problems from the mouth of the union, our local union leader stood up and asked something like, "So you're saying these financial problems are true, and our district really is dealing with a huge budget shortfall?"

The UniServ director said, "Yes."

Then our local leader did what I've witnessed loving teachers do my entire career. She said something to the effect of, "Well, then, do we need to take a cut in pay? How can we help?" The UniServ director got a sinister smile on her face and told us we should not compromise at all. She said we should, "Take the district for all its got!"

I'm sad to report that many teachers in that room started cheering and clapping in support of sticking it to the district. I was stunned and sickened by this response. I cannot say how many teachers were cheering, but I can say they did not represent the heart of the true and great teachers in that room. Many of us who wanted to do what was right for our students and community sat silently—for me, the room was spinning. I was overwhelmed by the noise and base self-interest encouraged by the state union, which created an atmosphere of confusion and left many caring teachers feeling alone, voiceless, and outnumbered.

The memory of feeling helpless that day, mixed with the union's disgraceful treatment of the great teachers whose jobs were on the line, joined in my heart with the many other times the union had made me feel totally voiceless and undermined as a teacher. I finally figured out that it didn't matter how much evidence I had, how much sense I made, or how much good I was trying to do for my colleagues and our students, I could not make any difference by serving as a union leader.

Every one of those fantastic teachers was laid off at the end of the school year. One told me she couldn't understand why the district didn't appreciate her hard work to bring up test scores. Another was pregnant and was terrified to lose her security. A third said through tears, "I guess I was wrong about God's calling on my life."

The rest of us were demoralized. Even though our situation was the fault of union leadership, the unions found a way to blame the layoffs on the school district, and most teachers believed the deception.

State and national teachers' unions claim they care about children and represent the little guys, but thanks to them, class sizes went up in a lower-income district full of needy kids, and new vulnerable teachers lost their jobs. Aren't those the little guys? Remember the kids manhandled by the Witch? Those are little guys too.

During the last weeks of the school year, the topic dominating the teachers' lounge discussions was how wrong it was that those great teachers were losing their jobs. We all reassured them they were outstanding, offered them letters of recommendation, and I told them we wanted them as teachers in our district, but their union refused to allow us to vote on a small pay cut to save their jobs.

They'd been told their almost one-thousand dollars in annual union dues were a form of job protection. They were told the union represented their best interests and was looking out for them. The union never bothered to tell them they have no power to protect new teachers who lack tenure, and they never took responsibility for silencing those of us who wanted to save their jobs. These teachers, and multitudes like them across our country, paid an organization to literally destroy their jobs, and our government not only sanctions this infuriating relationship, but for decades has allowed teachers who refuse to pay the fees to be fired. This is wrong on so many levels, and teachers are not the only ones being hurt. In fact, as a parent, I would have to face this same issue years later when the two best teachers my son Ben ever had were laid off and the two worst teachers he ever had, including one who didn't like boys, kept their jobs.

Teachers with few scruples learn to take advantage of union rules like LIFO. They know their jobs are secure as long as they stay friendly with union forces, so they put forth little energy, often care little about student achievement, and many stick around long after their patience for kids has worn off while growing their retirements using other union-inspired pension rules that reward longevity without regard to performance.

Now I want to make clear: I am not placing all veteran teachers into this category. I know many outstanding teachers who have been serving America's children with excellence for decades, and their wisdom and experience is a blessing, but they are people with good character, strong work ethics, and a genuine love for the children.

My friend Larry Sand, retired teacher and president of California Teachers Empowerment Network (CTEN),[5] witnessed many incompetent teachers during his career as a teacher in New York City (Harlem) and Los Angeles. In the nineties when Larry was working in Los Angeles Unified, he worked with a physical education teacher who had an obvious problem with alcohol.

"The guy was a lush," Larry told me. "We all knew he was heading out to his car several times a day to enjoy his libations between classes." When I asked Larry if the faculty complained or if anything was done to protect the kids, he said, "All the teachers knew he was drinking—everybody knew it. People even jokingly said, 'If you want booze, go to M—'s car.' The principal never did anything to stop the problem." Can you imagine how dangerous it was for every one of that man's PE students to be under the supervision of a drunk every day?

It would be so easy for us to rid our schools of bad teachers and protect America's kids simply by using commonsense and allowing educators and parents to run our schools instead of labor unions. If you came onto a school campus for one day, you'd figure out in a nanosecond which teachers have given up, don't care, lack energy and passion, or are even abusive.

Larry worked with a middle school teacher in LA Unified who was a terrible teacher and was always nasty to the kids. He told me, "One day she decided to head out to the athletic field during lunch. Kids were all over the field, but this teacher didn't care. She laid out her blanket and started sunbathing—topless!"

Another teacher witnessed her nude escapade and called on the plant manager to act as a second witness. When the administrator confronted the offending teacher, her excuse was, "What was I thinking?"

Larry told me, "Even the union knew better than to back her up on this behavior, so she blamed the union for not standing by her in solidarity."

The local union leadership may not have agreed her behavior was appropriate, but since the union mentality dominated the school's culture, her job was saved. Larry told me, "Instead of firing her on the spot for indecent exposure on a school campus, they simply sent her to another school with a really wretched principal."

Years later, Larry's campus received a new principal who really cared about the kids and worked hard to create a positive atmosphere. One day Larry and the principal were talking about this troubling phenomenon in our schools called "The dance of the lemons." This is when bad teachers or administrators, who've misbehaved in some big ways, are moved around and assigned to new schools instead of being fired. She and Larry commiserated because they'd heard of or personally witnessed this miserable problem over and over for years.

Larry understood that the union was the culprit when it came to being stuck with bad teachers, but he couldn't figure out why bad administrators were being protected too. The principal explained to him that union work rules have so completely overrun our schools that even administrators, who are supposedly "at will" employees, are not always fired when they're incompetent. The unions' collectively bargained grievance procedures are so detailed and convoluted, they allow tenured teachers to make all sorts of egregious mistakes before they lose their jobs, so these processes, which were originally created to protect good teachers who were falsely accused, are now being used to protect the indefensible and that negatively impacts the entire school culture.

Larry told me, "It's a serious problem. The union mentality rules. We don't get rid of the dirt in America's unionized schools; we just move it around and sweep it under the rug."

I've seen this throughout my career in districts across my state and the nation, but there's another problem too. The unions' culture of fear has created a combative relationship in most districts today. Great administrators try to remove bad teachers all the time and live with constant frustrations because union work rules not only force them to keep bad teachers, but administrators who try to improve the situation discover quickly that messing with the status quo can get them crushed. So like teachers, most administrators go along to get along.

My good friend Eileen Blagden was one of the best principals I know, but her entire career was destroyed because she dared to protect children and good teachers from a dangerous teacher in her school. Eileen was principal at an elementary school in Southern California. A teacher in the district had been on leave after a 2008 arrest for indecent exposure and lewd and lascivious behavior, and a subsequent charge of trespassing for which he pled guilty. Though he was found not guilty of the sex-related charges, a restraining order forbade him from going within one hundred yards of public parks, beaches, schools, and bathrooms in the city of Long Beach.

In 2009, Eileen's employer, a school district located in a neighboring city of Long Beach, allowed the man back into the classroom but transferred him to Eileen's school as a kindergarten teacher. Eileen was not permitted to know the man's history, but she could tell from the start that he was emotionally unstable, and he was even falling asleep during class. His colleagues described him as "a ticking time bomb," so Eileen watched him closely.

The mere fact a man with this record was placed in charge of vulnerable kindergarteners is the first thing that gave me major pause when I heard about this situation. I've taught kindergarten, and those little kids are as innocent as they come; they get confused easily and have a difficult time articulating things to adults, so I was genuinely worried about the kids. Eileen was too.

In early 2010, this teacher shared his desire to kill his grade-level colleagues and talked of suicide too, so Eileen contacted district leadership and asked them to remove him immediately. The district sent out the teachers' union representatives and assured Eileen the man would receive psychological support. But Eileen was concerned about the safety of kids and teachers, and she's a mandated reporter of possible threats to students in her care, so Eileen told the district she was going to inform the other kindergarten teachers of the threat against them and call the police for the safety of the children and staff. She was shocked when she was told by a district administrator, "If you report this, you'll be sorry."

Eileen was never sorry for doing the right thing. She went to the Sheriff's Office and reported the issue. She told the detective she would likely lose her job over reporting the situation. She told him about her administrator's threat.

Three days later, she was placed on five months administrative leave for not following a district administrator's directive, but she had clearly followed the directives of the law by informing the police. In fact, when the detective called her later after looking at the unstable teachers' rap sheet, he asked her how in the world this man was in the classroom. He followed it up by saying the situation didn't make sense and wondered aloud if he needed to check out all of his kids' teachers. Eileen was later stripped of her role as principal and reassigned as a teacher.

When the district was questioned during a lawsuit brought by Eileen alleging retaliation for whistle-blowing, district officials suddenly cited Eileen for poor performance. The district claimed there were complaints against her, but they could produce no evidence, couldn't even remember who made the complaints, or the conduct that generated the complaints. The judge said, "This evidence raises an inference that the defendant's claim of receiving complaints against [Blagden] is false."

The detective brought the unstable teacher's rap sheet to court exposing a long list of infractions making it clear the man didn't belong in a classroom full of vulnerable kids, and he shared Eileen's comment that she felt she'd lose her job over reporting the man because a district official had threatened her. It became clear Eileen was suffering retaliation for doing the right thing. The deposition videos of district officials are very telling and as my friend Larry Sand puts it, "Their evasions made for a stark contrast with the tough and forthright questioning of Blagden's attorney, Ron Wilson. Sieu's [assistant superintendent] hemming and hawing for twelve minutes in response to *one question*...is downright painful to watch."[6]

A trial was set, but the district agreed to a settlement before trial. Unfortunately, part of that settlement is a confidentiality agreement, so Eileen cannot even talk about what happened to her. Thankfully, before that confidentiality agreement was imposed, Eileen gave many interviews and said in a press statement, "All I want is for the truth to come out. This is about protecting our children and the staff on the campuses of our schools. I did the right thing in reporting the threats to the police. The children come first—not the union, and not the school district's reputation."

I've noticed something sinister throughout my career. Whenever an "at-will" employee like Eileen is demoted, fired, or mistreated, all of the teachers get scared and say things like, "See, that's why we need the union."

27

Teachers are on constant high alert, and the union has convinced them the administration is out to get all employees, and it uses administrators like the ones who harassed Eileen to make its case. Somehow teachers don't see it's the union work rules, protection of bad teachers, control of many of our schools and administrators, and culture of fear that allow dishonest administrators to flourish. Even more sadly, teachers stand by quietly and watch good leaders like Eileen take the ax because they're so afraid of losing their own jobs they don't even speak out in defense of their own protectors.

As you can imagine, working in a district in which she was treated so unkindly was incredibly disheartening, so Eileen resigned. According to news reports, the unstable teacher was offered a cash settlement to leave the district quietly. Anyone can log onto the Commission on Teacher Credentialing (CTC) to see the status of any teacher's credential, so before the confidentiality agreement was imposed upon Eileen, she kept watch on the status of the teaching credential awarded to the dangerous teacher. Even though Eileen knew her career was ruined, she still wanted to protect the children across the state of California.

To Eileen's dismay, the man's credential remained active, so Eileen submitted a report. The CTC sent her a thank you letter and informed her that they had launched an investigation and had publicly reprimanded the teacher and revoked his credential. Thanks to Eileen placing the safety of children and teachers above her own best interests, that dangerous teacher will never be allowed to hold a teaching credential again.

But why hadn't the school district or the teachers' union reported the man's dangerous behaviors and cash pay-off to the CTC? We have laws in place that require school districts to make such reports, so why weren't they followed? Why did the topless teacher and the drunken teacher keep their jobs at the expense of the children they were hired to serve?

I cannot answer those questions with any certainty. I have my assumptions, but only district leaders and union leaders can answer those questions. My guess is we won't get a straight answer.

I can tell you this though: Eileen and I both agree we have plenty of laws in place to protect kids from dangerous teachers, but thanks to the culture of fear dominating our public schools, those laws are often ignored or rendered useless. There's one other thing Eileen and I know. School boards are the only ones with the authority to hire and fire superintendents, and teachers' unions spend mass quantities of money and resources across the country to get their favored candidates and union activists onto local and county school boards, so the unions can control district high officials. You'll discover in later chapters that the unions even slander and lie about honest neighborhood candidates who try to run against the unions' chosen candidates.

This is why so many high officials running school districts kowtow to union desires and the protection of teachers who don't belong in the classroom. It's a corrupt arrangement, and I'm saddened that so many educators in high position don't have the courage to speak out about the abuse. I guess I can understand their fear; they just want to pay their bills and feed their kids, but their silence is part of the problem.

School board members who dare to speak out about this corruption are slandered and crushed during the next election cycle, and since unions coerce teachers to be boots-on-the- ground campaign workers for the unions' chosen candidates (and use the trusted reputation of teachers with messaging like "Teachers Support…"), voters fall for the attacks on honest board members and candidates all the time.

Voters beware. When your local unionized teachers call you urging support of certain candidates; they are calling on behalf of union leadership, and most are calling because they've been coerced into doing so.

You know, when unions defend incompetent teachers to ensure that all teachers have access to fair treatment, I can sort of understand their motives. When the unions fight against commonsense education reforms, harass those who speak out in opposition to the union agenda, and deceive the public with clever messaging to build up more power and amass more wealth, I can understand those motives too. I don't agree with them, and I think they're immoral, but I understand them as a reality of human behavior. But I cannot for the life of me figure out why the unions and school district officials would stand together and keep quiet about abusive and dangerous teachers at the expense of children. It just doesn't make sense.

The district leaders are always worried about their reputations, and you'd think the union would want to be seen as the "good guy." You'd think they'd realize that defending the defenseless is bad for public relations, but they don't seem to get it. My guess is that the hearts of these leaders have become hardened. Constant focus on power and money at the expense of goodness and truth always hardens the hearts of those enslaved to influence and greed.

The public school administrators who falsely accused Eileen of poor performance have nonchalantly gone on with their jobs. One retired with a nice pension, another is now the superintendent in a neighboring school district, and another was promoted to the highest position in the district.

Meanwhile, Eileen's family struggles to get by. The culture of fear branded her "demoted" in 2010, and to this day, Eileen is still unable to secure a job as a principal.

"My career was stolen from me," she told Larry Sand in one of her interviews. "They pulled a part of my heart out; physically stabbing me would have hurt less."[7]

CHAPTER 4

— ⸎ —

CULTURE OF FEAR

"They caught a teacher red-handed putting an emblem on the board member's car window. It was a picture of his family being blown up."

In 1993 during my fifth year of teaching, a school voucher initiative was on the ballot in California. It would provide parents the power to choose the schools that were right for their children, and it seemed like a terrific solution to the varied needs of teachers too, but every time our faculty met for mandatory staff meetings, the teachers' union representatives told us we had to defeat vouchers.

According to those union representatives, vouchers were a personal attack on public school teachers, and if the initiative passed, the entire public school system would fall apart. Every single time they spoke against vouchers, they put pressure on all of us teachers to become boots-on-the-ground campaign workers to defeat the voucher initiative and speak against its supporters whom they labeled "radical right-wingers."

I was confused about vouchers, so I studied both sides of the argument to make an informed decision. Now, I wasn't a parent at this time, but I was anxious to be one, and the parents with whom I'd spoken saw vouchers as a godsend that would give them the ability and authority to rescue their children from low-performing public schools and the increasingly politically charged social agendas invading classrooms and overstepping their parental authority.

During every staff meeting, the unions terrified teachers with emotional arguments that went something like this:

Vouchers are being pushed by radicals who want to destroy public education, our public schools will be annihilated; children will be hurt and forced to attend schools with teachers who are unqualified. You will lose your jobs and pensions. The wealthy special interests are behind this initiative.

I heard various forms of that hysteria every week, but no one ever gave me substantive proof or intelligent responses to any of my sincere questions. Instead, they shut down debate and frighten teachers into submission. Every word the union representatives shared was designed to incite fear in teachers—fear for their own families and fear for their students—and to label anyone who stood in favor of vouchers as a pariah standing with evil against all that's good for American schools.

I'm certain the teachers representing the union stance genuinely believed the scary union talking points because I knew they were decent people. But educators, like everyone else, have bills to pay, children to feed, and worry about job security, so the state and national unions play on those fears and take advantage of the vulnerabilities and naiveté of workers. Teachers who fall for union rhetoric get pitted against teachers like me, against taxpayers, and against education reformers who really want the best for kids.

The majority of our faculty members were conservative-leaning politically, and many were people of faith, so I knew I wasn't the only one offended by the slanderous term "radical right-wingers." Several of my teacher friends had their own children in private schools and were struggling to make tuition payments, and several were secretly using the addresses of family members to get their children into better schools. I knew those families could use the extra assistance vouchers would offer them in their personal freedom to have school choice for their children.

When I suggested children would be protected from failing schools with horrible teachers because parents would be given the power of choice, the union leaders told me that even though parents are sincere in their desire to choose good schools, they don't have the expertise to make the right choice for their own children. They said only teachers know best. I thought that was the most condescending and ignorant statement I'd ever heard.

In my opinion, parents are the number one experts on their own children, and teachers are hired to serve them—we are not hired to lord it over them and behave as if we know better. We are the third corner in the Education Triangle offering teaching expertise as a compliment to their parenting—in whatever school environment *parents* believe is best for their children.

My husband's Aunt Julane started her forty-six-year teaching career in a one-room schoolhouse and ended it as the principal of that same school after it expanded. She was a wildly successful educator and beloved by her community. Every time I ask her the secrets of successful teaching she gives me the same one-sentence answer: "Parents supported me one hundred percent."

She says she never had any discipline problems in her classroom because parents backed her at all times and Judeo-Christian values were universal in the culture and the classroom. Unlike teachers today, Julane never felt overwhelmed with negative issues in her classroom, and she never felt blamed for society's ills. Disruptive students were not permitted to undermine her teaching efforts, and teachers were well-respected members of the community.

Aunt Julane and I believe parents are the *key* to educational success and we're not alone. According to research done by Charlene Haar, an award-winning teacher and PTA member, "A 1987 Harris survey for the Metropolitan Life Insurance Company (MetLife) purported to show a wide range of benefits from parental involvement in their children's education. Parents who were more involved developed more positive attitudes toward school personnel. Likewise, teaching improved when parental involvement was prevalent, and teachers were more satisfied with their work."[8]

In my experience, parental involvement is the single greatest factor in the educational and behavioral success of students. In fact, Charlene shares another bit of information in her book, *The Politics of the PTA*, that gives teachers a voice far better than I can provide. "When the Carnegie Foundation for the Advancement of Teaching surveyed 22,000 teachers in 1988, 90 percent of them cited a lack of parental support as a problem. Elementary and middle school principals agreed."[9]

I'd be remiss if I didn't add that parents who come at teachers with combative, accusatory, or defensive tones and defend their children at all costs, instead of holding their children accountable for learning and maturing, are undermining teachers and the Education Triangle.

Here's a note we received from one of Ben's teachers that illustrates the encouragement teachers feel when parent/teacher unity is strong.

> *Thank you so much! Can I just tell you how refreshing it is to have parents who are supportive and see the parent/teacher relationship as a team rather than an opposition?! It was great meeting with you guys yesterday. I hope that Benny knows it was out of support rather than reprimand.*

The Education Triangle in action.

Since it's not debatable that the Education Triangle is vital for success, it's hard to understand why parental involvement and parental choice aren't given the highest priority in America's schools, and why the education authorities continually tell teachers like me that it's inappropriate and not permissible to require parental involvement. School is mandated, but parental support is not? That's a pretty dizzying intellectual conclusion. One of the reasons so many charter and private schools do well is they require parental participation, and shockingly I've heard teachers' unions cut them down for that requirement.

I believe strongly in parental rights and inclusion, so instead of blindly accepting the union arguments against vouchers, I started researching and attending debates. I heard arguments on both sides but noted the arguments on the pro-voucher side were more principled, reasoned, and even documented, and the arguments on the anti-voucher side were highly emotional, lacking in documentation, and matched the arguments I was hearing in my staff meetings. But I kept an open mind.

At our next staff meeting union representatives continued harassing us with their divisive messaging and reminded us of the Armageddon-like public school destruction coming our way if we didn't defeat vouchers. They convinced many teachers that vouchers were a threat to our jobs and pensions. Because I was only a fifth-year teacher, I hadn't yet figured out that the unions use these same talking points to defeat every commonsense education reform that good people try to pass, and teachers and millions of citizens fall for them year after year. At the time, I was still pretty naïve.

As our union representative was preaching her latest sermon on defeating vouchers and passing around her sign-up sheet again, I quietly passed it on without signing it. Apparently, that was an unpardonable sin because the representative stopped mid-sermon, looked right at me, and pointedly asked me why I hadn't signed up to work the phone bank. When I said, "No, thank you," she pushed the issue, so I told her I'd been researching the voucher initiative and was leaning toward supporting it. Right there, in front of my colleagues, she looked at me as if I were Judas Iscariot himself and shouted, "You're a radical right-winger!"

I felt my face flush, my mouth parch, and my heart raise its beat. Though I never looked around the room, I knew every eye was on me. I was isolated, marginalized, and labeled an outsider during a mandatory staff meeting from which I could not escape. The shunning was powerful.

Their slander of me stifled all civil discussion about vouchers, and the non-verbal cues directed at me sent a message to everyone that they'd better not even think about joining me in my independent thinking. I had honestly thought union leaders would appreciate my efforts to be thoroughly educated and informed on the issues impacting our schools—like I said, *naïve*—but they were threatened by my desire to seek truth and silenced me.

This is the day my eyes were opened, and I learned that the union leadership's job was to squelch dissenting opinion. It became apparent to me that arguments used by the union to demonize vouchers and those supporting them were carefully crafted talking points meant to scare the hell out of teachers and parents, distort the truth to voters, and shut down principled arguments, so unions could continue controlling our schools and making money off of educators. They had no intention of answering honorably or giving me the respect I deserved as a trusted teacher and forced supporter of *their* political agenda.

Right there on the spot, the unions converted me, and I became a believer in school choice.

You know, I don't expect unions to agree with me on every issue, and I have no problem with them having different opinions, but I do have a problem with their outright bullying, their silencing of debate, and their intrusion into teacher autonomy. Why is it that teachers, who come with varied experiences and expertise, are not allowed to disagree on issues within education? Why am I ridiculed because I, as an *education* professional, see a different solution for students than state and national *labor* unions? Why are teachers with independent thoughts and ideas attacked for genuinely desiring to do what's right for kids? Why do *labor* unions have so much power over *education* policy anyway?

The year-long punishment I received for refusing to help defeat vouchers was the beginning of my education on the way unions manipulate and control our educators, public schools, and culture. Their negative impact is so pervasive the culture of fear is now dominating our nation's character and discourse, so crass and unjust attacks on good people seeking to serve others are now commonplace.

I have several friends who've run for school board in districts across the country because they really care about kids, and in every single case, they've been bullied because they dared to put the needs of students ahead of the desires of unions. One of my fellow plaintiffs, Karen Cuen, a gifted music teacher, was a school board member for a time. Once the unions found out she wouldn't kowtow to their demands, they slandered her in print during the re-election campaign and convinced teachers to campaign against her. One of the insulting flyers showed Humpty Dumpty holding his rear end under the headline, "In the end...what you don't know could hurt our kids." It then lied about Karen claiming she didn't support counseling, school lunch programs, gang and drug intervention, and that she was unable to work with parents and teachers. She *was* a parent and a teacher, but she was defeated—with her own dues money! A union-dominated board member took her place.

Union militants mistreated Julie Williams for her values too. Julie has two sons, one is gifted and the other has special needs. After years of dealing with issues in their educations in the massive Jefferson County School District in Colorado (Jeffco), she was getting fed up. "They put a ceiling on my gifted child and a floor on my special needs child," she told me. "My gifted child spent most of his years doing another worksheet and tutoring other kids, and my special needs son didn't even have an appropriate math program for his needs."

Julie ran around advocating for her special needs boy from the time he was in preschool, but she wasn't making any progress. She and other parents had to fight for every little thing. She served on the Special Education Advisory Committee for about five years, but she felt parents' voices were ignored. At one point, she reached out to the instructional coach in her son's school. In Jeffco, there are coaches assigned to support teachers so that all students' needs are met. Julie asked the coach if she could help obtain a more appropriate math curriculum for her special needs son, but she was shocked by the response to her request. The coach told her, "I have lots of friends in high places in administration, but I am not willing to help you. If you really want to help the kids, then you need to work on the campaign of these two [board member candidates], and go door to door to help them, and that's how you'll get it."

Julie told me, "That's breaking the law!" She complained to the superintendent who responded by talking to the teacher and apologizing to Julie, but the teacher was never disciplined. Julie noticed that the district had coaches for coaches and more coaches who were supposed to be helping teachers, but when Julie helped in the classroom she said, "I didn't see them do much of anything." She noticed a very bright young man was being allowed to fail because the school refused to deal with his learning issues. That kid's parents had the resources to remove him and placed him in a private school where he did well, but Julie didn't have the money to move her kids, and she wanted to be the voice of the voiceless, so in 2013, Julie ran for school board and campaigned on doing what's right for kids.

She won with almost 64 percent of the vote, but as soon as she and two other new members who also supported the students were democratically elected by the community, the teachers' union started and supported a national coalition called "Stand Up for All Students" to lead a recall effort.

As soon as they were sworn into their positions, the attacks on Julie and her two colleagues began. According to Julie, the union coalition immediately launched five hundred people on the ground and brought in two individuals from Chicago to be community organizers who would host house parties through PTA parents, block parties, visit the homes of every single teacher in the district, organize events, protests, and other disruptions. At the gatherings, they indoctrinated people with union messaging telling them that Julie and the new board members wanted to cut teacher salaries, raise class sizes, and misuse district monies. None of this was true. Everyone was trained with union talking points on how to talk to neighbors, students, parents, and people at the grocery store. They even provided an online toolkit.

At their first official board meeting in December 2013, hundreds of teachers showed up against the new board members. Julie told me, "They were very vocal, very mean, and some of my kids' teachers were there. They weren't just coming and listening. They came to disrupt, to stand up, to yell at us, to point their fingers at us and say, 'You, you're the one. I'm gonna get you!'"

In January, the superintendent announced her early retirement, and during a Saturday meeting that was supposed to be a training for board members, Julie told me, "Teachers showed up in droves. The superintendent told the crowd we [the new board members] pushed her out of her seat and it wasn't what she wanted, and she cried." Julie said all of this was completely untrue. The superintendent was moving to a job working for CASE (Colorado Association for Superintendents), and Julie later discovered the superintendent could help the union coalition with the recall effort in her new job. After the superintendent's talk, Julie said, "They basically shut down our meeting because it became so aggressive and mean. The three of us had police escorts out to our cars through the back door to avoid the angry mob."

The protests against Julie and her colleagues went on for two years, and because the teachers get out of school early, they were able to arrive much earlier to school board meetings than community members working nine to five, so parents who supported the new board members and their stance for the kids couldn't even get into the building. The union coalition also filled up all of the public comments slots, so no one else would be able to make their voices heard at board meetings, and Julie told me, "If you did get in, it was flat scary, so no one who didn't agree with them would go to the meetings because they were fearful and they were scared for retribution for their children."

The organized disruptions were so well orchestrated, the protestors against Julie and her colleagues didn't just fill the boardroom, they filled several floors and the outside of the building as well.

What was it about Julie and the new democratically elected board members that raised the ire of the unions and their allies? They were people with conservative values, and they were advocating the district opt out of Common Core because of serious concerns about much of its contents; in fact, Julie campaigned on this promise, and that's why parents voted for her. At one meeting Julie brought in national Common Core experts Sandra Stotsky and the Fordham Institute to speak on the resolution to opt out of Common Core. Instead of respectfully listening to their well-researched concerns, or having a fair and reasoned debate, the union coalition of parents and teachers booed, hissed, and made fun of Sandra and the other presenters as they spoke.

This is precisely the culture of fear unions push in every district they dominate. Their angry rants and loud shout-downs make it impossible for communities to engage in thoughtful discussion. The hysteria and terror they create give the unions complete control while stifling the voices of those who don't agree with them.

Millions of parents and teachers across the country are deeply concerned about issues with the Common Core. So why would unions inspire protests against duly elected community members who were putting the desires of families first? Well, I'm not sure how unions would answer the question, but after being forced to use Common Core resources that push the same political agenda the unions push and after reading up on grants offered by the Gates Foundation, my guess is they have about ten million reasons. That's about the amount of money NEA and American Federation of Teachers (AFT) accepted from the Gates Foundation to support Common Core curriculum development.[10] In fact, in 2013, the year the organizations received that money, *NEA Today* published an article titled "Six Ways the Common Core is Good for Students," which states: "Common Core will ultimately be good for students and education."

Now I'm not questioning the motives of the Gates Foundation; after all, I know some terrific teachers (like Nathan Strenge) who've offered wonderful advice through Gates run organizations, but unfortunately, they trusted teachers' unions in their Common Core process. Perhaps they didn't know that the teachers' unions work to push their social and political agenda into everything they touch, and they don't represent the values or educational expertise of great teachers.

Money and politics are the reasons the unions worked to impeach Julie and her fellow conservative board members from the moment they were democratically elected. Julie said the unions started sharing on their websites that they were creating a blueprint on how to win school boards and how to get conservative leaders out of America's schools. Around this time Julie attended a school board convention for board members. She told me, "The entire thing was teaching school board members how to be progressive and how to lobby our legislators for progressive ideas and thoughts."

Every other school board member I know who has attended these trainings nationwide has told me the exact same thing.

Julie and her fellow new board members also believed taxpayers should not have to fund the collection of union dues through paycheck deductions, and they were standing for a balanced budget including equal funding for all children whether in traditional public schools or public charter schools. I agree with them completely, as do millions of concerned citizens, but instead of giving them opportunity to present their views, the union coalition responded by attacking parents and teachers who came to meetings seeking equal support for charters. During one meeting, as PTA parents and teachers inspired by union forces shouted down the charter families and drowned out their pleas, a Jeffco parent was caught on video flipping off the cameraman—with both hands. The following spring, according to Julie, she was voted in as PTA president.[11]

High school students in Jeffco were told they would lose all of their advanced placement credits if the new board members got their way. Julie told me, "This wasn't true. All we wanted was a curriculum review committee. We wanted to give parents a voice."

Julie added, "The teachers held a 'Wild Cat Sick Out'—said all the teachers had the bird flu—and it closed down three entire schools." They incentivized the students to participate in rallies and walkouts too. Julie said rather than receiving an absence for walking out, the students received excused absences, and there were golf carts filled with water bottles and snacks, which escorted them to the street to do their protesting. No surprise, kids protested every day before and after school for a year and even made national news—what indoctrinated kid would pass up those incentives?

The students started disrupting board meetings, they protested in front of Julie's house, and demonstrators threatened another board member. Julie told me, "They caught a teacher red-handed putting an emblem on the board member's car window. It was a picture of his family being blown up."

Every morning this man's little kindergartener had to go to school and see graffiti against her father on the school wall. "That's the kind of tactics they use," Julie told me. "He was able to pull his kids out and put them in private school. I don't have that kind of money, so that's why I fight for school choice."

Despite the attacks, Julie and her two colleagues fought hard for kids and taxpayers. They balanced the budget for the first time in decades, and even had enough cash on hand to build a school in a growing area. They raised achievement, and teachers got twenty-one million dollars in raises, but the unions were angry and continued their assault.

As shocking as the harassments were, the worst attack on Julie came at the expense of her special needs son. Every day, for well over a year, as he exited the school bus, he had to cross over the picket line. A teacher, who was a friend of his family, even asked him about his summer while picking out her sign displaying horrible things about his mother.

One day he came home crying and told Julie he didn't want to go to school anymore. When she asked him why he said, "Because they don't want you anymore. No more Julie Williams. No more BOE [Board of Education]. They want a new person." As if the repeated attacks he'd been hearing against his mom weren't enough, he told Julie that the picketers gave him a sign and had him lead the parade down the sidewalk protesting his mother. "He thought it was a parade," Julie told me through tears. "And then when he got down there and saw what those signs said, it crushed him. He will never ever be quite the same."

When Julie complained about the heartless mockery of her special needs son, the people involved denied the allegations. "They said my son was lying," Julie recalled. "There is no way my son could make something up like that, and to cry like he did and to have the details. This is a young man who has such a hard time expressing himself."

The school dedicated their newspaper to recalling his mom too. It was sent out to more than eighty-five thousand families several times with pictures of his teachers insisting on the recall of his mom. Julie and her two colleagues were recalled in November 2015—two years after they were democratically elected. Julie told me, "They smashed us into the ground."

Even after all of the harassment Julie and her family endured at the hands of teachers and the union coalition, she still had positive things to say about good teachers. "With my son having special needs, we've really had relationships that we'd built up over the years with these teachers. They came to our house for barbecues. They knew me as a person, but they all turned because of the pressure of the union." Julie understands the culture of fear and knows most people cower under it. "Our teachers who have put their hearts and souls into our kids should not be manipulated the way they are," she said. "The same progressive indoctrination that's happening to our kids is happening to our teachers as well. The unions want power, money, and control over our hearts and minds."

I agree with Julie since throughout my almost thirty years of teaching in America's public schools, the unions have incessantly worked to indoctrinate us in their "progressive" ideology (I put it in quotes because it doesn't feel like progress to me, and I think regressive would be a better word for their behaviors). After being beaten down for many years, most teachers just shut their mouths and obey so they won't be the ones isolated and harangued.

After I was slandered as a radical right-winger for refusing to defeat vouchers, a few teachers caught up with me on the way back to our class-rooms. They shared they agreed with me and were tired of being brow-beaten during every meeting. I asked them why they didn't speak up and remove their names from the anti-voucher sign-up sheet so we could stop the bullying together and stand up to the harassment. All three of them did the same thing I've witnessed throughout my career every time I ask teach-ers why they don't speak up against union abuse—they lowered their heads, shrugged their shoulders, and said nothing.

They were so terrified of union forces, they would not speak up or stand up for the interests of their students or even their own children. I've witnessed this same stifling fear among educators hundreds of times throughout my career.

I've given a bit of thought to the personal attacks and outright bullying I endured during the voucher campaign season (and during many other seasons since), and I've come to a decision. I feel rather complimented by the slanderous term "radical right-winger" now. If it's radical for me to stand up for the best interests of the students I was hired to serve, and if I'm a right-winger for diligently researching both sides of an issue and choosing to support the principled position, then I hope I'll be a radical right-winger for the rest of my life.

Throughout the voucher campaign and the entire year, I was shunned and treated with disdain by union leaders. Other teachers who agreed with me noted the shunning and were sure to avoid speaking out about their true feelings, so debate was silenced again. Our mandatory dues were used to produce beautiful campaign flyers with cleverly worded talking points warning voters of the evils of vouchers. These were dispersed to voters throughout the state along with phone calls and active campaigning provided by the pressured assistance of California teachers.

(I thought my colleagues and I had it bad, but I met another teacher who had it worse. She stood in line to tell me her story after I spoke at an event. When she refused to sign up to work the phone bank to call people in her community on behalf of a union campaign against her beliefs, she was told by her union representative, "If you don't show up to phone bank, you'll have to pay someone to do it for you.")

Just like every single campaign season since the beginning of my career, union leaders took it upon themselves to make political statements on behalf of teachers with our money but without our input or approval, and they posted signs declaring the supposed political opinions of all teachers on the bulletin boards in the teacher's lounge where parents can see them every day. They said something like: *Teachers Vote No on Prop 174*. How the heck did they know how each of us was voting? They also convinced PTA parents that vouchers would ruin their local public schools and got many of those parents to participate in the efforts to defeat vouchers too. For many of those parents, vouchers could have been the greatest gift to their children, but thanks to clever union messaging, and teacher union domination of the state and National PTA, many parents unknowingly worked and voted against their better interests.

The unions and their allies spent eighteen million dollars against the measure.[12] The parents and their supporters, attempting to help children escape lousy schools, had a fraction of the resources at their disposal, so as usual the government unions dominated the airwaves with my forced dues and fought viciously against the best interests of kids and families. The voucher initiative was soundly defeated, and once again, Californians voted against their better interests in favor of union domination of our schools.

The teachers' unions and their allies defeat school choice in California and across the nation because unions don't dominate teachers in choice schools. Trapping more kids in public schools provides unions more teachers already stuck in union shops. Unions don't want to let go of teacher monies funding their political agenda.

According to a report, "Big Money Talks: California's Billion Dollar Club: The 15 Special Interests that Spent $1 Billion to Shape California Government," compiled by the California Fair Political Practices Commission, the CTA tops the list. Of the fifteen, the top two are government unions. Here are highlights of the top four. I find it interesting that everyone talks about "Big Pharma" as a problem, yet the CTA spent more than double that of "Big Pharma."

CALIFORNIA ORGANIZATIONS AND BUSINESSES THAT SPENT THE MOST TO INFLUENCE PUBLIC POLICY AND ELECTION OUTCOMES 2000–2009

Top Spenders in Order	Organization or Business Name	Amount Spent to Influence Policy or Elections
1	California Teachers Association (Affiliate of National Education Association—NEA)	$ 211,849,298
2	California State Council of Service Employees (Affiliate of Service Employees International Union—SEIU)	$ 107,467,272
3	Pharmaceutical Research and Manufacturers of America	$ 104,912,997
4	Morongo Band of Mission Indians	$ 83,600,438

Source: "Big Money Talks: California's Billion Dollar Club: The 15 Special Interests that Spent $1 Billion to Shape California Government." California Fair Political Practices Commission, March 2010.[13]

SPENDING BREAKDOWN FOR CALIFORNIA TEACHERS' ASSOCIATION 2000–2009

Ballot Measures	$144,116,835
Candidates	$16,716,386
Political Parties	$6,613,834
Other Campaign Committees	$5,885,936
TOTAL SPENT TO INFLUENCE VOTERS	$173,332,991
TOTAL SPENT LOBBYING OFFICIALS	$38,516,307
GRAND TOTAL SPENT	$211,849,298

Source: "Big Money Talks: California's Billion Dollar Club: The 15 Special Interests that Spent $1 Billion to Shape California Government." California Fair Political Practices Commission, March 2010.[14]

After spending eighteen million dollars to defeat that 1993 voucher initiative, CTA spent even more in a future battle against educational choice. According to the report, "The biggest expenditure, 26,366,491 dollars, was made to oppose Proposition 38 on the 2000 ballot. The measure sought to enact a school voucher system in California. It was defeated 29.4 percent to 70.6 percent."

I learned a fundamental truth about teachers' unions from my experience with the voucher initiative, and this truth has held true throughout my almost three decades in America's public schools. The truth? The teachers' unions claim to put the needs and safety of children first, but they do not. They use the adorable faces of children, the vulnerability of children, and the innocence of children within their messaging to grab the hearts of empathetic voters so they can get what they want from the American taxpayers, but they are *not* in the business of doing what's *right* for America's school kids (or their teachers). They're in the business of promoting themselves, pushing their one-sided political agenda onto the American people through our schools, and gaining widespread power using the billions they've collected for decades from educators' forced fees.

The ranting of a radical right-winger? Nope, this comes directly from top union leadership:

> *"And that brings me to my final and most important point, which is why, at least in my opinion, NEA and its affiliates are such effective advocates," Bob Chanin, NEA's top legal counsel for 41 years told thousands of teachers at an NEA Representative Assembly meeting. "Despite what some among us would like to believe, it is not because of our creative ideas. It is not because of the merit of our positions. It is not because we care about children, and it is not because we have a vision of a great public school for every child. NEA and its affiliates are effective advocates because we have power, and we have power because there are more than 3.2 million people who are willing to pay us hundreds of millions of dollars in dues."[15]*

CHAPTER 5

IT'S ALL ABOUT THE MONEY

"Union leaders are making thirteen to fourteen times more than the average American starting teacher, and six or seven times more than the average California teacher."

About three years into my career, I received some unsettling news. My doctor told me I'd never have children. I was devastated. I'd been praying for my future children since I was nine years old, and the only thing I ever wanted to be more than a teacher was a mother. My heart ached over my reality.

My husband at the time (I'm no longer married to him) was working on his MBA. He was busy with school and work travel, so I threw my energies and passion into my students and they became a huge part of my life. I served on all sorts of committees, earned my master's degree in education, took a bunch of neat classes, and made some games to help me inspire kids to love learning. I was very fulfilled in the classroom, but I desperately wanted to be a mother, so there was an empty place in my heart.

Around Christmas time during my seventh year of teaching, I awoke one night in a horrible sweat. Then it happened another night and another. A week later I received the astonishing news that I was pregnant. I was overjoyed, but my doctors were concerned. My infertility had been caused by serious scar tissue on my cervix; the result of emergency surgery because of early stage cancer. They'd removed all of the dangerous cells, but they'd taken most of my cervix too, so getting pregnant and carrying a baby to term was considered nearly impossible. I'd begged God for a child, so concern or not, I was going to protect my baby and bring him into this world.

At four months along, my doctors stitched up what remained of my cervix, and I had to leave the classroom in exchange for six months of strict bed rest. It was at this time that union work rules and I came face to face.

You'll recall that I had refused to join the union because they protected the nasty Witch while children were abused, so I was an agency fee payer. Remember that fee payers are punished for daring to refuse to pay the overt political expenditures of the union; even though we still pay 100 percent of the collective bargaining fees, which amount to hundreds of dollars a year. Well, one of the punishments I faced was the inability to purchase disability insurance through my employer because disability insurance was a benefit provided only for union "members in good standing." As a fee payer, I wasn't in good standing, so I was without disability insurance when I was placed on bed rest and had to go on something called "differential." That means I received my wages, but I had to pay my substitute every day as well. I was only a seventh-year teacher, so I was low on the pay scale. After taxes, paying my substitute took up the bulk of my pay. My husband was working, but he was also going to school, so this was a huge burden on our modest budget.

Now, I've never in my life expected anyone else to pay my bills or give me any special treatment, but when I look back at the way union rules and "benefits" left my family and me so incredibly vulnerable when I was trying to bring life into the world, I almost gag at their hypocrisy. You see, the teachers' unions and their favored politicians are the ones who lead the battle cry against what they call our nation's "war on women." They advertise, help organize, and support the Women's March on Washington DC in cities all over the globe, give money to Planned Parenthood claiming it's going to women's health, and continually pat themselves on the back for being warriors for women fighting for family leave and other perks to support women and families in the workplace.

Yet, there I was, a woman lying flat on her back for six months trying to bring a precious baby into the world, and because I wouldn't become a member of their political club, they denied my family and me the right to disability insurance and the funds we needed to properly nourish and protect an innocent child. I was being penalized for being a woman with an independent mind, and the pressure and financial woes my union created added great stress to an already very high-risk pregnancy. I was paying them hundreds of dollars a year to be represented, but when I really needed work-related support, they bullied my baby and me.

By God's grace, my Benjamin was born healthy and weighed in at nine pounds, but the memory of my vulnerable pregnancy stuck with me so profoundly that when I became a single parent when Ben was four, I joined the union as a full member specifically so I could purchase disability insurance. Without another income to lean on, Ben and I were way too vulnerable for me to go without insurance, so I had to set aside my own deeply held values and pay additional monies to union politics (including abortion and attacks on school choice) just so I could purchase disability insurance to protect my son and me. These sorts of "for members only" arrangements are precisely why so many teachers who are offended by union politics continue to remain as union members and pay for union politics against their better interests.

When I became a single parent, union politics damaged Ben and me again. My single parent status meant Ben had to attend preschool for nine to ten hours a day. Thankfully, he had loving teachers, but our reality was difficult. Every morning as I dropped Ben off at 6:30 a.m., I'd walk him in, get him settled, give him hugs and kisses, and then cry myself all the way to work. It was awful.

Good Shepherd Preschool was nestled inside a small church that sat on the corner of a busy street, and part of the playground looked out onto that city street. Directly across the busy street in full view of the playground was an elementary school.

The very first day Ben started attending Good Shepherd full time, one of the teachers saw him trying to climb the chain-linked fence surrounding the playground. She ran over to stop and protect him and found him crying as he tried to climb what was a gigantic hurdle for such a little guy. She asked him, "Benjamin, why are you climbing the fence? That's a busy and dangerous street." Ben looked at her with his determined and tear-stained face and said, "My mommy works at a school. I want to go see my mommy."

That wasn't my school, but to a desperate four-year old any school is Mommy's school. They were understanding and caring with Ben, but he made a few more escape attempts with his cute buddy Victor who was also missing his mommy. Ben eventually settled in, and felt secure at Good Shepherd, so I was really concerned about his transition to kindergarten.

This is when Ben and I suffered another wound courtesy of the union that was supposedly "representing" our best interests. Thanks to teachers' unions' massive spending against school choice, most families don't have school choice in California, and we certainly did not. Because we were moving a lot after divorce, I was worried about Ben having to change schools every time we moved. I knew that would create more insecurity for him, and it would be a lot more challenging for me to get to know his teachers. I also had no safe before school or afterschool childcare options. With the many dilemmas, I felt the best thing for Ben would be to come to my school district. I'd been teaching in my district for a dozen years, and I knew a family I trusted who offered childcare in their home right next to my school. It seemed like the perfect solution to a very stressful situation.

We didn't live within my district boundaries, and without school choice I did not have the right to bring Ben into my district, but my superintendent had been permitted to bring her children into our district for their kindergarten experience, so I was hoping Ben and I would be offered the same blessing. I went to my site administrator and explained my dilemma. She said she didn't want to mix the personal with the professional, so Ben could not attend our school. I asked if he could attend a different school inside of our district, so I would not be on the campus, but she again said no. I begged (and even welled up with tears I was unable to control), but she did not relent. I tried going to the next level in the chain of command to see if I could find some empathy for our situation, but I was told the decision was up to the site administrator, so I was out of luck.

Besides being devastated and facing the extreme stress of finding the right school and childcare situation for Ben, I couldn't understand why it was a negative to allow a family to teach and learn in the same school (or district) together. I know countless private schools that encourage teachers' children to attend, and many even offer free or reduced tuition for teachers' children, and the Master had always been permitted to bring her grandchildren into her first-grade class even though they lived outside of her district. Aunt Julane taught her younger siblings, her future sister-in-law, and every kid who grew up in the neighborhood, so everyone felt safe and secure in

Aunt Julane's class. Ben and I didn't live in a small town, but I felt like having Ben at my school would give us a sense of community and safety, and because of my single-parent status, it would have relieved Ben and me of untold grief and stress.

Fortunately, I was able to find a high quality private school for Ben that offered excellent childcare staffed by loving and qualified young women. The school was forty minutes away from my school though, which made every morning a challenge, and we had to be on an incredibly tight budget for me to afford the tuition and childcare, but Ben was safe, and he was in a school that embraced parents into the Education Triangle.

During this time, I often thought about how unions slandered me as a "radical right-winger" for daring to support school choice. Here I was eight years later, and my child and I were directly and negatively impacted by laws I was forced to fund against our better interests. It didn't escape my attention that those with power and connections in our public schools were given special privileges that were denied to my child and me, so they couldn't possibly understand what it was like to fight the system.

We were no different than millions of other families across the country whose lives are weighed down by laws that prohibit or limit school choice, but because I was forced to fund the attack on my own family, I was motivated to do some research into why unions, who use teacher monies to promote "pro-choice" when it comes to abortion, are so vehemently against choice when it comes to educational options for families.

It took me years to figure out exactly what was going on, but you know what I discovered: *it's all about the money.*

The teachers' unions have monopoly control and exclusive representation privileges in public schools that are unionized. They gained their control decades ago, so most teachers in classrooms today have never been given the opportunity to vote on whether or not they even want the union. My union was certified in my district when I was a child, and many of the teachers I know weren't even born when their unions were certified. All of us have been forced to accept union representation for decades, so the collective unions have raked in billions in forced fees. For my entire career, if I didn't pay up, I'd lose my job.

The teachers' unions spend millions each year on something called the "Great Public Schools" campaign. When teachers are agency fee payers, the unions are required to send us a financial document each year called the *Hudson Notice*, which highlights broad categories of state and national union spending so we can see our "chargeable" and "non-chargeable" expenses. Teachers who are full members never see this financial document.

Many of the spending categories are worded to make them sound innocuous, but most are highly political—like "human rights" and "great public schools." When the unions fight for a great public school for every child, what they really mean is they're fighting to defeat school choice. In my most recent *NEA Hudson Notice* (agency fees for 2014–2015), the NEA reports spending over fifty-eight million dollars (in one year) to promote "Great Public Schools."[16] This is just the expenditures of one national union. The American Federation of Teachers (AFT) spends heavily to defeat educational choice too, and the state unions, which receive the greatest percentage of dues, also spend millions defeating school choice.

Millions of people are manipulated by the talking points created with this massive amount of money, and they believe the unions' claims of protecting the kids. But we'd be wise to listen to what teachers' union leaders have already told us about their reasons for promoting public schools and defeating choice, so we can understand the real reasons they dump tens of millions into their "great public schools" campaign denying parents like me choice, and students like the first graders in the Witch's class the right to safety in their own classroom.

Don Cameron, the NEA's executive director during the nineties can help us to understand union motives. He was very candid when he said, "NEA's future is inextricably linked to the well-being of public education… [O]ur job is to continue advocating for our members, and the surest way to protect their jobs is to protect public education."[17]

Why is NEA's future "inextricably linked to the well-being of public education?" Because public schools are the only schools in which the unions already have a stronghold and the only way teachers in union dominated districts can rid themselves of state and national unions is to decertify them with a 51 percent majority vote, which is nearly impossible within the union's culture of fear. Teachers in the great majority of charter and private schools don't belong to unions, and don't desire to join. In other words, the more school choice is available, the fewer unionized teachers will be forking over a grand a year to unaccountable and abusive unions.

Charter school teachers and families beware; the unions have their sights on you. Adopted in the NEA's 2017 Resolutions is New Business Item (NBI) 47: "NEA will develop and promote resolutions that local associations can introduce at school board meetings calling for county-wide and state-wide moratoria on new charter school authorizations in every state that has legislation authorizing the creation of charter schools." They also adopted NBI 56: "Using existing resources, NEA will support state and local affiliates to organize and implement the NEA Charter School Policy." And NBI 133 has been sent to the appropriate committee so the unions can figure out how to organize all charter schools "…to reach a goal of full charter unionization."[18]

The problem is most charters were created as an alternative to the union-controlled schools model, so why would unions work so hard to push themselves onto schools that purposely left union control?

A stroll through union tax returns provides some of the information we need to know. According to the NEA's 2013 Form 990 tax return, the NEA is a 501(c)(5) tax-exempt organization, and in 2013 alone its gross receipts almost exclusively from member dues and fees were *392,586,438 dollars.*

What's equally eye-popping are the salaries of the union leadership (including housing allowances for the highest officers), especially when compared to the salaries of the American teachers forced to fund the largess.

NEA LEADERSHIP COMPENSATION 2013

Position	Name	Reportable Compensation	Other Compensation	Total Compensation	Housing Allowance for Residence or Personal Use
President	Dennis Van Roekel	$381,762	$145,024	$526,786	Yes
Vice President	Lily Eskelsen Garcia	$325,457	$122,311	$447,768	Yes
Secretary & Treasurer	Becky Pringle	$322,922	$131,952	$454,874	Yes
Executive Director	John Stocks	$356,563	$150,272	$506,835	No
CFO	Michael McPherson	$255,625	$129,432	$385,057	No
State Affiliate Executive Director	HT Nguyen	$247,012	$155,044	$402,056	No
Gross Receipts for 2013 (tax exempt) $392,586,438					

Source: NEA Form 990 Year Ending 2013, GuideStar.org[19]

NATIONAL AVERAGE TEACHER SALARIES FOR 2012–2013

Source	Teacher Position	Average Salary	Housing Allowance?
National Education Association, NEA.org[20]	National Average Starting Teacher	$36,141	No
National Center for Education Statistics[21]	Estimated average annual salary of teachers in public elementary and secondary schools in California	$69,324	No

We don't want to leave out the American Federation of Teachers. According to their 2014 Form 990 tax return financials, their 2014 gross receipts totaled *196,337,148 dollars*. President Randi Weingarten made a total compensation of *439,825 dollars*, and Secretary-Treasurer Lorretta Johnson brought in total compensation of *336,072 dollars*.

I don't want to mislead anyone about teacher pay. During this same year, teacher pay in my district topped out at *103,000 dollars* annually, so some teachers are making very generous salaries, but these union leaders who are clearly making thirteen to fourteen times more than the average American starting teacher, and six or seven times more than the average California teacher, live limousine lifestyles off the backs of middle-class educators. Then with a straight face, union leaders slander private CEOs as "greedy," and "the wealthy one-percent," because those executives make much larger salaries than their employees. The irony increases when we consider that unions pay no taxes on the income they coerce from teachers like me, and then vilify corporations for seeking tax breaks.

And these are just the amounts that make it to the national level; the state level unions keep the lion's share of the purse. Hardworking boots-on-the-ground public school educators fund all of this and union politics too, yet full union members are never given the opportunity to challenge union expenditures.

As a full union member serving on my local union board, I never even saw state and national union financials, but in 2012 when I became a non-member fee-payer again, a friend who volunteers at the National Right to Work Foundation taught me that fee-payers had the legal right to challenge the amounts the unions deemed "chargeable" for non-members. Even though I'd been a fee-payer for ten years at the beginning of my career, I never knew I had that right. Sure enough, once I knew to send a request for a rebate and to ask for information on the challenge, I received a letter from my state union letting me know I could challenge their fees before a "neutral decision-maker" at an arbitration hearing.

Those "neutral" audits are often held at state union headquarters and are on school days, so non-member teachers have to enter unfriendly territory, often travel great distances, and take off personal time leaving students with substitutes in order to attend. We're permitted to pay a CPA to help us wade through the financial documents, but our CPA must be pre-approved by the union. Thanks to these barriers, very few fee-payers ever attend the arbitration hearings, but I have three teacher friends who've attended, and one of them went twice.

Meet Barb Amidon. She challenged the Washington Education Association (WEA) at their arbitration hearings in the nineties. After entering the opulent union headquarters, which boasted a stunning staircase adorned with plants and flowing water, and an in-house locker room and gym, she was led into a room and the door was shut behind her.

The room was filled with two large tables completely covered in multiple stacks of union financial documents. Each stack was two to eight inches tall. Barb was given one hour to go through them—though a thorough inspection would require weeks—and then she had to listen to the "hearing," and attempt to ask questions without the benefit of reviewing the records.

In Barb's case, the "independent auditor" (neutral decision-maker) was clearly what Barb called "a friend of the union." She said, "Their department employees were laughing and joking with him between sessions, and the same guy served as the 'independent' auditor both years I attended."

I'm very sad to report that Barb, and the two other teachers I know who attended these union hearings, all told me that while they were exercising their rights to review union financial records, union employees were rude to them, mocked them with their intimidating body language and facial expressions, were impatient, and talked over them when they asked questions. Barb told me, "The challenge was a sham."

I once sought advice from another friend who attended a CTA arbitration hearing at their headquarters in Burlingame, California. I was thinking about driving the over 400 miles to challenge my "chargeable" fees, but I never went because my friend said, "Rebecca, it's not worth your time. It's a kangaroo court."

Teachers serving our children deserve better.

CHAPTER 6

DEFICIT AND DISORDER

"They'd look at me as if to say, 'You're an idiot.'"

Right around Christmas in 2002, Ben and I were finally moving into our cute little home in Huntington Beach. We had moved six times in a four-year period, so the relief of finally settling into our new home was profound. Ben was only seven, but together we'd already been through years of physical and emotional upheaval, so this little house represented freedom and stability for us.

Ben and I lived in all sorts of different places after divorce uprooted our lives. The worst place was an apartment in a low-income neighborhood in Huntington Beach. Our ugly apartment was upstairs on the corner of the building, so I'd hoped having only one wall touching a neighbor would help with the stress of having a small, active child in an apartment, but as Murphy's Law would have it, the young woman next door worked nights and slept all day. If we so much as made a peep, she would complain to the manager and bang on the wall. When she was awake, she'd glare at us and make hateful comments while Ben rode his tricycle in the small patio.

The city bus stop was right outside of our window on the other side of the apartment, so bus noise and fumes were an annoyance, and interesting characters loitered at the bus stop beneath our living room window both day and night. But the worst part was the gunshots I heard some nights while trying to sleep. I was terrified living in that apartment alone with a small child, but since our life changed suddenly, it was the only place I could afford at the time.

Single parenting is not only the hardest job I've ever done, it's the most emotionally draining as well, and many of us who find ourselves in the unenviable position of parenting alone often experience stress far beyond normal limits. Add to this a lack of convenient school and childcare options, and anxiety dominates. As hard as I tried, I made many choices through a cloud of emotions and stress, and it's embarrassing to admit that by the time Ben had reached seven years old, he had been through some unnecessary upheaval and hurt because his mother made some very stupid decisions. People naturally pour out empathy and care onto widows and their grieving children, as they should, but grieving single parents overwhelmed with strong-willed youngsters navigating the anger that naturally comes over them as they learn to cope with the realities of divorce are often further damaged by other's careless comments and attitudes.

Long story short, some key people in my life continually told me that Ben was doomed to a life of discipline problems because a single mom was raising him. One went so far as to repeat over and over, "This kid's going to end up in juvenile hall."

It was a huge misjudgment of the facts, but since Ben really was hurting and acting out his anger and our lives were in constant upheaval, the ongoing ridicule discouraged me to the core. Through years of challenges in life, I had remained strong and able to cope, but feeling alone, isolated, and without positive options, this situation took me to a very low place. I had never been depressed in my life before this circumstance, and I've never been depressed since. But during this time, I experienced hopelessness, and in my very dark place, I even lost my faith in God.

It was during this awful time that I found the home in Huntington Beach. I'm thankful that even though I'd lost my faith in God, He hadn't given up on me. He poured out His grace; we found exactly the kind of house we needed—with a big backyard and a gigantic tree in the front, and our days of physical instability were finally over.

The first thing Ben said when we walked into the home was, "Mommy, this is the perfect house for us. We can cozy up by the fireplace with hot chocolate, and I can climb that big tree outside every day." Ben has always been a kid with his priorities straight.

Ben and I experienced a lot of healing in our little home. He and his Nana even planted a Victory Garden, and things were looking up, but the following fall when I attended Ben's parent–teacher conference my concerns started growing again.

Ben was in second grade. He was never in trouble for negative behavioral issues; in fact, he was known as the young man who held the door open for the girls and carried their lunch pails out to the lunch benches each day. (How I wish I could have witnessed that scene!) However, he struggled greatly with sitting still and paying attention to direct instruction. Ben's teacher, who was a lovely young woman, was growing more concerned about his lack of focus. We had tried several plans to help him improve, but the school was now putting a lot of pressure on me to have Ben placed on stimulants for ADHD (Attention Deficit Hyperactivity Disorder).

Ben had been diagnosed as severe ADHD before, so I knew the educational and psychological world saw him as "deficit" and "disorder," but as his mother and a long-time educator who'd worked with dozens of boys labeled ADD or ADHD, I was wholeheartedly against labeling and drugging wiggly little boys who struggled to pay attention while sitting at desks for six or seven hours a day. I was the only teacher I knew who was against drugging and labeling the children at that time, but I'd seen the relief on many a parent's face when I was sitting in the teacher's seat at the parent–teacher conferences and told them their wiggly little boys didn't seem "deficit" or "disorder" to me, and no, I didn't want to drug them. There was (and still is) so much pressure on parents to put their active children on drugs, so they can better fit into the narrow classroom model we offer families in our current industrialized educational system.

I guess I've always been sensitive about labeling kids because my father was labeled when he was a boy. Daddy was born in abject poverty in Arkansas. He was the youngest of seven children. His mama died of tuberculosis when he was only three months old, and his father mourned so heavily, my daddy told me, "When Mama died, half of Daddy died with her."

When my daddy was young no one ever read to him and there were no books in his home. When he started attending school, no one ever helped him with his homework or encouraged him either. Daddy was yearning to excel in school—he dreamed of being a lawyer, a police officer, or a pastor, but his father thought Daddy's learning was the job of the educators. My grandfather, LeRoy, passed many outstanding values to my daddy, and it wasn't that he despised education; he just didn't understand his vital role in the Education Triangle. Instead of explaining his critical position to him, the education establishment chose to judge him as too poor and too ignorant to care.

Daddy was bright and able to learn, but his school wasn't equipped to help him, and most of his teachers were so overwhelmed by his circumstances he told me, "They just passed me along." He remembers the feelings of shame when teachers gave up on him. "They'd look at me as if to say, 'You're an idiot,'" Daddy remembers. He's always quick to tell me that he values and respects teachers and doesn't want to disparage them in any way; in fact, he's married to one, and two of his children are teachers. He believes most teachers do their best in some tough situations.

Daddy had two special teachers in middle school who saw through his poverty and believed in his abilities so much he earned an A in both of their classes, but Daddy earned straight F's throughout elementary school. Every time he brought home his report card, LeRoy would sign it without saying a word.

It breaks my heart to report this to you, but when Daddy was a boy some of his teachers called him "dumb" and "dunce," and he was literally crowned with a tall pointed dunce cap. I wish I could have rescued Daddy from that fate. It makes me nauseated every time I think of it. He silently endured all kinds of ridicule and shame in the name of education. It's shocking that teachers would do something so cruel, but Daddy told me matter-of-factly: "They were always calling me dumb and dunce."

I asked my daddy if he could tell me how it felt to be singled out, crowned with a dunce cap, and labeled such debilitating names. I expected to hear a heart-grabbing story of the deep shame he endured, or the gut-wrenching ache he carried in his stomach after being mocked and ridiculed, instead I heard a story of acceptance. "It's just how it was," Daddy told me. "People don't realize, unless they were raised in that situation; I just accepted it."

We could dismiss this cruelty committed in a bygone era as ignorance on the part of the culture and pat ourselves on the back for being so much more enlightened, but if we're honest with ourselves, we have to admit we're still pinning hurtful names onto millions of children today—names like the ones pinned on my Ben—"deficit" and "disorder," and kids and parents today are accepting it as well.

Though our culture seems comfortable with these characterizations, I'm offended by these labels we place on wonderful kids who've been created outside of the norm, and I was against drugs for Ben and my students because I'd done my research on them. They are forms of speed that are so toxic they're highly regulated. At that time, parents had to visit the doctor's office multiple times a year just to receive refills. I know teachers think the drugs help because they make kids sit still, but I struggle with the constant push by the educational community to medicate children.

Though I had been able to fend off the push for Ben to be drugged for quite some time, the pressure from his school to put him on medication was getting unbelievably strong. Reluctantly, I took Ben for a thorough diagnosis (which added more stress to my budget), and no surprise, he was labeled severe ADHD again. It breaks my heart to think of the way we label children "deficit" and "disorder," and it was an agonizing decision to place my son on medication, but after the pressure reached extreme levels, I finally agreed to try out the medicine.

It was a nightmare.

I suppose Ben's wiggly classroom behaviors improved since he was an absolute zombie during the day, but at night, he couldn't sleep at all. As a single parent, I had a very disciplined schedule including homework, playtime, dinner, packing lunches for the next day, bath time, and bedtime stories all by 7:00 p.m. Almost every night Ben would fall asleep while I was reading to him, and I'd often fall asleep right next to him from total exhaustion, only to wake up around ten and drag myself into my own bed. My alarm would go off at 4:00 a.m., I'd do my exercise, get myself ready for work, get Ben up, make breakfast, drive Ben to childcare and myself to work, and we'd do the whole routine again the next evening and morning. This schedule worked great for a hardworking single mom, but losing sleep was not an option.

When Ben was on the ADHD medicine, we lost almost all of our sleep every night. The doctor tried changing the prescription, adjusting the dosage, and prescribing things to help with sleep, but every option we tried was just as disruptive. In addition to sleep deprivation and zombie behavior, Ben started to act forlorn. He was extremely sad, and he was a shell of the little boy I knew and loved.

During this time Ben's school had an awards day. As I sat in the parent section and watched the children, I observed Ben sitting among his peers with his shoulders slumped and a frown on his face. When his teacher called his name to come up and receive his award, Ben didn't even smile. She read a long paragraph about his character qualities and presented him a beautiful certificate. He stood next to her the entire time with a down-hearted look on his face and his shoulders rolled forward in a depressive stance; I noticed dark circles surrounded his eyes, and he looked like he was ready to burst into tears. My normally social little boy would not make eye contact with the crowd, and he stood there looking like he'd just lost his best friend. The uncomfortable looks on the faces of the other parents told me they could see the hurt too, and many of them looked at me with condescending stares that made me feel judged as a mother, as though Ben and I were abnormal and social outcasts.

Tears welled up in my eyes, a lump caught in my throat, and my heart broke because I'd allowed supposed "experts" to tell me there was something wrong with my child, and he'd been hurt in the process. I took him off of those pills immediately, and my super-active, fun, loving little boy returned. Our sleep returned too, and I determined never to allow anyone to talk me out of my deeply held beliefs and gut feelings again.

Since Ben still needed help with focus, I continued researching and discovered a wonderful psychologist named John Rosemond who specializes in old-fashioned parenting ideas. I read several of his books and found a fantastic home to school behavior plan in a chapter titled "When to Motivate," in his book *Ending the Homework Hassle*.[22] This plan gave me hope because Mr. Rosemond shared that he and his wife had been frustrated by the same sorts of issues with their own son and discovered that they'd bought into some modern parenting ideas that were exacerbating their son's problems; in fact, they were the very parenting and "self-esteem" ideas so many in the teaching profession were espousing, promoting, using in our schools…and that I was believing.

Ben's school agreed to the plan, so we started him immediately on a daily contract. The first two weeks, as Dr. Rosemond had warned, Ben didn't take us very seriously, and lost his privileges almost every day. During week three, Ben saw the light. He discovered that if he paid attention in class, he got to enjoy his regular fun life at home. If he chose not to focus in school, he did not get to enjoy his regular fun life at home. It was that simple. Once Ben realized his Education Triangle was serious and on the same page, he dubbed the behavior plan, "The System," and told me, "Mommy, I hate The System." Now we were getting somewhere.

Ben's third-grade teacher said he was the most distracted and "off-task" child in her class, but when I attended Back to School Night the following year, his fourth-grade teacher sought me out. She said, "I just want to tell you that I love teaching your son, Ben. He's by far the best student I've had in my class throughout my nine-year teaching career," and she never once mentioned *any* problems with focus. My jaw dropped, and I questioned if she was referring to the right Ben, but thanks to an outstanding parenting plan implemented by all members of the Education Triangle (student, teacher/administrators, and parent), the most off-task child in the class transformed into the top student of a teacher's career.

All without drugs or labels.

In my mind, an ADHD diagnosis was not an excuse for misbehavior; in fact, I never even told Ben of the diagnosis until he was out of high school because I don't believe in telling children they are "deficit" and "disorder," and I don't believe they are those negative assessments. Ben's situation presented a challenge to help him to learn self-control and to help him to direct his wiggly body and wandering mind toward his lessons during class. It was all about holding him accountable, not making justifications for his off-task behavior, and you know what? Helping Ben made me a one thousand times better teacher. I asked Ben the other day if he could offer a comment to my readers about the impact of "The System." Without skipping a beat, he said, "Dang, Mom, it was effective. I'm using it on my kids someday if they don't listen in school."

Even though I loved that school, and Ben improved dramatically with the highly structured "System," I have to pause a moment and share my thoughts on the way we, as a society and especially in our schools, have accepted the practice of placing negative labels on wiggly little boys and then filling them with stimulants. I believe (from my decades of personal experience with family and friends, and in my classroom) that our current educational system is bringing great damage to very gifted and bright children by labeling them as "deficit" and "disorder," instead of making learning more engaging and intellectually stimulating, and that's a real tragedy. According to the Centers for Disease Control, diagnoses of ADHD have increased considerably since 1997 to 11 percent of children by 2011.[23] Shouldn't we be asking ourselves why?

Everyone knows that children labeled "deficit" and "disorder" either lack focus, are unorganized, or are full of boundless energy, and they don't like to focus on boring stuff, but they can focus for hours on video games, building blocks, and other interesting activities. I've noticed in my classroom that the wiggly little boys (and girls) who struggle with pen and pencil work and can't sit still at the carpet, are totally focused and they even shine as leaders when we do hands-on science experiments, work on computers, engage in debate style conversations or Socratic seminar, act out a story with costumes, or work with building materials.

Could it be that these kids are just wired differently than the kids who can sit still for hours? Since most of our school days are structured with children listening instead of learning through experimentation, could it be that it's not the kids who are "deficit" and "disorder," but it's our schools that have the deficit because we insist on educating every child—no matter his talents, energy level, learning style, or intelligence—the same way? We ask boys to sit still, to fold their hands on their desks, and to thrive in environments void of adventure. If we're honest with ourselves, we'll admit we're asking active boys to go against their very nature, and then we label them with inaccurate labels when they can't live up to our unrealistic expectations.

Ben and I are the first to admit he's loaded with bundles of energy and in constant motion even now in his twenties, but we know he's not the "deficit" or "disorder" that teachers and psychologists labeled him.

Our educational system also puts tremendous pressure on all kids to follow the same narrow university path, but not all kids are wired for another four years of classroom lectures and sedentary learning. Ben spent two years working toward his bachelor's degree and held a solid B average, but he hated almost every minute of it and learned very little. During a heart-to-heart conversation, he told me that throughout his education the message at school was clear: "You're a lesser person if you choose trade school or other hands-on work instead of the university. My friends and I love working on cars, but we're considered stupid at school."

Because of this, Ben was ashamed to follow the path he dreamed of pursuing. Finally, in his second year of college, after teaching himself to weld fender flairs onto his car, Charles and I convinced him to make room in his schedule for two welding classes at a local community college. He found his passion, and the coerced university plan took a backseat.

Ben loves welding, and he's really good at it. I find it ironic that so many people labeled him with ADHD because welding requires high levels of focus while doing intense work, wearing heavy clothing, and using flames in the thousands of degrees. While welding four to five hours at a time, Ben is laser-focused, and he's a top student in the program. Ben comes home from welding each day talking up a storm about all of the new things he's learning, and he already has a business plan created using his out-of-the-box thinking and entrepreneurial spirit.

Ben was wired for a different kind of education. He still listens to lectures and reads assignments, but they lead to his hands-on work, and I'm amazed at the knowledge he quips out as if it's something simple. He'd likely earn a D- in handwriting because his penmanship is so awful, but do you care about the penmanship of the guy who builds the bridge on which you drive every day or the building in which you work? I doubt it. Ben is not "deficit" or "disorder," he's just wired differently. God was wise to bless Ben with constant motion and other abilities not appreciated in one-size-fits-all classrooms. His "deficits" are the gifts necessary for him to fulfill his calling. And once he was released to be himself, his confidence rose, and his incredible leadership skills that lay dormant for years came shining through.

My father had a similar circumstance. When he joined the Navy at age seventeen, he found the discipline and structure that was missing in his motherless home life, and he grew as a learner while serving as a cook and storekeeper. He told me he has no idea how he passed the entrance exams, but he's grateful he had a second chance. Ben and my daddy are a lot alike. Well-meaning educators labeled them both, and those labels held them back. Both were just in need of different teaching styles, discipline structures, and encouragement from mentors who believed in them.

So why do we resort to labeling and drugging kids whose parents prefer to have them in schools that are more suited to their learning styles? Why do we fight against and limit school choice when so many parents and kids would benefit from the options it provides? One answer is teachers' unions. As the NEA's Executive Director Don Cameron told us:

NEA's future is inextricably linked to the well-being of public educa-
tion.... [O]ur job is to continue advocating for our members, and
the surest way to protect their jobs is to protect public education.[24]

So looking out for their own interests funded by dues paying members in traditional public schools, they pour hundreds of millions into defeating parental choice, dominate school boards with union friendly trustees, and undermine parents attempting to create schools better suited for all sorts of kids—including those labeled dumb, dunce, deficit and disorder.

Many of my friends have written incredible charters to create schools suited for kids like Ben only to be met by angry union inspired mobs shouting them down as they presented their charters to local school boards for approval. No surprise those school boards—heavily influenced by unions and unwilling to grant charters that would create competition for students attached to tax dollars—rejected the charters, and then when my friends appealed to our county board of education (which was union heavy for years), they were rejected again.

In addition, union leadership hurled hurtful names onto the benevolent folks (parents and community members) who worked hard and donated their own resources to create choice schools for kids like Ben. The unions label education reformers as "education deformers," "greedy special interests," "anti-public school," "anti-teacher," "anti-student," and even "public school deniers."

I'm an education reformer. How in the world can I be anti-teacher, anti-student, or a public school denier when I've taught in America's public schools, serving students for twenty-eight years? I'm for school choice because both of my sons, my daddy, and hundreds of children I've taught over the years would have benefitted from more innovative school options, my own education was compromised in some public schools, and I believe parents are far more qualified to choose the right learning environments for their own children.

This is not a put-down to public schools or the teachers serving in them. Many teachers are doing a fine job, and some children are served well by their public schools, and their parents are happy with those schools, but too many families across the country need something different.

One-size-fits-all doesn't work for every kid, just like one teaching situation isn't right for every single teacher. Can you imagine forcing an English teacher to instruct Trigonometry or a History teacher to teach Biology?

No one is attacking teachers here. It's the teachers' unions that have turned a sincere desire to do what's right for all kids, parents, and educators into a knock-down, drag-out political fight because their future is "inextricably linked to the well-being of public education." It's my deep hope that good public school teachers will begin to understand they are valued and desired by those of us who work for choice. We just want them and the kids they serve to have real options.

There's one other thing. My boys and their friends tell me that students on their high school campuses were selling their prescription ADHD meds for twenty to thirty dollars a pill. It provided the prescription holders a lucrative business. Ben told me, "Even some goodie-two-shoes kids would buy them." They say it was very prevalent with kids in their advanced placement classes—especially during finals week.

Ben told me one of his good friends (a student with an above 4.0 GPA) was really out of it one day. Once Ben finally got his attention the student said, "Sorry, Dude, I took Adderall before this test so I could get a better grade." His parents didn't know he was buying drugs from classmates.

The pressure to drug our children, and the pressure for them to drug themselves, discourages many of us. We'd prefer to place our children in educational environments in which their advanced kinesthetic (hands-on) abilities are valued and developed; discipline standards are suited to their strong wills; and their active minds are encouraged toward adventure and deep understanding instead of filling in bubbles on tests.

I support the right of parents who see things differently than I do, and I realize there are some children with serious challenges who may benefit from medications, but I've talked to thousands of people (men especially) who resent the encumbering labels that were pinned onto them when they were children and onto wiggly little boys and girls who are forced to sit still for hours at a time in our industrial style classrooms. It's important to realize that to us "deficit" and "disorder" feels a lot like "dunce."

Thanks to God's Grace, my father overcame his debilitating schoolroom label and took on his true identity as a gifted businessman. But at eighty years old, he still wears the scars of the thoughtless schoolroom label.

The sting of that label has made my daddy insecure about writing a personal letter to anyone. One of my most cherished possessions is a personal note he sent to me when I was on a forty-day wilderness adventure and in need of comfort from home. My homesickness motivated him to write to me, but he asked his teacher wife to proofread his draft before transferring it to the lovely card he chose for me. A "dunce" can't spell you know, and he was so nervous about writing it in his own handwriting that he asked my stepmom to draw lines on the card to keep his writing straight. Sixty-five years removed from the classroom, Daddy still had to ask a teacher for approval.

His card was the highlight of my summer, and I'm so glad he found a way to overcome the label given to him by well-meaning educators who couldn't see past his circumstances to his potential. The message of his letter to me is timeless, and I'm so proud of Daddy for finding the courage to write it; I'd like to share part of it with you.

My Dearest Darling Daughter!!

I have not had the great pleasure of talking to you for such a long time!! Maggi and I went to see South Pacific and visited with Charles and Ben. [They were playing in the orchestra.]

I told Ben I was proud of him and how he made the decision to stop playing football. He will take heat from his peers and the coaches, but I am so proud he was able to think it out and come to the right decision for him. I can remember a young girl who went through a similar situation. That's a wonderful gift you gave to your son—the character to make a decision and stick to it no matter what some people say.

Just this short portion of his letter is full of so much love, wisdom, and encouragement to Ben and me, and I know we'll receive blessings from it many times throughout our lives; especially once my daddy is gone. It's so tragic that a schoolroom label has kept him from writing letters like this to everyone he loves. I'm hoping and praying he'll find the courage to write a personal letter to each one of his children and grandchildren because we all need the benefit of his love and wisdom for our lifetimes, and we all need the connection of reading our letters in his personal handwriting too.

I'm always asking Daddy about his childhood. His oldest sister, Melba, mostly raised him—she was fifteen when their mama died, so in lots of ways, Daddy raised himself. He picked cotton when he was little; had a shoe-shining business at age ten; and at twelve and thirteen, he sold newspapers on the street. He earned four cents for every paper he sold, but his entrepreneurial spirit dreamed up the idea to allow customers to rub his baldhead for good luck for an extra fee.

I often well up with tears when we talk about his childhood, and I know things would have been drastically different if his mama had lived. Maybe if she had advocated for him, the teachers wouldn't have labeled him dumb and dunce. He's always quick to remind me that his circumstances taught him a strong work ethic, his family passed on good moral values, and Jesus has blessed him richly, yet there are two things in his life he admits still make him sad: The first, he's never seen a picture of his mama, and I'll let him share in his own words the second thing.

"I only have one regret in this life," Daddy told me while choking back tears. "I didn't get a good education."

CHAPTER 7

BULLYING 101

"The caption in the dirt read, 'Rotten Apples,' and directly under it sat one oversized, rotting apple with my name on it."

In 2004, I was talking with my friend Shelly about my lousy relationship history. She'd met her fiancé on eHarmony, so they took me out for dinner one night, snapped a picture of me and talked me into signing up on eHarmony too. I'm glad I listened to them because Charles and I met on eHarmony in 2004 and married in 2006. Charles has served as a university music professor for decades, taught middle school band before that, and we both come from large families with strong Judeo-Christian values, so we're a terrific match.

However, because state and national teachers' unions have bullied conservative educators to keep our mouths shut; making us (and the American people) believe that most professors and teachers agree with union politics, we both assumed we'd butt heads politically, so our first conversation was about politics figuring that would be our last. Delightfully, we discovered we lined up politically too, and were equally frustrated with being forced to support union politics. We learned a valuable lesson that day that we'd like to share with you—many professors and teachers share our values and disgust for state and national unions; they're just too afraid to speak out.

When I became Mrs. Friedrichs, I gained a terrific new stepson as part of the deal too, so Ben gained a big brother. Kyle is four years older than Ben, and he's Ben's exact opposite, so since opposites tend to attract, Ben and Kyle got along pretty well from the beginning.

Though blending a family brought major challenges, the burden of single parenting was lifted for both of us, so we were able to take on some additional service projects we'd been unable to do as single parents. I had my focus set on helping to improve the very low morale amongst teachers and staff in my school district, so I stepped up as a union representative in hopes of making a difference from the inside.

As part of my service as local union secretary, Charles and I attended a 2008 California Teachers Association (CTA) annual leadership conference. We'd both been to many different teachers' conferences throughout our careers. He'd attended several full of instruments, sheet music, computer beats, music texts, and more, and I'd enjoyed countless conferences full of brightly colored books, hands on "manipulatives" for use in math and science lessons, and other items for making lessons come to life for kids. But walking into the registration area of this CTA conference was nothing like either of us had ever seen in all our years educating American students.

Flanking the registration table and encircling the entire room were EXPO booths. There was nothing odd about that, but what was troubling to us was the difficulty we had finding a booth that actually related to our jobs or our needs as educators trying to teach students. Instead, we carefully surveyed booth after booth full of one-sided information on abortion rights, transgender and homosexual rights, gay students' rights, gay teacher rights, gay students' clubs information, and a variety of other topics—almost all of which were politically charged social agenda issues favoring the Far Left portion of the Democratic Party. To say we were totally shocked is an understatement. Indeed, we felt like we'd wandered into the wrong convention room because almost nothing in this room resembled a conference for teachers seeking to become better educators or hoping to make connections to other teachers across the state to improve educational outcomes for students.

After checking in that evening, we were invited to attend several gatherings the union was hosting in various guestrooms throughout the hotel. We stopped in at two of them but left both quickly because the only things going on in those rooms were a lot of heavy drinking and tons of political pressure by union operatives who made us feel very uncomfortable. Teachers' union leaders assume that all educators agree with union politics, so they speak disparagingly about those of us with more conservative values and cut us down right to our faces.

Besides feeling personally attacked, we were shocked at how much teacher dues were being abused. The hors d'oeuvres plates overflowed with high-priced luxury foods, a bartender was making mixed drinks at an open bar, and the scene was repeated in several rooms throughout the hotel. I talked about this with a few of my teacher friends who attended with us, and some of them dismissed it by saying, "Well, we volunteer our time; at least they can treat us right at a conference." Though I agree volunteers should be thanked from time to time, teachers' dues had already covered our conference fees, mileage, food, and luxurious hotel rooms, so I felt sick to my stomach that hard-working teachers were also funding high-priced parties without their knowledge. State and national teachers' union leaders host scores of conferences like these all year long across the country, so it seemed over the top and an abuse of funds to Charles and me.

I also attended several seminars at the conference and was further disturbed by the union's almost total focus on politically charged social issues and its leadership's resistance to answering the many sincere questions of teachers on behalf of our students and colleagues. One of the reasons I attended was to participate in a seminar on special education. I was hoping to find support from my union because throughout my entire career, I had great difficulty obtaining help for children who were desperately in need of extra assistance or special education services.

Many other teachers like me attended the same seminar and had the same goals as I did. We all felt frustrated by our inability to obtain services for students we felt genuinely needed them. We'd all experienced administrators who required us to jump through hoops to obtain testing for kids, only to be put off again and told we needed to jump through more hoops. We all felt some unknown policy or unseen power was undermining our efforts and squelching our ability to do what's right for kids with special needs, but no matter how hard we all fought, we were unable to find the support we needed for many of our students.

Though it was eye opening to hear teachers from across the state share the same frustrations, we were discouraged when our concerns were dismissed. We were told there was no way the union could help us because the federal government doesn't put enough funding behind its special education laws. We already knew that. We were hoping our union would use our massive dues and its collective power to actually *help* us change the status quo so children in need could be served and teachers could be relieved of great stress—at the time we hadn't figured out that our union *is* the status quo.

It was at this conference that the three hundred other teachers and I sat terrified as CTA and NEA leaders berated us from the stage. You'll recall that one brave California teacher asked how we educators could gain a voice on how our money is spent, so union leaders harangued her, isolated her, and shut her down so completely that she withered into an emotionally distraught heap in her seat while the rest of us sat immobile and stunned.

You'll recall those union leaders educated us on the only "right" way to think and told us if we did not agree with *their* expenditures of *our* money we were backward and bigoted. We learned that no debate is permitted—*ever*.

State and national union leaders harass independent minded teachers all the time, so that's why most teachers just go along to get along, and that's why so many Americans believe that teachers as a group agree with union politics. The fact is, like any other institution in America, teachers come from all political categories. Indeed, as the NEA's own internal studies reveal, teacher union members actually skew slightly conservative.

NEA STUDY RESULTS: POLITICAL PHILOSOPHY PUBLIC SCHOOL TEACHERS

Year Study Conducted	Percent Conservative	Percent Tend to be Conservative	Percent Tend to be Liberal	Percent Liberal	Total Percent Lean Conservative	Total Percent Lean Liberal
1971	17	44	28	12	61	40
1996	20	41	31	8	61	39
2006	23	32	32	13	55	45

Source: NEA's Status of the American Public School Teacher 2005–2006 (most recent study available)[25]

Yet despite this, the majority of union money, human resources, power, and influence are directed toward liberal candidates, policies, and politics as highlighted below.

TEACHERS UNIONS: TOP CONTRIBUTORS TO FEDERAL CANDIDATES, PARTIES, AND OUTSIDE GROUPS 2016

Contributor	Total Contributions	To Candidates And Parties	Percent to Democrats
National Education Association	$20,912,909	$2,379,658	87.6%
American Federation of Teachers	$9,000,041	$2,400,527	99.5%
AFT Solidarity 527[26]	$2,818,742	$0	
California School Employees Association	$121,197	$121,197	100%

Source: Center for Responsive Politics[27]

Percent to Republicans	Total Contributions To Outside Groups	Percent Liberal	Percent Conservative
12.3%	$18,518,000	100%	0%
0.3%	$6,599,514	100%	0%
	$2,818,742	100%	0%
0%	$0		

Knowing this, the "offending" teacher's question was completely valid, and it was the union leadership that was totally out of step and out of line when they abused her and misuse our dues. But they harassed and bullied her for questioning them because that's how state and national union leaders keep their power, even though they love to play the victim.

But don't take my word for it. At his retirement farewell address in front of the NEA Representative Assembly, Bob Chanin (longtime NEA counsel) said:

> *Why are these conservative and right-wing bastards picking on NEA and its affiliates? I will tell you why. It is the price we pay for success. NEA and its affiliates have been singled out because they are the most effective unions in the United States, and they are the nations' leading advocates for public education, and the type of liberal, social and economic agenda that these groups find unacceptable.[28]*

Just what is this agenda that good people find unacceptable? My friend Chalone Warman, retired high school English teacher, attended a May 5, 2018 CTA-sponsored seminar titled "Social Justice Forum." It was advertised as training for teacher and student CTA members to learn how to "Help students become leaders in the fight for educational justice." Her summary is revealing.

> *Throughout the day I felt as though I had walked through a portal into another time zone--50 years ago. They were complaining about white supremacy, structural inequality, the tyranny of the one-per-center's, etc.—even reaching back to the "culture of lynching" in the early 1900's and the Japanese internment camps during WWII to underscore how poorly America has treated minorities.*

> *The speaker was the worst kind of demagogue. Clearly his mission was to "fire up the base" while dropping lines such as "Trump is sucking away the goodness of our souls." He continuously preyed on the attendees' insecurities by igniting their own prejudices. The "social justice" mantra was hammered all day long without ever identifying specifically what it is or what it looks like. It hovered over the event like poison gas.*

I was sickened to see how teachers' dues are being misused. CTA has strayed so far from issues that are important to all teachers—class size and salary—and has entered the murky realm of "recognizing the inequities within the system."

Using this kind of vitriol and constant focus on envy and division, state and national union leaders *divide* teachers, the public, and bully good teachers into silence.

In January 2015 I was the keynote speaker at the Redland's Republican Women's luncheon. My stepmom, Maggi (a retired California public school teacher of thirty-nine years), was a member of the group. Her club was excited about our case in support of teacher freedom because many of them were retired teachers and had endured the abusive culture of fear in America's unionized schools, so I received a warm welcome. Sadly a few union operatives showed up, which made some of the ladies apprehensive.

At the end of my talk, I chatted with ladies who'd lined up to share their own stories of abuse at the hands of unions. I'll never forget the woman at the end of the line. A lovely woman retired from teaching for many years, but even though her trauma occurred decades ago, her voice shook, and she checked our surroundings for union allies before laboring to tell me her story.

When she was a young teacher, the unions came to unionize her school. She didn't want to join, but the union workers were persistent and intimidated all of the teachers on her campus. She told me, "They were insisting on 100 percent participation."

She recalled that to put pressure on all of the teachers, union leaders put up a big paper tree on the bulletin board in the teachers' lounge. The caption above the tree said "Golden Apples" in bold print, and every time a teacher joined the union, they would add a large, paper apple to the tree with the teacher's name on it. For weeks they put pressure on every teacher, and although many of her teacher friends told her they didn't want to join, the tree was filling up because everyone was afraid of losing their jobs if they didn't join. She felt strongly about not joining and didn't trust union motives, so she refused no matter how much union leaders harassed her.

One day this dear woman walked into the teachers' lounge and experienced abuse that still hurts to this day. That big tree was covered with every teacher's name—all printed proudly on large golden apples situated up in the branches of the tree. She told me, she was the only teacher missing from the branches. But union leaders weren't using the tree just to encourage membership; they created it to mistreat those who declined membership, so they'd added a new section down at the base of the tree as well.

The caption in bold font declared unmistakably how the union felt about teachers who chose independence over their oppression—dissenters would pay a heavy price. The woman told me, "The caption in the dirt read, '**Rotten Apples**,' and directly under it sat one oversized, rotting apple with my name on it."

The tree and its message of shame remained up for weeks. She was branded "Rotten Apple," all day, every day—just like she was wearing a scarlet letter.

I wish you could have seen this precious woman. Think of the best teacher you ever had—one who was kind, patient, loving, and who hugged you when you were feeling down. That fun teacher who understood your wiggles, could laugh at herself, and told your parents you were a good kid. She was *that* teacher. I could feel the love coming out of her, and I knew kids felt safe in her class many years ago. This loving woman who should be one of America's greatest treasures and should have been thanked and supported for her efforts with children, was instead abused, shunned, and marginalized by a government teachers' union that claimed to represent her best interests.

What's really stuck with me—and placed a permanent pit in my stomach ever since I heard this retired teacher tell her story—are the visible signs of stress she was under while recalling the memory. Our teachers' unions abused this woman to such a degree that the pain is still palpable several decades later. So I promised her that day I would do all I could to share her story with anyone who would listen.

I've met many other teachers of all ages since that day, and most of them are too afraid to share their stories with their names attached because unions harass people who speak out. Thankfully, I've met a few fearless teachers from across the country who've given me permission to share their stories.

In 1949 Ruth Finnegan started her teaching career in North Carolina, and she spent some time teaching in Atlanta, Georgia, too. She absolutely loved being a teacher. Several years into her career in 1968, Ruth started teaching in Hershey, Pennsylvania. From her first day on campus, union officials hounded her every single day to join the union, so she asked them, "What do you do for us? What service do you provide me?" They responded, "You should not ask any questions, just join."

Ruth informed me, "I didn't join."

About a week into her new job in Hershey, Ruth was working alone in her classroom long after school hours, grading papers. As she poured through the children's work, there was a knock on her door. Ruth answered the door and five large men in black suits pushed their way into her room and started pressuring her to join the union. Not intimidated (but terrified), Ruth asked again, 'What services do you provide for me?'"

As they moved toward her, the men in black suits informed Ruth that they could provide a lawyer for her if someone sued her. As a loving teacher, it never once entered Ruth's mind that she'd be sued, but the men in black suits surrounded her and implied she would definitely need a lawyer. She answered them, "I'm here to teach. I don't expect anyone to sue me." The men in black suits insisted teachers were sued all the time and needed their protection. Ruth felt immediately that if she ever had legal troubles these were the last guys on earth she'd want fighting on her side, but she couldn't get rid of them and they were interrupting her work, so she reiterated her position. "I'm here to help children," she said. "I'm not here to damage them in any way."

The men in black suits would not take no for an answer, and even though Ruth was buried in work, they would neither leave nor back off from their aggressive approach. They just kept trying to force her to sign a paper to give them the right to take money out of her paycheck for union dues. Ruth said in exasperation, "I'm really busy now. I'll think about it."

Ruth told me, "Since I said I'd think about it, they finally left."

Ruth was really upset about the interaction with the men in black suits, so she asked a teacher colleague what she thought about the union. Her friend said, "I joined the union, but I didn't want to. I don't think they offer us anything we need." Ruth couldn't understand why her friend joined if she thought the union useless, so she asked, "What would happen if I refuse to join?" Her friend said, "You'll probably lose your job."

"I was new on the job," Ruth told me, "I couldn't lose my job."

She had another teacher friend whose husband was a principal, so she asked them how they felt about unions. "We don't think the union provides us a service either, but we joined because we don't want to be fired from teaching. The unions really have it in for a person who tries to refuse to join." They followed their statement with, "We would appreciate it if you don't tell anyone what we said."

Ruth told me, "So I kept my mouth shut."

When Ruth talked to her husband about the five men in black suits he told her, "You might as well join because they will be after you, and if you don't join, they could just say, 'Goodbye, we don't want you teaching here.'"

Now before we move on with Ruth's story, I'd like to point out four psychological manipulations used by those who force power and control over others: fear, intimidation, isolation, and ignorance. You'll note that Ruth and her friends were afraid of losing their jobs (fear). The unions were so adept at creating a culture of fear that no one wanted to talk openly about their aversion to the unions' takeover (isolation and intimidation), so they hunkered down, avoided talking about the issue and made themselves vulnerable to hearing only the unions' message (isolation and ignorance). The union leaders used those psychological manipulations to convince teachers their jobs would be on the line if they refused to surrender to union wishes.

Even though many of the teachers had huge reservations about the union, and Ruth was fighting for their liberty, since the culture of fear reigned, and the workers refused to engage in healthy debate, ignorance clouded their judgment, and the unions got their way. Once they've captured you through fear, intimidation, isolation, and ignorance, they take over.

Ruth was very put off by the idea of joining a union, but her friends said, "It has to be 100 percent membership." That made her mad, so Ruth continued talking to many other teachers. "I discovered there was a lot of resentment of the union just coming in and taking that money out of our salaries before we even saw our paychecks. If you said something, your job was less secure, so you just kept your mouth shut, which is not my way of living."

Ruth told me she had an intense desire to stand firm and not join. "I gave them a fit that first year and didn't join right away, but nobody wanted to talk about the union, so I couldn't get anyone to stand with me."

Pretty soon, the five men in black suits showed up in her classroom again and putting heavy pressure on Ruth intimidating her with their actions and presence. They came when she was alone again and just like the first time, they wouldn't take no for an answer. Ruth shared, "I was at the point I realized it's either lose my job or sign on their dotted line. I wish I'd have fought them. Maybe it would have helped others to stand up and fight." Even though this occurred over fifty years ago, Ruth choked back tears, "I'm sorry now that I have that on my record."

Ruth and I talked a little about our experiences with the sweet children we loved to teach and some of the frustrations we've experienced because of administrators who get emasculated or corrupted by bully unions. She shared from the heart and told me, "I still believe from the number of teachers I talked with in the Hershey school, if we would have gotten together, we could have done something to stop unions. But I just couldn't even get my good friends to speak up. They were too afraid. It's sad that we have unions in our schools. I don't think they have any interest in helping teachers or the children. *'We'll give you a lawyer free of charge'*—I think that's a sorry excuse for them being in the school, period."

State and national teachers' unions offend great teachers like Ruth who really love students and want to serve their communities because abusive unions don't represent our values. I'm sure you noted the way they forced Ruth and her friends to sign over the authorization for unions to garnish wages directly from their paychecks. Today they've managed to get the courts to enforce laws allowing them to work with school districts for union dues and fees collections. The taxpayer-funded school district employees provide the man-hours to arrange automatic paycheck deductions from unionized employees' checks. The district then hands the money over to the unions. Unions are tax-free 501(c) organizations, so they pay no taxes on the hundreds of millions in dues and fees they collect from workers, and taxpayers fund the collection of the dues.

You've gotta hand it to them; they've figured out a lucrative system. It's a cushy arrangement and works out nicely—if you're not the employee who'd rather be free from union harassment and misrepresentation.

Ironically, at that CTA leadership conference Charles and I attended in 2008, a highlighted seminar was "Bullying 101." In that seminar, we learned about the evils of bullying, how desperately we all needed to work to end the trend of student bullying on campus, and we learned about the union's pride in its high profile national programs to end bullying in schools. Ending student bullying is a noble goal, but it's hard for me to believe the union leadership really gives a care about stopping bullying.

Union leadership will likely attack me for this stance, but I ask them to explain this to the American people: if they're so benevolent and worried about student bullying, why on earth is bullying acceptable when the victims are innocent parents, teachers, and students who espouse different values than unions?

Given the way unions mistreat loving teachers like Ruth, the brave woman at the CTA conference, and the one they branded "Rotten Apple," I have to wonder if their "bullying" seminars are actually "how-to" classes: "how to" shut down caring teachers seeking answers from representatives; "how to" be brutal so you can be raised up into the highest state and national union positions; "how to" use fear and intimidation to scare the hell out of teachers and brand someone for life as a Rotten Apple.

CHAPTER 8

SeXXX EDUCATION—
TEACHERS' UNION
STYLE

"As I continued reading the Making Proud Choices! teachers'
manual, I felt sexually violated."

Yes, the teachers' unions are experts at bullying teachers who dare to question their agenda, and they've perfected the art of oppression for a very good reason: they have to keep us quiet, so they can use our good reputations and hard-earned money to push and fund their political strategies and sexual agenda without question. Most people are unaware that the teachers' unions use teacher dues without our knowledge or permission to fund a massive social and political agenda, but a few wise parents and teachers across the country are starting to catch on.

In 2013 a dear friend sent me a most shocking email message. She forwarded it from a young mother living in Northern California. The email's subject was: *The Latest Horror!*

The horror the young mother articulated was the fifth-grade sex education program at her eleven-year-old daughter's public school. She felt a strong desire to educate other parents on the scandalous lessons within the curriculum, and our mutual friend thought I could help her spread her message to a wider audience. She sent me a link to the teacher's manual for the entire eight-week Planned Parenthood-designed curriculum called *Making Proud Choices!* And I was shocked.

The first activity to which she alerted me was "The Condom Relay Races." In the lesson plan, the teacher is told to instruct the boys and girls on condom use and demonstrate the steps in using one. She's then directed to set up two anatomically correct, fully erect adult penis models and to put her classroom full of pre-teens into two lines.

She's told to make it a fun activity.

The two teams of children have to race—each child has to put a condom onto the penis the proper way and verbalize the steps involved in mixed company. The team who finishes first, wins.

My immediate reaction to this "fun" lesson? This is child abuse, and I would resign my position before being forced to teach this deplorable lesson to children. It's more suitable to a drunken fraternity party than a classroom full of vulnerable kids. I remember vividly what it was like to be eleven years old, and I've worked with eleven-year-old children for three decades. I can assert with authority that most eleven-year-olds forced to touch fully erect man-sized penis models and discuss condoms, penises, and sex would be profoundly traumatized.

The initial page of the teachers' manual would give a person the idea that the program simply focuses on preventing sexually transmitted diseases, AIDS, and unplanned pregnancies (which, by the way, is too much information for eleven-year-olds), but as soon as you turn the page, the overt sexual indoctrination of children begins.

Even the rules, which are to be posted throughout the eight weeks of lessons, are a form of indoctrination and could lead to the abuse of children. The second rule, "Don't Yuck My Yum (WOW)," states, "If someone feels the need to make a noise about a specific thing which may be a sexual activity we say, 'WOW.' We don't say, 'eww' because we don't want to say anything bad about something someone else likes. This would take away the safe space of the classroom and not everyone would feel comfortable sharing."

Safe space? Are they kidding? Never mind that almost every single word and activity the teacher must present is excruciatingly uncomfortable for the teacher and an assault on the innocence and privacy of every child in the room, and "Eww" is the only appropriate response.

As I continued reading the *Making Proud Choices!* teachers' manual, I felt sexually violated, and I had to repeatedly get up to pace the room because I was fuming that children and teachers are being abused with this sort of inappropriate curriculum. The lessons started out telling the eleven-year-olds: "Proud and responsible behavior includes protecting yourself by using a condom when you have sex. By sex, we mean vaginal, anal, or oral sex (VAO)."

Vaginal, Anal, and Oral sex (referred to casually as VAO) come up and was normalized in every single lesson, and in one lesson, in which they discuss a thirteen-minute "Hawaii Video," kids are taught to protect themselves during anal and oral sex by using a "dental dam." I had no idea what this meant, so I had to look it up. I was so shocked by what I saw in the search results, I couldn't bring myself to open any of the links, but I was able to understand enough to know dental dams (originally created to help dentists during oral surgery), are now being used between the mouth and anus or vagina during oral sex, and our school leaders feel this is appropriate information for eleven-year-olds. I'm thoroughly embarrassed to share this information with you, yet any day now a curriculum like this could show up in your child's school, and all children would learn it and teachers would be told to present it, so I feel duty-bound to educate you.

Imagine if you, as a parent, invited your child's teacher to your home for dinner, and the teacher showed up and you were having a marvelous time together. Then, during dessert, she started talking about VAO, dental dams, and overt sexual ideas, and then whipped out her fully erect penis model, put it on the table and said, "I have a fun idea! Let's have a condom relay race!"

I know this sounds ridiculous—because it is ridiculous! If a teacher behaved this way in your home, I imagine most of you would kick her out, report her to the authorities, work to remove her from the school, and prosecute until she was listed as a sex offender. So why is it suddenly okay for teachers to behave this way in the classroom with thirty vulnerable kids looking on and no parental protections? And why isn't it a violation of the constitutional rights of teachers when they're forced to turn a blind eye to this misguided form of child abuse?

Most people understand that childhood innocence is precious and needs to be cherished. But *Making Proud Choices!* and other union-promoted curriculums like it, indoctrinate children with a nonchalant attitude toward all sexual ideas at any age.

In one activity, "Tell it to Tanisha," an adolescent girl casually mentions having sex with a boy and that she's now considering having sex with a girl; her only concern being "that I might be infected with HIV." A thirteen-year-old boy considering having anal sex with his boyfriend is never advised to seek the counsel of his parents but rather is told, "Talk it over with your partner and use a condom." A twelve-year-old is advised to use a dental dam while having oral sex because, "That's the proud and responsible thing to do." Can you even imagine if your child or grandchild had to endure these lessons, and what about the health implications and affront on religious beliefs?

This was all so over the top, bizarre, and abusive I thought maybe it was limited to just one misguided school district in Northern California, that is until a mom reached out to me about a story of a very similar sex education program for sophomores at a high school in the suburbs north of Chicago, and a teacher friend sent me an entire website created by parents fighting the same sorts of lessons confronting children in Massachusetts. Then a teacher in my home district, Capistrano Unified called me in a panic. She told me she and her teacher colleagues were required to attend teacher trainings in February 2017 on a very similar sex education curriculum called *Teen Talk*.

From the moment this teacher contacted me, she was eager to share her story in protection of children and families, but a lawyer friend cautioned her. She said, "He advised me not to put my name out there given that I'm still a teacher within the district. He felt that I would be opening myself up to a very high potential to be hassled and/or axed. He cited a teacher in Florida who was dismissed just for writing a letter to the editor of her paper sharing personal opinions but stating she was a public school teacher."

The culture of fear strikes again.

Thankfully, she did allow me to share her story to enlighten all of you, but I've changed her name for her protection. Let's call her Stella.

Stella is an eighth-grade physical science teacher who generally teaches chemistry and physics, but suddenly she and the other seventh and eighth-grade science teachers in Capistrano Unified were told they were required to teach a new sex education program. Teachers attended the training in February 2017 and were told they had to begin teaching the content that May.

Stella shared, "Our training session was the first any of us knew about the new sex education program. In the front of the room there were various tools for sexual use. I remember seeing about sixteen birth control methods including an 'insertive condom' that can be used in the vagina or anus, government approved birth control methods we'd never even heard of or seen, and a large erect penis model.

Stella and her colleagues were told that to be in compliance with the law, they needed to teach all of the methods for birth control and safeguarding against communicable, sexually transmitted infections, and they had to use language that embraced all relationships. She said, "They told us the law says that we don't just tell the kids these tools are available, but we need to use 'age appropriate' lessons to instruct the children in their proper use. We were also told that we had to use the word 'partner.' We could not use 'he,' or 'she,' or 'boyfriend,' or 'girlfriend' any longer."

Stella continued, "There was also a big, pink rectangle of vinyl—maybe ten inches long—called a dental dam. Most of us didn't know what it was. The trainers explained that we would be teaching the kids that the dental dam is for use during oral sex and it is to be placed as a shield between the students' mouths and their partner's vulva, vagina, or anus. At that point, our mouths and jaws dropped on the floor. We knew right away we weren't going to be doing that. We were like, 'No, no, no!'"

Stella said, "We were all floored by the content in *Teen Talk*. It had really extreme and explicit sexual content and graphics, a lot of detailed discussion about intercourse, anal sex, oral sex, and really immature handling of it with games and activities that demonstrated sexual practices. You're using these inappropriate childish games to teach something that is far beyond age appropriate. This was not family life or teaching kids how their bodies were changing or what to expect with hormones. This was straight up training them to partake in various sexual acts."

Stella told me the most common response from teachers during and after the training was, "I cannot teach this stuff to my students," but most seemed too terrified to say anything for fear of losing their jobs. She told me, "They showed us pictures with actual lessons taking place with students putting condoms on fully erect adult male penis models. They had the penis models in their classrooms at different table groups, with girls and boys, seventh and eighth graders, twelve and thirteen-year-olds, in mixed company, and they were showing the photographs to show us what we should do in our classrooms with the kids."

Stella said that within the first ten minutes of the training, she asked to see the parent letter the district would send home to see how parents would be notified of the new curriculum, but the trainers had nothing to show her except a generic form. She told me, "We were saying, 'Oh my gosh. You've gotta be kidding me. This is not going to fly in our community. This is not what our students are ready for. We have children in our classrooms; this is not something their families are going to want.'"

Stella knew parents needed a warning about the extreme changes in the curriculum. She told me, "Parents are going to automatically assume their children are having the same instruction as their older siblings in the past, and then their kids will be exposed to this really extremely explosive curriculum, and not only are the kids going to be shocked and go through a kind of abusive curriculum, but their parents are going to be up in arms when the kids come home and share what we've done to them in class. Then we'll be dealing with the fallout."

Stella told me the *Teen Talk* presenters never answered her sincere questions, but they did explain that the new law has what Stella calls "a sneaky provision" in that the parents don't "opt in," they can only "opt out" of participation in the program. She told me, "When the letter goes home, and nothing comes back, then the children are automatically in the instruction, which is ridiculous because kids very often don't get letters home. How do we know if the parent got the letter? There was no way of assuring us that parents' wishes were being upheld."

The old union "opt out" trick.

Stella told me that once some parents found out about the curriculum, they put a lot of pressure on their schools and the district, and some parents were even told they could not view the curriculum. Stella said most could not view it; but once some got a hold of it, those parents came unglued. She told me, "Teachers couldn't sleep at night because they were so horrified. They started telling their neighbors about the curriculum and trying to gain support for removing it. A teacher I know was planning on taking an entire month off of school just to avoid teaching it."

Stella and her colleagues showed the curriculum to their administrator who Stella told me was, "super supportive of us. I remember the words, 'No, no, no. The kids cannot see this.'" Stella believes the administrators did what they could, but she doesn't know if it helped much because she said, "It's a very weird situation. They have their feelings against this stuff, but no one wants to be the one who steps forward. They all step backward and don't take a stand."

Stella told me that once parents got involved and teachers felt supported, the district started backtracking immediately, and Stella started researching the process. Stella said, "Fortunately, we have a woman, Dawn Urbanek, who attends every board meeting and posts her detailed notes on CUSDwatch.com,"[29] so Stella researched Dawn's notes and listened to the audio of the meeting on which the curriculum was approved. She told me, "The staff presented the sex curriculum to the school board saying a teacher review committee had gone over the curriculum and chose it, approved it, and recommended it to the board. And they said this curriculum also went in front of the district instructional review committee, which reviewed, approved, and recommended it." She said the school board approved it based on those reports, but no committees had ever reviewed the curriculum, and teachers were mortified and shocked by the adoption of the traumatizing curriculum. "Why wasn't anyone given a heads up?" Stella asked. "The whole thing was fishy."

Additionally, Stella told me, "To make it even more sneaky, they called it a 'pilot program,' and were able to dodge some of the legal requirements of a textbook adoption. In a pilot, only a few classrooms try out a curriculum, so you don't have to follow the entire instructional review process, which includes making the curriculum open to the public to review, publicize, and challenge before a textbook adoption."

Pilots are supposed to be used sparingly just to test the program for a short time, but Stella said, "We were told explicitly at the teacher training in February 2017 that this program was to be implemented district-wide in all of the middle schools by the end of the school year. That seemed very illegal without following the protocol."

Thanks to parents supporting the teachers, the detailed notes of community watchdog Dawn Urbanek, and vocal teachers like Stella, teachers were permitted to go through the curriculum page by page to see how they could modify it. Stella told me, "After the parents and teachers put on all of the pressure, the district agreed to keep the old curriculum for the 2017 school year, but this was completely contrary to the law. In order to do what was right for our community, we had to break the law."

Stella, her colleagues and their group of informed parents were able to keep *Teen Talk* away from the kids in our district in 2017, but the curriculum reappeared in 2018. Thankfully, more parents and grandparents have joined the fight, and as I write, we're forming committees and working with some school board members in hopes of protecting the children from the new curriculum, but we're told the ACLU is putting pressure on districts that try to avoid these curriculums.

During all of this, more horrifying information came my way through another teacher, and union member, who's served children in America's public schools for over twenty years. Let's call her "Priscilla" in protection of her identity.

In addition to teaching, Priscilla also serves as a school board member. As part of her due diligence as a trustee tasked with voting on the selection of a new sex education curriculum that's compliant with the new California laws, she asked the publisher of *Teen Talk* for information on other districts already using their curriculum and for respected organizations that support *Teen Talk's* contents. They sent Priscilla their list of seventy-two districts and twelve independent schools or charters across the state of California that are already being trained in or using the *Teen Talk* curriculum. They also informed her, "The ACLU is a big supporter of our curriculum because it is one of only a few that meet the California Ed Code mandate." According to Priscilla, another curriculum that meets the mandate is APEX, which is an online health class currently being used in fifty-three districts in California.

Priscilla told me according to the law all students are required to take part in sexual orientation/gender identity lessons, and according to current interpretations of the law, parents cannot opt out of these lessons. She told me, "In my district nearly 1,700 ninth graders have completed the 'gender identity / sexual orientation' pilot of the APEX online curriculum, which is imbedded into the new health requirements for graduation because of the new California Healthy Youth Act. In the course, gender identity is defined as a 'continuum'—it's the way a person 'feels' about their gender, regardless of biological sex. Transgenderism is introduced. Concerning sexual orientation, students are taught they can either be heterosexual, bisexual, homosexual, pansexual, asexual, or questioning. Pansexual is defined as attracted to many different genders."

Using data from the CDC, Red Cross, FDA, and HIV.gov, Priscilla has been challenging these curriculums because while teaching risky sexual behaviors, they are withholding vital information that would protect students from contracting or transmitting HIV. She told me, "The law says its purpose is to provide pupils with the knowledge and skills necessary to protect their sexual and reproductive health from HIV. However, given the critical knowledge they are *withholding* from students, it seems the real purpose is to promote various sexual orientations."

So why do we have laws that force teachers to instruct students in dangerous and abusive sex education curriculums their parents abhor? Once again, we can thank the state and national teachers' unions and their political allies who push something called "Comprehensive Sexual Education" (CSE) including intense indoctrination in gender identity, gender expression, and sexual orientation.

According to the NEA Resolutions number "B-53. Sex Education," in the 2016–2017 NEA Resolutions document, "The National Education Association believes that the developing child's sexuality is continually and inevitably influenced by daily contacts, including experiences in the school environment…that the public school must assume an increasingly important role in providing the instruction. Teachers and health professionals must be qualified to teach in this area and must be *legally protected from censorship and lawsuits.…* The Association also believes that to facilitate the realization of human potential, it is the right of every individual to live in an environment of freely available information and knowledge about sexuality.… Such programs should include information on…b. Diversity of culture and diversity of sexual orientation and gender identity; c. Sexually transmitted diseases including HIV and HPV, incest, sexual abuse, sexual harassment, and homophobia; d. Age-appropriate, medically accurate information including lesbian, gay, bisexual, transgender, and questioning (LGBTQ) issues. This should include but not be limited to information on sexuality, sexual orientation, and gender expression."

The trouble is, the unions' idea of "age-appropriate" and "medically accurate" are far removed from the understanding, professional expertise, scientific evidence, and deeply held beliefs of most teachers and parents. Under the guise of protecting LGBT students from bullying, the unions and their allies sneak in these curriculums that in turn bully mass amounts of children, teachers, and parents into accepting and participating in activities and ideas that are an attack on their personal, religious, safety, and privacy rights.

Look, bullying comes in all shapes and sizes. I've been in the classroom for a long time, and I've seen all different forms of bullying on school campuses. Kids bully others about weight, glasses, braces, birthmarks, freckles, long toes, ear size, nose shape, and so much more. It doesn't matter the topic, the pain is visceral and deep because the victim gets isolated and the bully terrorizes and dominates him—mocking and rejecting the victim until he feels hopeless and too powerless to stand. Mean girls called me "ski slope nose" and chased me home from school threatening to beat me up every single day for months when I was in fifth grade, and the teachers' union has been bullying and isolating me for over three decades, so believe me, I understand bullying.

As a school board trustee and teacher, Priscilla wants to understand our union's efforts and learn more about education laws and their impact on teachers and kids, so she and some of her colleagues regularly attend teachers' union conferences, youth conferences, and other union-sponsored events.

Priscilla told me, "During a CTA 'Equity and Human Rights Conference' in 2016, I attended a workshop titled, 'We Must Engage Charter Schools.' A CTA legislative advocate (a union lobbyist) was the presenter." In a sincere desire to properly follow her legal responsibilities under the new California Healthy Youth Act and to more fully understand CTA's stance, after the presentation, Priscilla detailed the following classroom situation to the CTA lobbyist:

"I used to teach high school. I had a transgender student, gay students, and students of faith in my classes. In the context of a class discussion a Mormon student expressed his personal beliefs about marriage being between a man and woman. He shared his views respectfully." She then asked the presenter the following question: "As a teacher, how do you think I should have handled that situation in order to respect the diversity of all of my students?"

The CTA lobbyist replied, "You should treat that student as though he said, 'Black people should be burned at the stake.'"

Priscilla was stunned. She already knew the constitutionally protected religious rights of students were under serious threat in our public schools, but now she knew her union dues were funding the attacks.

In an effort to make certain this was truly the stance of the CTA, she and two friends attended a CTA LGBT Conference in 2017 and joined a workshop titled "Creating a Safe Place—Legal Obligation" led by the LGBT CTA caucus chairman. Priscilla recounted her story to this union leader, and he affirmed that his colleague was right to say the Mormon student should have been treated as though he had said, "Black people should be burned at the stake."

The man's words brought chills to her spine, and she told me, "The LGBT caucus chair is also the teacher advocate for our entire state, so how are California teachers going to be represented if they don't agree with union ideology? And how will students be protected from the prejudice that brings with it accusations of hate speech and the unfair consequences that follow?"

My boys and their friends have suffered horrendous attacks on their free speech rights throughout high school and college and have been disparaged for being white male Christians. Beginning in middle school and through college, Ben's science teachers told him, "Your Christian faith is a fairy-tale." One of Ben's teachers even harassed him in front of the class because his political science tests revealed his conservative values. Priscilla told me, "Secondary education kids I'm talking to say they are terrified to say what they believe. They say it's 'social suicide.' One young man stated in a class conversation that he believed that according to his religion marriage is between a man and a woman. Later he got text messages from kids saying, 'You're a hater. Why don't you just kill yourself now?'"

NEA's 2017 New Business Item (NBI) 30 states: "In partnership with the Southern Poverty Law Center, NAACP, ACLU, GLSEN [Gay Lesbian Straight Education Alliance], National Center for Trans-Equality Human Rights Campaign, and any other legal and human rights groups of related concerns, NEA will track incidents of discrimination, racism, homophobia, and transphobia, as well as anti-Semitism, Islamophobia, and all other forms of religious discrimination, and bigotry in our public schools. The data will be shared with districts to educate and eradicate hate through the development of programs that include, but are not limited to, training on unconscious bias, culturally responsive instruction, and the anti-defamation league."[30]

You may recall in 2017 (shortly after this NBI was passed), The Southern Poverty Law Center released its "Hate Map" of 917 organizations it claims are hateful. Many of them are groups with Judeo-Christian values simply living out their deeply held beliefs and defending the constitutional rights of religious persons. They're categorized on the "Hate Map" by headings such as "Christian Identity," "Radical Traditional Catholicism," and "Anti-LGBT," to name a few,[31] and the teachers' unions are "in partnership" with these folks.

Dr. Linda Gonzales, an education expert who's taught elementary, middle, and high school, has served as a principal, a superintendent, director of state and federal projects, and has served fifteen years as a school turnaround specialist. She has personally witnessed the way teachers' unions are living out these resolutions and can corroborate Priscilla's testimony. She was with Priscilla when both CTA leaders stated the student of faith should be treated as a violent hater, as though he had said something equivalent to "Black people should be burned at the stake."

Dr. Gonzales told me, "I believe we can practice tolerance and debate issues and beliefs without mocking, insulting, disparaging, or offending one another. What I found difficult about the CTA position is that it disparages and disrespects divergent ideas by mocking, insulting, and dismissing the speakers of different persuasions, especially Christians, with labels such as 'Hate Speech.' My takeaway is that the First Amendment, in their view, applies only to sanitized ideas and beliefs. In my view, this is anti-American and not aligned to the Constitution. I value open debate and religious freedom."

The unions, as usual, are complicating matters because their real motives are not to combat the bullying of all students; instead, their motivations are to push their social and political agenda onto every single child, parent, and educator in every single school across America, so they can fundamentally change our culture. It's obvious because unions initiate, condone, and promote bullying when the victims are teachers, parents, students, or Christians who dare to question the union agenda. Once again, they're intruding on the Education Triangle here and trampling on the constitutional and human rights of millions.

Aunt Julane already gave us instruction on how to combat bullying in all forms: "Be kind." The way to protect vulnerable groups—like all children, LGBT individuals, women, minorities, Christians, the poor, *every human being*, is to teach kindness and provide opportunities for people to practice kindness by putting others ahead of themselves.

Good teachers already know this. If we have great administrators backing us up, and strong discipline policies on campus buoyed by constant examples of kindness, bullying issues are nipped in the bud. As teachers, we're legally charged with protecting children from physical and sexual abuse, and any teacher worth his weight knows the protection of children is our number one responsibility. Any teacher who doesn't know intrinsically to protect children at all costs doesn't deserve to be called a teacher and should immediately be fired…but of course, the unions protect teachers who push their social and political agenda—union activism and tenure rule.

CHAPTER 9

SOCIAL, SEXUAL, AND POLITICAL WARZONES

"Teachers like me are trying to protect the kids, but they call us racists, bigots, haters, and homophobes. I want people to hear and see firsthand that the teachers' union leaders see anyone who does not agree with their ideology as Ku Klux Klan's and Nazis."

The NEA Representative Assembly (RA) is the governing body of the teachers' union that creates NEA New Business Items and Resolutions. Though the unions claim all teachers have a voice in NEA policy decisions (like the Sex Education resolution), I didn't even realize the NEA RA existed (even after serving as a local union leader) until I met several teachers across the country who've been abused and silenced serving as teacher delegates to the NEA RA. They taught me about the politics of the NEA, and I finally understood why my colleagues, students, their parents, and I are constantly thrown into a social, sexual, and political warzone.

The NEA claims its RA is the "world's largest democratic deliberative body," and that its "delegates debate the vital issues that impact American public education and set Association policy and activities."[32] Jeralee Smith, a former teacher delegate, told me the NEA RA annual convention is massive and organized a lot like a political convention. There are great big state signs, and you sit with your state.

Their claims of democracy all sound good, but I discovered from the testimonies of Jeralee, Diane Lenning, Judy Bruns, Sue Halvorson, Ruth

Boyatt, and several other teachers serving as delegates that true to the deceitful roots of most union messaging, the union's definitions of "democratic," "deliberative," and "debate" are far removed from the ideas of fairness, respectful discussion, and compromise most Americans would attach to those three words. According to those teachers, the NEA's claim of being the world's largest democratic deliberative body is a total sham, and the reason inappropriate sex education curriculums are entering our schools is that the NEA RA operates more like a political action committee for the Democratic party's social agenda than a teachers' association, and when teachers object, they get squashed.

During her first NEA RA meeting, Jeralee stepped up to the microphone to speak to a crowd of over eight thousand delegates, and thirty-three television screens transmitted her face throughout the hall. All she wanted was to teach, and she really had no desire to fight a political battle, but she loved her students so much she spoke out for more balance and wholesome values in school curriculum. Teachers like Jeralee, her friends, and me are terrified to speak out at massive union meetings, but since the unions' sexual agenda is pushed onto students as young as five, and the teachers and parents we know are outraged, Jeralee put herself out there and asked for consideration of the needs, privacy, and safety of all children, respect for teacher rights, and honor for the authority of parents. She would have much rather kept her private business to herself, but in an attempt to protect children, Jeralee shared her personal story of her own struggle with sexual issues. But the NEA RA harshly rejected Jeralee's plea.

Jeralee told me, "I made it personal. Even though there were a lot of people who were supportive in a silent way, they didn't want to hear anything; they just wanted us to shut up and go away. They blackballed me because I was an ex-gay. I was never electable again after that."

Why would a teachers' union care if Jeralee is an ex-gay? Isn't that her personal prerogative? And why was she blackballed when the union claims to be democratic, tolerant, anti-bullying, and protectors of the vulnerable? Jeralee and her friends decided to start an Ex-Gay Educators' Caucus because the union bullies ex-gays. They wanted to make the voices of ex-gay students and teachers heard. They've been working hard for years to provide verified medically accurate information and empathy for ex-gays and all children, but at the 2017 NEA RA, to silence Jeralee and her friends even more, New Business Item 86 was presented and "adopted as modified."

It reads: "For the 2018 RA, NEA will thoroughly review and evaluate RA exhibitors' materials for information that is offensive, obscene, or in bad taste. Based on the findings of the review the NEA will enforce its standing rules 12.B (b) and 12.B (d) as they relate to exhibitors found in violation of the aforementioned rules. Because of concerns brought by 2017 RA delegates, special scrutiny will be made to the following exhibitors:

1. NEA Ex-Gay Educators

2. Creation Truth Outreach

3. Creation Science Educators[33]

It's troubling, but according to multiple teachers I've interviewed, ex-gays and Christians who ask for respect, student safety, parental authority, and balance in the curriculum presented in America's schools, are singled out and bullied regularly at NEA RA meetings.

Sue Halvorson and her friend once attended an NEA RA preconference talk called, "The Rise of the Religious Right: The Implications for Democracy." Her friend told me, "They started characterizing us Christians with inflammatory rhetoric. They described us as 'those people think they have the divine spark.' They said the religious right was so intolerant, have an intolerant spirit, a willingness to condemn everyone, have no regard for true diversity. [They said] we're dangerous; we're causing this crisis in democracy."

Two dear teachers from Washington, Barb Amidon (also a middle and high school counselor) and Cindy Omlin, told me they attended several Washington Education Association conferences, and at one of those conferences, they discovered a document and class called, "What's Left after the Right." Barb shared, "It was a workshop against 'right-winged conspiracy' nuts. Apparently, I'm one of them."

Sue Halvorson also dared to ask for balance in the sex curriculum in protection of children. As a result, she was blackballed from serving on sex education-related committees, so she and her friends spent personal time and money reproducing verified medically accurate information and educationally sound materials to share with teachers at the NEA RA. Since their values and ideas don't fit the narrow sexual agenda of the NEA, Sue and another friend (who can't share her name in protection of her colleagues) are brutally attacked every year at the booth they set up to share their information providing a balanced perspective. Her friend told me, "We were passing out pamphlets and there were delegates who actually crumbled up our pamphlets and threw them in our faces and told us, 'There's a special place in hell for people like you.'"

The majority of teachers have no idea our state and national unions are involved in pushing a politically-charged social and sexual agenda. Many run to the unions for protection from these issues with no idea their unions are the proverbial 'fox in the hen house.' Most believe the teachers' unions gather to improve workplace serenity and teacher pay, so most will be shocked to discover many of the topics dominating discussions at the NEA RA. To give you a brief look at the kind of efforts the NEA believes are in the best interests of teachers and kids, here are highlights of some of the 159 New Business Items (NBI) and Resolutions acted upon at the 2017 NEA RA convention.[34]

- NBI 1 asserts the NEA will provide on its website, "an ongoing updated list of companies and organizations that the NEA is boycotting."

- NBI 18 articulates NEA's refusal to cooperate with ICE (Immigration and Customs Enforcement).

- NBI 49 calls for homosexual advocacy in schools using materials from GLSEN (Gay Lesbian Straight Education Network).

- NBI 62 states, "The NEA will publicize our opposition to the travel ban imposed by the current presidential administration, and will join with other organizations in actions to defeat it."

- NBI 55 focuses on a "Gender-Inclusive Schools Toolkit" for use in affirmation of gender diversity.

- NBI 94 asserts, "The NEA supports sanctuary cities and schools and opposes any attacks and attempts to penalize and prohibit such sanctuaries…NEA members and local associations will take an active role in helping to create and defend sanctuary efforts."

- New Resolution C was to be amended by adding: "The National Education Association believes that all transgender students should be able to use the bathroom or locker room of their choice."

- Amendment 8 added to the NEA's "yellow book," "The association encourages its affiliates to educate members about the ways race privileges certain people."[35]

And Amendment 19 is so unbelievable, I'll share it in full or you likely will not believe it. The words that are struck out are those the NEA wants to remove from the long-held definition of the scientific method. The underscored words are those the NEA wants to use to change the scientific method.

> *Amend by deletion and addition on page 8, lines 40–43 of the yellow book: The National Education Association believes that the content in science education must be based on* ~~empirical evidence derived from valid scientific experimentation. Science, although inquiry-based, is verified through repetitive experimentation using the steps of the scientific process.~~ *scientific theory that incorporates empirically collected evidence, scientific methodology, and other accepted scientific processes. This entire process leads towards scientific consensus.*"[36]

So, the teachers' unions, which claim to support teachers in our efforts to present truth and "medically accurate" information in our schools, overtly abuse teacher leaders who (in protection of children and families) produce scientifically proven medical facts. Then, using money they claim educators are paying them for "representation," they are attempting to obliterate the scientific method while validating *opinions* as facts. They're heavily funding highly controversial political battles, attacks on teachers and kids with Judeo-Christian values, bullying ex-gays, and working overtime to bring sexually inappropriate lessons into our classrooms against the wishes and deeply held beliefs of parents and teachers.

Why the heck is a *labor* union allowed to do any of these things to our teachers, against our families, and in our schools? Why the heck does a *labor* union have so much power over *educational* laws and school curriculum?

Thanks to union interference and collaboration with many other groups that undermine parental rights continually in our schools, "The California Healthy Youth Act" requires schools to provide "comprehensive sexual health education" (CSE) for pupils in grades 7–12. Now that we're aware of the abuse and silencing suffered by loving teachers desperately trying to protect children from this law and the ideology behind it, it's easier to comprehend why every single curriculum I've seen under this new law is an attack on religious rights, parental rights, and childhood innocence.

Several things are worthy of note when reading the "California Healthy Youth Act." First, it asserts that parents "overwhelmingly support" comprehensive sexual education. I don't recall filling out that survey, but the culture of fear controls objectors by making them feel they're the only ones who aren't on board—*isolation*. I have news for them. Millions of parents are outraged!

Second, instruction using "medically accurate" curriculum in schools is required, and if teachers choose not to teach it, "experts" will be brought in to present the information.

Third, the law states:

SEC. 14. Section 51938 of the Education Code is amended to read:

51938.(a) … A school district shall not require active parental consent ("opt-in") for comprehensive sexual health education and HIV prevention education.[37]

Even if a school district wants to warn parents and proactively protect children from sexually explosive topics, they are not permitted to do so.

Finally, as Priscilla pointed out earlier, according to many experts interpreting the law to school districts, parents may not opt out of (or protect their children from) the following topics if they're presented outside of the sex education classroom during other times throughout the school day or year.

SEC. 4. Section 51932 of the Education Code is amended to read:

51932. (b) This chapter does not apply to instruction, materials, presentations, or programming that discuss gender, gender identity, gender expression, sexual orientation, discrimination, harassment, bullying, intimidation, relationships, or family and do not discuss human reproductive organs and their functions.

It's the old opt-out trick again: teachers' unions and their allies controlling people using confusion, isolation and ignorance.[38] [39]

A teacher in Rocklin, California read a book to her kindergarten students that taught them about transgenderism. A child in the class wanted to change from a boy to a girl, so the teacher read the book, and then the boy went into the bathroom and changed his clothes and emerged a girl. The children were told they had to now refer to the child by her new feminine name. Because this was a lesson on gender identity, parents were not even notified, even though many children were traumatized, confused and frightened because of the lesson. A huge controversy ensued with parents simply asking for parental rights and authority, but they ran head on into activists pushing their agenda into schools at the expense of innocent kids.

Citing California law, the school district stood by its decision to allow these sorts of lessons at any age level, even though parents begged them to protect their children.

The teacher who taught the lesson was awarded Teacher of the Year.

The "Healthy Youth Act" was sponsored by the ACLU of California; California Latinas for Reproductive Justice; Forward Together, whose mission statement reads: "A multi-racial organization that works together with community leaders and organizations to transform culture and policy to catalyze social change"; Equality California; and Planned Parenthood Affiliates of California.[40]

The coalition of supporters included the California School Boards Association, the California Teachers' Association, and the California State PTA.[41]

Why is the legislature heeding the advice of highly controversial, one-sided groups like Planned Parenthood, ACLU, and CTA, and allowing controversial and inappropriate sex education curriculums to be snuck into kids' minds without active parental ("opt-in") consent? Why are families prohibited from opting out of gender identity lessons, why are caring parents ignored, why are concerned teachers bullied, and why did the PTA, a group charged with speaking up for parental rights and the protection of children, agree to such an attack on parental rights and child safety? You'll discover the answer to my last question in a later chapter.

Educators like Priscilla, Stella, Judy, Jeralee, Sue, Diane, Dr. Gonzales, and I grieve over the way the teachers' unions have silenced us, undermined parental authority, and left children vulnerable to abuse. Priscilla articulates our feelings best: "Teachers like me are trying to protect the kids, but they call us racists, bigots, haters, and homophobes. I want people to hear and see firsthand that the teachers' union leaders see anyone who does not agree with their ideology as Ku Klux Klan's and Nazis."

With passion, Priscilla continued, "Our union has betrayed the sacred trust of teachers, families, and parents. These laws cause youth to question their faith, and to harshly bully each other, even suggesting suicide. And the CTA has endorsed all these laws and has even written many of them."

Priscilla has a message for all of us, "I've met a lot of LGBT people throughout my research, and they've become my friends. They're just people who want to be loved like the rest of us. But CTA leadership has gone too far. Instead of truly protecting students from bullying, thanks to union behavior and ideology, the bullying is increasing. We're just changing who's in the closet."

CHAPTER 10

WHAT THE HECK?

"We're inclusive, inclusive, inclusive...'That's a bald-faced lie!'"

Whenever I ate my lunch in the teachers' lounge, the new teachers in my school dominated our conversation by sharing their extreme discomfort with sexual topics pushed upon them during their Beginning Teacher Support and Assessment (BTSA) training classes. The teachers were so traumatized by the BTSA trainings (that they were required to attend) they shared their shocking experiences every single day. They informed us they were being told how to think about sexual identity issues and sexual acts. They were expressly told they were intolerant if they didn't agree with and accept the LGBT agenda and lifestyle without question, and when they tried to express their own beliefs, they were immediately shut down and treated as bigots. Every one of them had a sick look on her face, and each one expressed outrage at the topics and attitudes imposed upon them. They couldn't figure out why in the world elementary school teachers should have to be bullied and indoctrinated during beginning teacher workshops, and neither could I until I met the women serving in the NEA RA.

During the time these teachers were sharing their distressing experiences, I was learning more about *Making Proud Choices!* I read the lesson on birth control in the teachers' manual. After scaring the kids to death with lessons on every STD known to man, hands-on games with fully erect man-sized penises, and nonchalant talk about anal sex, the producers of *Making Proud Choices!* made sure the kids knew they could take part in this high-risk behavior with no real consequences by obtaining free birth control and abortions (at age twelve) without their parents' knowledge or consent. Here's their advice:

> *So just to let you know all these methods are available to you confidentially and for free once you reach the age of 12. This means that you can access these services and no one will find out. Not your parents or teachers. Even if your parent(s) call the clinic, they can not [sic] tell them you were there or received any services. It's against the law for doctors, hospitals or clinics to tell your parents. There are many youth clinics that offer all of these services to young people. This includes any reproductive health services you may need; including information on pregnancy options."*

What the heck? I was knocked off my feet again. It's now against the law for parents to "opt in" to protect their own children from sexually explicit lessons, or even support them with decisions like abortion, and doctors are no longer permitted to protect children either.

I knew my teachers' union used Charles's and my money to lobby for these laws and placed in office the foolish politicians who passed them, and I was infuriated. The health risks alone are enough reason to hold these reckless people accountable for placing kids in serious danger. Two of the things that make a woman a candidate for cervical cancer are sex before the age of eighteen and multiple sex partners, so presenting sexual acts as some casual, no big deal, natural part of growing up, can set girls up for cancer, infertility, and early death. What sort of doctor, who lives by the Hippocratic Oath of ethical standards beginning with "Do no harm," would feel good about allowing children to blindly walk into high-risk, life-threatening behaviors without the knowledge and support of their parents? I have to wonder how many fantastic doctors this law frustrates.

My friends serving in the NEA Representative Assembly have been speaking out for decades for balance in the curriculum, safety for children, and for parental and teacher rights. As you know, they produced verified medically accurate information in protection of children, but truth was shut down. My teacher friends have been abused every single time they've spoken out on behalf of childhood innocence.

One of those teachers, Diane Lenning, told me what I already suspected. "The NEA is the right arm of the Democrat Party, and I believe this because I've observed it to be." Just like my experience, Diane and her friends always knew what was coming in the Democrats' political landscape and discourse. Diane told me, "The teachers' union is writing the talking points for the Democrat Party. We heard everything first in the NEA Representative Assembly and thereafter we knew it was coming out in the political forms of Democrats controlled by the union. The NEA is their Petri dish."

I wasn't surprised, but I was mad. I thought about the thousands of dollars the unions were garnishing from my paychecks and from Charles's, of all of the times the unions sent us their magazines full of voter's guides and campaign rhetoric that was all against our values, our desires, and our strongly held beliefs as experienced educators, loving parents, and Christians. And I thought of all of the ways they've abused us and our outstanding teacher colleagues, students, and their parents over the years.

I was so dumbfounded I had to let the information sit with me for a while, and I thought:

The unions' political agenda backed for decades by teachers forced to fund them.

The unions' political agenda runs roughshod over the innocence of childhood.

The unions' political agenda stands against the will of parents who wish to protect their children from sexually provocative ideas and information.

The unions' political agenda robs American citizens of the rights to freedom of thought, expression, and conviction.

The unions' political agenda is forced at all costs—rights, privacy, and safety of others be damned.

Then the irony hit me: the very organization charged with protecting our academic freedom was using our compulsory fees to force us to teach an agenda utterly anathema to us, to sneak their social agenda in through the back door disguised as bullying prevention, to coerce us into teaching things we knew were harmful to children, to gag and manipulate our students and their parents, to persecute our fellow citizens with despotic mandates and oppressive "safe zones," and to bring about a judgmental atmosphere that feels more like a police state than a free Republic.

I want to be really clear about the personal agenda of the union leadership. I have no objections to individual folks pursuing their political and social agendas legally and peacefully; they should do what they believe is right in their hearts. But they have no right to use teachers—against our wills and behind our backs—to fund their politics and provide them unfettered access to our students, schools, and our trusted profession for their political and social gain. And they certainly have no right to persecute us for disagreeing with their underhanded exploitation of teachers and kids.

It's ironic to fathom that teachers standing up for our students and profession are the ones being attacked as intolerant and hateful by a group that's been forcing a thousand bucks out of our pockets each year and beating us up for disagreeing with them.

Sue Halvorson sat in a committee meeting about sexual issues at the NEA RA and she told me the co-chair kept repeating how "tolerant, tolerant, tolerant" they were. Sue shared, "She kept saying, 'We're inclusive, inclusive, inclusive'—like ten times at least." And Sue told me she thought to herself, "That's a bald-faced lie!"

After the meeting Sue went up to the "tolerant" co-chair, and she told the woman, "You know, you kept saying how inclusive, inclusive, inclusive, you are." Then Sue looked right in her eyes and said, "I don't believe you."

She let that sit with the woman for a while, and then reminded her of all of the times her "tolerant" group had come by Sue's booth to harass her and her friends, to throw things at them, to tell them they belonged in hell, to treat them with utter disdain and disrespect for simply having a different opinion, and all the times they'd booed Sue's friends off the stage, blocked their passage down a row in the assembly, or shouted at them to sit down while voting their conscience during standing votes, and then Sue told her, "No, you're really not inclusive."

Sue's right. The union is not inclusive or tolerant of anyone who dares to question union-think. Unions have co-opted the teaching profession for their own gain. They highlight and empower union activists who have no qualms about instructing children in intrusive, inappropriate sex education curriculums and who are flat-out vindictive toward genuinely loving teachers and parents who disagree with them. They totally ignore the many passionate and caring teachers—whether homosexual or heterosexual—who would never bring harm to children with such abusive curriculums, ever. The teachers' union activists are giving the entire world the idea that all teachers agree with their divisive rhetoric and sexualized agenda aimed at children, yet most teachers are offended by it and just want to educate and protect children.

Sweet Nicole is one of those vulnerable children who's been abused over and over by the unions and their allies; you'll learn more about the unions' devastating impact on her education in a later chapter, but they've damaged her with their sex education curriculums too. About a year after that mom sent me the *Making Proud Choices!* teachers' manual, Nicole approached me as soon as I walked in the door of a family gathering. She had a lost look on her face, and her body language told me she was feeling stressed. She took me aside and said, "Rebecca, my teacher made me learn some sex stuff, and it was *disgusting*." Nicole was eleven at the time, and I could tell she was not only looking to me to empathize with her disgust but to somehow protect her; after all, that's what teachers do. How could I tell her that it was *my* union that had put her in that disgusting situation? How could I face her and say, "Sorry, Sweetie, I can't protect you because I can't even protect myself"?

I could relate to Nicole's uncomfortable feelings too because I have graphic memories of the day the "experts" first came to visit my ninth-grade health class. Our teacher sat to the side, and the sex expert took over. She talked to us—in mixed company—about all sorts of sex acts, and then she gave a demonstration about condoms. My friends and I felt painfully uncomfortable the entire time the sex lady was in our room because she was crass and treated a sacred gift like it was something cheap and blasé. At the end of her lesson, she passed out free condoms to every single one of us, and it was so awkward. I'm not foolish; I knew some kids were having sex but bringing this lesson into our health class felt like indoctrination, and even as a teenager, I knew my parents and our family values were being undermined by my school.

It just so happened that our lunch break was after my health class, so all of the kids headed to the commons area. I was so glad the inappropriate sex lady was gone, and we didn't have to feel uncomfortable any longer, and then my friends and I walked into the commons. The boys, from every ninth-grade health class, had taken their condoms, blown them up like balloons, and they were passing them above all of our heads like volleyballs all over the commons area. I don't recall how the adults dealt with the disruption—some of them probably laughed—but as young girls walking through a commons area with hundreds of condoms flying over our heads with boys and men all over the place, we were agonizingly mortified. We girls were dealing with the trauma and awkwardness of the inappropriate sex lesson through silence and escape; the boys were coping by making a joke out of the situation. Either way, we'd all been hurt and exploited.

I remember that sex lady telling us some stuff that gave us kids the right to sneak around behind our parents' backs to obtain birth control, and I knew that was wrong. I wasn't even old enough to get a driver's permit, and my parents had to give me permission to go on a field trip, but this lady was telling me I could run around having sex with a bunch of boys and no one should care. It was bizarre.

While I was writing this very chapter, I received a phone call from Nicole's mom, Kim. Nicole was in ninth grade at the time, and that's when our union leaders and their favored state politicians decided kids should get another round of inappropriate sexual education. This time Kim was informed, so she was looking for the "opt-out" paperwork. I told her she had the right to request to see the curriculum, so she went down to the school and spent two hours looking over the three-inch teacher manual binder. She told me she wished they would have allowed her to view the curriculum in a private location instead of the school office because the contents were so disturbing Kim felt deeply embarrassed to be reading them while others walked in and out of the lobby. The curriculum is called "Sexual Health Education for America's Youth: for High School and Community Settings." California health and education offices approved it in collaboration with the Federal Offices of Adolescent Health, so don't think you're safe if you live outside of California.

Kim told me the lessons were intensely pushing the gay and lesbian lifestyle throughout the entire curriculum—not informing but indoctrinating and aggressively promoting. Kim said they continuously pushed messages like, "You don't know if you're a homosexual until you try. Don't be closed off to it," and suggesting that kids try it out. Every single example of student scenarios was disturbingly similar to the "Tell it to Tanisha" letters in *Making Proud Choices!* In fact, Kim said out of twelve scenarios, one-third were examples of boy-with-boy homosexual sex, one-third were girl-with-girl lesbian sex, and one-third were representative of out-of-wedlock heterosexual sex. None of the scenarios Kim saw in two hours of reading mentioned kids talking to their parents about these ideas even though the parent letter made it seem like kids would be constantly encouraged to talk to parents.

This was deeply disturbing for Kim. Her reaction was visceral and resembled the way she would feel if someone were going to physically harm her child. She reacted instinctively and felt a strong need to protect Nicole. She was sickened that her parental right to protect her child from harm had been trampled.

Kim said the school letter also made it sound like kids would learn a lot about abstinence, but that was a deception too. She said she saw only one sentence throughout her entire two-hour reading session that mentioned abstinence. The section on abortion and the morning after pill was huge, and Kim said they talk to children about the morning after pill as if it's "no big deal saying it's a 100 percent viable option," and she said they talk about pregnancy as if it's something horrible and inconvenient. Kim said they even insinuated pregnancy makes girls fat.

The portion on adoption was miniscule and more like an afterthought. Kim told me, "There was an entire section on all of the teen health centers available to kids without parent knowledge or approval, so every single kid is taught where they are, how to get there, and how to obtain help paying for the services without their parents' knowledge." You'll recall they can obtain these services at age twelve.

The downloadable materials for parental and teacher review were on a site called positivepreventionplus.com, but when Kim and I downloaded them, they were a highly redacted version of what she saw in the huge binder, and they included only the few things that were less offensive to parents, so those reading the downloaded information would have no idea what's really in this curriculum.

I couldn't shake the thought that if someone talked to our kids about these subjects in a public park, the person would be arrested and labeled a pervert. Why is it acceptable to bring these mishandled, age-inappropriate lessons into our classrooms as if they're suddenly safe because they've been approved and mandated by some politicians, ideological political groups, and union leaders with serious boundary issues?

I asked Nicole if she could remember how she felt when the sex lessons were pushed onto her and her classmates in fifth grade, and she told me, "I was disturbed. I felt scared, confused, and weirded out, and I thought during the lessons, 'Thanks a lot for the inappropriate information; I'm a kid!'" Her feeling of being violated and the look of robbed innocence on her face stuck with me in my gut and haunts me to this day.

I had already decided, if forced to teach it, I would resign, but who would protect my students from the lessons if I left? I know the natural response for all of us is horror for the kids who have to learn this stuff—that's a given. But I'd like you to consider the horror of the teachers who are faced with presenting this abuse to the children. This isn't just a disagreement about best practices for math or reading instruction, this is borderline criminal behavior, but teachers are being forced to do it or to look the other way while "experts" abuse their students.

Many times over the years my teacher friends and I have been horrified by rumors of these sex education curriculums and asked each other while rolling our eyes, "Where are all of these crazy ideas coming from?"

Well, teachers, after three decades in the dark about the origin of these intrusive ideas, we finally understand how the agenda is being financed and pushed into our schools and onto our country. We're all paying for it behind our own backs through our union dues.

Teachers' unions are using teachers who abhor these inappropriate curriculums to fund and promote something that is not only against our conscience, but in our professional opinion, is harmful to the students we labor to protect. The number one responsibility of teachers is to protect children, and that's the number one concern of parents too. We're mandated reporters of child abuse, but our union-controlled legislature has created laws that force us to allow the sexual abuse of children, and if we stand up to protect them, we're labeled bigots, homophobes, Nazis, and Ku Klux Klan members.

This is a moral outrage.

No wonder so many parents and teachers keep reaching out to me with their horror stories. They're hoping I have some way to help them end the nightmare, I guess, but I have no power to change things. Jeralee, Sue, Diane, Barb, Cindy, and I have been blowing the whistle on union abuse for three decades, and we've been pummeled for doing so. We've been verbally beaten up for questioning our unions' support of Planned Parenthood and other abortion industry standards and practices too.

For many years teachers' union leaders at the Ohio Education Association Representative Assemblies and the NEA RA, mocked and shunned Judy Bruns for daring to represent the voices of pro-life teachers as a teacher representative at the OEA RA and the NEA RA. She told me abortion was the reason she became a delegate at the NEA RA. She wanted to speak up for the babies, and she came prepared with observations and facts. At her first NEA RA, she went up to the microphones and asked three specific questions about the union's stance on abortion because just like I'd experienced, union leaders kept lying to her about the NEA's involvement with abortion.

She knew the union leadership would twist her words if she didn't use specific language in her questions, so each question started out the same, "Through the words 'reproductive freedom' in our resolutions document, does the NEA support," and then she'd add on the detail. She asked if the NEA supports abortion in the first trimester, if the NEA supports abortion up to viability (and she spelled it out as that point at which the fetus is capable of surviving outside the womb with assistance), and she asked specifically if the NEA "Supports the woman's choice or decision to abort up to and including delivery, commonly termed by the media a partial birth abortion." The answers to all three of her questions was, "Yes," and the last question received an additional response of, "We have no *restrictions*…" or "We have no *limitations* [on abortion]."

Judy couldn't remember if they said "restrictions" or "limitations," but it doesn't really matter which word they used. The stance they take on behalf of millions of teachers is clear. Teachers forced to fund the union's extreme full-term abortion agenda disagree on moral, psychological, religious, and personal grounds, but just like we're forced to support their sexual agenda, we're coerced to fund their position on abortion; even though our country is totally split on this issue, and teachers are too. The union leadership makes moral and political decisions on behalf of all teachers, and then they abuse us for daring to disagree.

Recently I received an article highlighting a video secretly filmed by an eleven-year-old child during his classroom sex education lesson in a Florida school. The contents of the video are so disturbing, yet precious little kids were forced to watch the live presentation in their classroom. The "expert" was demonstrating the use of strap-on sex toys to vulnerable children. She wore a very large adult male penis, and then propped her buttocks in the air and showed the children where to insert it; thankfully she was wearing clothing. It's certain to me those horrified eleven-year-olds' parents had no idea that sexual abuse of their children was part of the curriculum, but it's too late now. It's doubtful any of those children will be able to erase that memory from their minds and hearts.[42]

These "experts" will be called in more often because when real teachers see these sex curriculums, they will never in a million years agree to abuse children with the lessons, but our "California Healthy Youth Act," which "impose[s] a state-mandated local program," permits experts to provide instruction when teachers are not "trained in the appropriate courses…with knowledge of the most recent medically accurate research on human sexuality." That's the unions' version of medically accurate too.

So, teachers, you and I can escape the abusive curriculum and emotional trauma of these lessons by allowing an "expert" to take over our classrooms, but what about the kids? Who's going to protect them? I hope great teachers will rise up and fight alongside parents, but so far, I've noticed that teachers feel they will lose their jobs, so most are silent while parents fight alone. Teachers, isn't the protection of children worth the risk? And have you ever asked yourself why your union isn't protecting you, so you can protect the children in your care?

And parents, won't you go inform the teachers you know that their union is involved in this outrage? We must restore the Education Triangle and stand together for the protection and safety of our children before it's too late. It's the only way we'll regain our authority.

The Florida school didn't allow the "expert" to return after the pornographic video of her lesson appeared, but according to news reports, the "expert" claims she's a victim of "bigotry" because she's a "proud member of the LGBTQ community." Bigotry? What does the abuse of children have to do with bigotry? What about the eleven- and twelve-year-old children now permanently scarred by her outrageous behavior? What about the rights of their parents and promise of safety for children in our schools?

I know you're starting to see more of this sexual abuse of children in school districts across the country, so I want to offer a gentle reminder of the NEA Resolution "B-53. Sex Education," which I shared with you earlier. Remember it? "The National Education Association believes that the developing child's sexuality is continually and inevitably influenced by daily contacts, including experiences in the school environment…that the public school must assume an increasingly important role in providing the instruction. Teachers and health professionals must be qualified to teach in this area and must be *legally protected from censorship and lawsuits.…* The Association also believes that to facilitate the realization of human potential, it is the right of every individual to live in an environment of freely available information and knowledge about sexuality."

So, I'll ask again, why does the teachers' union want to ensure these experts are "legally protected from censorship and lawsuits"? This situation feels a lot like watching as the Witch manhandled six-year-olds and no one in authority did anything to stop her.

Diane Lenning started a Republican Educators Caucus in the NEA RA to try to give a voice to the millions of teachers and parents who are deeply concerned about the inappropriate sexual lessons and divisive political agenda in our schools. In fact, Diane and other concerned teachers submitted an objection to the NEA president because the NEA gave their coveted professional Human Rights award to a teacher who revealed in his book that he chose *not* to report a 16-year old minor male student's sexual relationship with a grown man. Diane told me, "As education professionals, we are mandatory reporters of abuse or sexual inducement to students. Many education leaders felt it went against teacher ethics to present a human rights award to a teacher who ignored his required duty to protect students."

In response to their concern for child safety and professional standards, Diane told me some NEA member-teachers threw a giant fit, recruited new members, staged a coup, and tried to oust Diane as leader of her own caucus. They failed by only one vote. Later, dissenters accused these loving teachers of being biased against LGBT individuals, but their objections had nothing to do with the sexual choices of others. They stood against the award recipient choice because he was a mandatory reporter and failed to report the sexual exploitation of a minor under his supervision.

The experiences of the teachers serving in the NEA RA helped me to connect some dots in my almost thirty-year experience as a teacher abused by her union. I found out that the union really does have "how-to" classes on bullying with titles like, "How to Deal with Conservative Right-Wing Extremists." No wonder they called me a radical right-winger.

The personal experiences of Diane, Jeralee, Stella, Priscilla, Sue, Judy and others verified everything I thought to be true for many years. Diane sums it up best based on her experience with the NEA from the 1990s through 2006: "Anybody who's joining the NEA needs to understand that this is an organized group of teachers who will use your money against you and all the people in America who believe similarly to you, and *the money is the issue. They have the money.* The money brings them power."

CHAPTER 11

THE UGLY TRUTH
BEHIND A PRETTY FACE

"The PTA has credibility; that is why we always use the PTA as a front."

During 2009 and 2010, my home district, Capistrano Unified, was in a long battle with the teachers' union over necessary pay cuts and possible layoffs because of the extreme downturn in the economy. Many hard-working parents in our district ran a foundation to raise money for all sorts of support for our schools, and in 2009 those parents decided to support our local teachers with a massive effort to restore teacher salaries and save jobs. The parent efforts were downright inspiring.

Julie Collier, a dedicated parent volunteer and former elementary school teacher, served as the ambassador of the foundation's efforts. At the end of their campaign, they'd raised one million dollars and saved hundreds of teacher jobs.

Our entire community was proud of those heroic efforts, but do you know how the community was thanked for our extreme benevolence? The following year when the district was still facing monetary shortfalls and definite pay cuts, the teachers' union staged an enormous strike and drew parents and kids into the battle.

Julie recalls, "I was a strike substitute at my son's school. It was the same school where I was a PTA volunteer, and the foundation ambassador, but when I'd drive in, the teachers would yell at me and try to intimidate me."

Julie told me the teachers' union, Capistrano Unified Education Association (CUEA), instructed the teachers to take the teaching materials out of the classroom during the strike. She shared, "They took markers, books, and unplugged equipment. Whatever they had that was not anchored to the ground, they either took out of their rooms or locked in cabinets so the substitutes couldn't use them to keep on track with the curriculum." Once Julie realized the union was pulling this trick, she brought in lesson plans for other substitutes. She told me, "It was the kids' jobs to go to school, and there were parents following through on that. For teachers to take that away and for a teachers' union to have such a negative impact on students is extremely telling of their priorities."

Charles and I sent Ben and Kyle to school during the strike, and we can attest to Julie's stories. Ben was herded into the multipurpose room and shown videos for most of the week, and we were also treated with disdain for daring to cross the picket line. We pay thousands of dollars a year in property taxes to fund our schools and teachers' paychecks, but our kids were completely robbed of education, and our tax dollars were squandered.

Another friend of ours, Julie Dutton, sent her children to school during the strike too. Her son, David (whose name I've changed because Julie's afraid of additional reprisal), was in sixth grade at the time of the strike.

Julie told me, "Before the strike, David had straight A's in every class." The strike was in mid-April, so David had maintained an A average throughout the entire school year. She continued, "Within one week of the end of the strike all of his grades were still A's except his science grade was dropping dramatically. She discovered all of his test scores were A's, but he suddenly had several missing assignments.

David, a very dedicated student, had never had a missing assignment before, and he loved science, so Julie knew something was wrong. She emailed David's teacher, but she never received a reply, so she sent another and then another, but the teacher never responded. When Julie asked David to ask his teacher if he was receiving his mother's email communications the teacher said, "My room has really bad Internet connection, so I probably didn't get them." Julie (just like you and me) could see right through this excuse, so she wrote a handwritten note to the teacher and sent it to school. She still received no reply from the teacher, and Julie told me, "David's grade went from an A to a D almost overnight," so she emailed the principal and copied the teacher. After the principal contact, she finally received a phone call from the teacher.

Julie shared, "Unbelievably, he initiated a heated conversation, and he claimed that David had not been turning in his assignments," so Julie told him what she really thought was going on.

She said to the teacher: "I don't think it's a coincidence that my son had all straight A's and then after I sent him to school during the strike his grades suddenly went from A's to D's. I hope my son is not being retaliated against." The teacher started backpedaling and telling her how David did a great job on his volcano report and his tests and that he was a good student, but he still made David redo the work to bring up his grade.

Shortly before that strike, the other Julie (Julie Collier) was serving as the PTA legislative representative for her son Jack's school. As she studied the PTA's stance on all policy issues as part of her volunteer efforts, she was shocked that the PTA was in support of the teacher strike. It was also in support of every other political and social effort the teachers' union was supporting. She found this very odd because many of the teachers' unions' stances were in direct opposition to what she and many other parents believed were in the best interest of children.

A few years before the strike, in 2007, she started "Parents Advocate League" (PAL) to provide a voice for parents in our educational system.[43] Julie fights for all families, but her personal battle started when her son, Jack, was underperforming in elementary school. Julie and her husband worked with school authorities to discover how to help Jack. "We were told Jack had dyslexia," Julie told me. "We took him to the doctor immediately. After a full examination our doctor said, 'That's ridiculous. There's nothing wrong with him.' That's when we realized we needed to find a different avenue."

Because the teachers' unions have been able to dominate our school boards in Orange County, California for years, and the state PTA stands with the unions against school choice efforts, there are very few charter schools in our area, so Julie's family had no options. They could not afford private school tuition, so Julie and several other discouraged parents worked together to start a high-quality charter school.

They hoped their efforts would be embraced and appreciated (just like when they'd raised one million dollars to save teacher jobs), but their journey for the good of children led them into a battle that Julie described as "stepping on a hornets' nest." They knew the teachers' unions would harass them, but they also received a large amount of resistance from a small group of teachers and PTA parents in the district. They heard constant rumors that the group was having regular meetings to undermine the charter school.

One Friday night when Jack was ten, he had a buddy to the house for a sleepover. Early Saturday morning, the boys went outside to play, but they immediately ran inside to get Julie. She told me, "My husband and I followed the boys out to the front yard; we couldn't believe our eyes. Our entire front yard was layered with toilet paper, so we couldn't see any of the grass." Typically, Julie would laugh about something like this because kids love to sneak around and play tricks on their friends, but this wasn't child's play; it was something devious, and its message was seriously disturbing. Julie told me, "As we lifted the paper, we found hundreds of plastic forks stuck into our lawn. They were driven in by the handles, so the prongs were sticking up, and the toilet paper was carefully laid across them, so you couldn't see the forks at all. If those boys had run onto that lawn, their feet would have been cut to shreds."

Julie called the police who were also disturbed by the dangerous lawn forking, but their real concerns started when Julie showed them the flyers that were taped to their front door and placed on the windshields of their cars. "They left flyers all over talking about our charter school in derogatory terms," she told me. When the police officers saw the flyers in connection with the bizarre and dangerous lawn forking, they filed an informational report.

"The police understood it was a threat, so they stuck around and gave us advice on how to avoid nails in our tires and other attacks." They were never able to prove who was involved in the dangerous threat, but the hateful words on the flyers matched the insults the teachers' union and that small group of teachers and PTA parents were spreading about the charter.

Julie and her friends didn't allow intimidation tactics to stop them, instead, their charter flourished. "It was amazing. Jack not only loved school, but his standardized test scores improved by well over a hundred points, and his grades rose from D's and F's in his public school to A's and B's. His teachers and administrators were caring, everyone was accountable, and the other families were thrilled with the results too."

The charter went to only eighth grade, so Jack attended a private school for his freshman year and continued to succeed so well he was on the Honor Roll, but due to limited funds, he had to return to the public schools in his sophomore year, and his grades plummeted again. Julie recalled, "Jack was earning A's and B's at JSerra [private school]. Now he was working harder but getting D's and F's. It just didn't make any sense."

When Julie met with the principal to try to figure out how to help Jack, she says she was put off by the principal's body language and response, "He looked at me with his elbow on the back of his chair, shrugged his shoulders, and said, 'Our schools are far more rigorous than private schools.' He completely ignored the concerns I'd presented about my son and was basically saying that all private and charter schools are inferior."

Julie's family was hurt and honestly baffled by the situation, but they didn't stop fighting for Jack. Julie told me, "We started noticing on the parent portal that Jack was getting D's and F's on his tests, but his teachers never handed his tests back to him, and rarely went over them, so neither he nor we could look at them to discover where he was struggling and to give him additional help." Julie asked if she could see Jack's tests to support him with learning the material, but the teachers told her the only way for her to see the tests was to make an appointment during work hours to come into school and review them. The teachers told her, "We're afraid of cheating."

Julie had been a teacher for years, so she understood the issue of cheating, but she couldn't understand why the teachers didn't simply modify the tests each year to prevent cheating. She later discovered that the teachers' union fought so teachers would not be required to return tests so that teachers would not have to rewrite tests every year. Julie told me, "So instead of giving the kids the tests to use as a tool to relearn and master what they didn't get correct, it's just put in a file and no one can see it, and then they go on with the next lesson even if the children haven't achieved mastery of the skills needed to move on."

This was the start of Julie's long battle for the rights of kids and parents in Capistrano Unified, the eighth largest district in California. She spoke to the superintendent on several occasions, presented at multiple school board meetings, and even met privately with a school board member, but no one seemed to have the authority to fix this egregious problem. "I kept telling them, 'You're the bosses of these teachers; you're the trustees of parents' children and taxes, you should be able to tell them to give the tests back to the parents.' They always gave me the same answer: 'It's complicated,' and the superintendent always said, 'It's going to take a minute.'"

Although every district leader with whom Julie spoke promised to try to fix the problem, no one did. Their local PTA was one of the strongest in the state, but instead of helping, they stood with the union.

Julie fought so hard that her son, Jack, started taking heat for her advocacy. One of his teachers was so unkind and unfair that Jack's fellow students said, "Dude, that teacher hates you." Julie told me, "Jack started freaking out and feeling lots of pressure. It was a real shock to his system that a teacher would actually take out her frustrations with his mom on him. She hated him, not because he was someone to hate; she hated him because of me—because I dared to speak out."

Julie started receiving messages through her PAL's site from other frustrated parents. "There were so many parents who were angry about the policy but were too afraid to even show up to board meetings. They would call me and say, 'Please speak out on this. Thank you so much. I just can't do it. I'm afraid.' I'd say, 'You have every right to speak up,' but very few did because all of them received some form of subtle retaliation from some teachers, or they were shunned from serving at PTA events." The culture of fear reigned.

Julie discovered the problem had been dominating the district for a long time, and some teachers were even making extra money off the arrangement. Julie shared, "One parent told me that nine years before, when she demanded that she see her son's test, the math teacher said, 'Well, I can't let you see that test, but if you want to hire my colleague to be the tutor, I'll give her your son's test and she can review the test with your son.' This parent had to pay forty dollars an hour so her son could learn what he did wrong on the test. The parent went to the principal and was told there was nothing he could do about it."

Now I want to make it clear that this sort of arrangement, and the counterintuitive filing of tests without giving kids and parents feedback, frustrates the good teachers in Capistrano Unified. Many outstanding teachers throughout Capistrano Unified work very hard for the good of their students, and rework tests each year if cheating is an issue, but their voices have been silenced.

Julie fought tirelessly seeking help from school officials, "They were going through negotiations that year, so I asked them to please make the test policy part of the bargaining process." Although they told Julie they would try their hardest, it was never added to the new contract, so the opportunity to create a positive change for students was lost. The PTA never backed parental efforts either. Julie told me, "No one did anything, including the trustees who heard me month after month, and the superintendent who promised to fix it. Everyone did nothing to help us, so we realized Jack was in a system in a traditional public school that does not value parents."

It hit Julie that if the problems were this bad in Orange County, California, where many parents have the resources to fight, it must be so much worse in other neighborhoods. She told me, "This is an entire system with zero accountability to student success."

Julie ran for school board in an attempt to help change the problem as a trustee, and my family wholeheartedly supported her efforts and those of several other outstanding candidates over the years, but the teachers' unions waged a vindictive campaign against her, and the PTA supported the unions' candidates.

My friends who are teachers in Capistrano Unified gave me all sorts of intelligence on the hateful things the unions said about Julie and the other pro-student candidates. I heard many unsuspecting parents repeating negative things about our terrific candidates because they believed the deceptive union talking points. As usual, the unions got the teachers to make phone calls for the union candidates, and they poured all sorts of teacher dues into glossy flyers and a deceptive messaging campaign. I received those calls and flyers; they were misleading and trusting teacher voices were used to promote union candidates many of them had never even met.

We were scrambling to raise a few thousand dollars to promote our candidates, but our efforts paled in comparison to the union largess and PTA support. No surprise, the union-backed candidates won again, so the status quo remains, and last I heard, the parents and kids still have a tough process when desiring to review tests.

Julie and I have discovered through personal experience that the "P" in "PTA" has been undermined to such a degree that we can't make our voices heard. We're allowed to host fundraisers and break our backs to save teacher jobs, but whenever we ask for improved education policies, question curriculum, or insist on teacher quality for the good of our children, we have an uphill battle. I discovered the same thing during my years as a teacher serving in PTA, but I could never figure out what was driving the problem, until I met Charlene Haar.

Charlene, a thirteen-year public high school teacher, was the 1987 recipient of the Presidential Scholars Commission's "Distinguished Teacher of the Year" award in South Dakota. In addition to putting her full energy and tremendous talents into her students, she also served as a PTA member in her community and as a teacher-leader in the NEA Representative Assembly. Throughout her distinguished career, Charlene uncovered some very troubling facts plaguing the National PTA.

As part of her work as a research associate with Bowling Green State University, Charlene directed an in-depth study of the National PTA, which allowed her to spend time at the national offices in Chicago studying financial reports and interacting with officials at all levels of the PTA. Her study revealed deep concerns that are articulated in her book, *The Politics of the PTA*.[44]

Charlene uncovered that voices of parents have been drowned out at the national and state levels of the PTA because of intimidation by the teachers' unions. In fact, it was the unionization of the NEA that undermined the good work parents were attempting to do on behalf of their kids through the PTA, and because of the strong-arm tactics of the unions, parents were coerced into acceptance of teacher strikes and collective bargaining; even though they knew both had negative impacts on their children.

According to information she shared with me personally and in her book, when parents took policy stands in support of parents' and students' rights that were in opposition to the powerful teachers' unions, the unions called on teachers to boycott the PTA. When teachers won the right to collectively bargain, parents were completely shut out of negotiations and thus rendered voiceless in local school districts too.

In her book, Charlene shared an analysis of an actual teachers' union v. PTA kerfuffle. "[T]he state PTA and the powerful Ohio Education Association [OEA], an NEA affiliate, came to blows over three bills in the state legislature.... The state PTA actively—and successfully—opposed several of OEA's legislative proposals in these areas, and that was when OEA apparently decided enough was enough. At its 1976 state convention, OEA adopted a resolution asking its 85,000 teachers to drop out of the PTA, to boycott all its activities, and to encourage parents to form new parent–teacher organizations that are not affiliated with the PTA. Of the 217,000 members who quit the PTA in 1976, more than 50,000 were from Ohio, where entire units disaffiliated."[45]

The National PTA had been dealing with union bullying tactics and policies harmful to kids for years. It had even created a task force years earlier to develop policy in order to address the problems. According to Charlene's book, "At its September 1968 meeting the board first identified several 'dilemmas' that teacher strikes and negotiations posed for local PTA members." Here's a list:

1. If the PTA provides volunteers to man the classrooms during work stoppage, in the interest of protecting the immediate safety and welfare of children, it is branded as a strike breaker.

2. If the PTA does not take sides in issues being negotiated, it is accused of not being interested.

3. If it supports the positions of the board of education, which is the representative of the public in negotiations, the teacher members of the PTA have threatened to withdraw membership and boycott the local PTA activities.[46]

The National PTA was placed between a rock and a hard place and felt its only "option" was to support the teachers' unions in every instance. Those well-used and well-funded union tactics—fear, intimidation, ignorance, and isolation—overwhelmed them. Since volunteers run the PTA with far less organizing power or financial heft than the teachers' unions, the tactics worked. The PTA was forced to take a position of "neutrality," and it remains neutral to this day, even on those issues for which it would be uniquely qualified to advocate, like our current fight against Comprehensive Sexuality Education.

Charlene asserts, "Neutrality marked the end of the PTA's independence, because it prohibited the PTA from adopting positions that were opposed by the teacher unions."[47]

Charlene's book is loaded with multiple examples of union bullying, manipulating, and controlling the PTA, and because of her research inside the PTA and her service as a teacher leader in the NEA RA, she is uniquely qualified to expose the disturbing relationship that has silenced good parents in just the same way great teachers have been silenced by the unions.

Dawn Urbanek understands the silencing. She's the parent watchdog who attends all school board meetings in Capistrano Unified, runs CUSD-watch.com, and helped Stella expose the sex education nightmare in Capistrano Unified. During the awful teacher strike in our community, Dawn learned firsthand that her efforts as a PTA executive board member were being undermined by PTA's neutrality stance. In April 2010 she penned a detailed letter to her local PTA leadership that began: "CUCPTSA [Capistrano Unified Council of PTSA] position on PTA leader neutrality during contract disputes does not comply with the National PTA, California State PTA and the CUCPTSA Not for Profit Charter, By-Laws, Mission Statements or Advocacy Platforms. As a result, parents of CUSD have been severely handicapped in their ability to obtain information about contract issues that reflect the stated position of the PTA which is to advocate for 'What is in the best interest of children.'"

Among many other things, Dawn wrote:
The National PTA's stated mission is to be:

- A powerful voice for all children,

- A relevant resource for families and communities, and

- A strong advocate for the education and well-being of every child.

In addition to articulating many breeches of trust, she wrote, *"Parents need the PTA to be the one voice of truth—the voice that puts the best interest of children over everything else.…* The PTA has a legal, moral and ethical obligation to uphold its founding principles. The PTA's failure to do so has resulted in offending many of the PTA leaders in the District and has resulted in substantial harm to the families in CUSD who have always looked to the PTA to be a voice for the children."

Dawn ended her letter with: "As a result of the actions stated above, I am no longer going to be a member of the PTA. I have resigned from all of my positions on the Las Palmas PTA Executive Board and the CUCPTSA Legislation Team. I will begin to look for other ways to remain a strong advocate for all children in CUSD."[48]

Though Dawn was standing in the gap for parents and kids, ever since her departure from the PTA, she's been mocked for attending the board meetings and informing parents through CUSDWatch.com, and sadly, some people believe the deceptive name-calling. The unions' four psychological manipulations strike again. This time isolation and ignorance take center stage.

Dawn's letter and Charlene's stories reveal the union's overwhelming influence over the PTA to support coalitions and policies that are most definitely *not* in the best interests of children.

Most of the PTA parents I've worked with for decades desire a greater voice in our schools and would be totally offended by these intrusions into parental authority, so it's obvious that most parents at the local levels of PTA have no idea they are supporting union policies against the better interests of their families. Without knowing it, many parents are fully embracing and funding the policies that have left them totally voiceless in local negotiations too. Indeed, according to Charlene, "It matters little that many parents neither want, nor support, nor are even aware of the legislative agenda of the National PTA. One of the findings in a 1996 poll was that '[w]hile most parents have a favorable impression of the PTA, an overwhelming majority—82 percent—are ignorant of the organization's taking a stand or having a position statement on any issues.'"[49]

No doubt, that 82 percent would be shocked that teachers' unions not only acknowledge this relationship but crow about it. Witness Kim Moran, director of field services for the AFT's (American Federation of Teachers) Committee on Political Education, who, while encouraging members to form coalitions with the PTA, said flat out:

"The PTA has credibility. That is why we *always* use the PTA as a front."[50]

Because of this, unions often ask PTA leaders to head large alliances between multiple union organizations. For instance, the PTA was the face of a union-heavy coalition founded in 1997 called "Learning First Alliance." Though this coalition was billed as a group working for kids, public statements and operations revealed the true motives. Charlene shared, "Despite its protestations to the contrary, the Learning First Alliance was established for political purposes."[51]

In her book Charlene explained, "Although the PTA adopts the same position as the public education establishment, PTA leaders contribute very little to coalition strategy sessions. With rare exceptions, the public education coalitions do not rely upon the PTA.... Instead PTA support is featured mainly to forestall criticisms that a coalition position does not have parental support."[52]

Remember the PTA (along with the California School Boards Association and the CTA) was part of the coalition of supporters behind the "California Healthy Youth Act" that forbids parents "opt-in" authority before their children are indoctrinated by inappropriate sex education curriculums. Recall the "Healthy Youth Act" was sponsored by the ACLU of California, California Latinas for Reproductive Justice, Forward Together, Equality California, and Planned Parenthood Affiliates of California.[53]

I know it's hard to believe the teachers' unions have corrupted the PTA; after all, the PTA seems as American as apple pie. But the evidence is irrefutable. Charlene states, "PTA members and officials often bristle at the suggestion that the PTA is dominated by the teacher unions.... In practice, however, NEA domination is pervasive."[54]

Now you know why the state PTA stood with Planned Parenthood, the CTA, ACLU, and other highly political organizations to prevent parents from demanding transparency and protection for their children from sexually provocative and inappropriate content. It's troubling to consider the California School Boards Association was part of this coalition too, but as Eileen Blagden's, Julie William's and Julie Collier's stories revealed, the teachers' unions control many school boards as well, so why should we be surprised their association is controlled by the teachers' unions also?

It's quite a trick. The union uses the time, money, energy, and apple pie image of parents, teachers, and children to push forward their self-serving agenda while betraying the trust of America's most revered organization: the PTA, and very few are wise to it. Yes, quite a trick—like so many other cushy arrangements manipulated by teachers' unions. You've gotta give the devil his due(s).

CHAPTER 12

RACIAL EQUITY DISCIPLINE POLICIES

"A teacher almost got killed in one of our schools; the unions never protected him…They used him as a bargaining chip."

For years, the teachers' lounge was a place where my colleagues and I could hash out lesson plan ideas, organize student productions, or just relax and share funny stories of the hilarious things that happen regularly in classrooms full of little kids. But as discipline problems have increased, the teachers' lounge experience has become more like a daily counseling session full of deeply discouraged, battle-weary soldiers seeking help and relief. Day after day, each one of us seeks advice for how to deal with multiple behavior problems that are disrupting the learning and bringing chaos into our classrooms.

Although I could articulate dozens of stories of extreme discipline situations I've faced as a classroom teacher, I'll share one. I had a child in my class whose behavior was so out of control I had to stand next to his desk or have him sit with me at all times while teaching. If I turned my back on him, he would abuse the closest victim. He wreaked havoc on the playground too. He continually lifted the skirts of little girls and got into fights regularly. His extreme anger ruined every single game in which he participated. When I held his parent–teacher conference, his mother and grandmother cussed me out (including the "F" word). Obviously, I asked them to leave, but that abusive family and their child were permitted to harass and mistreat my students and me all year, and the child was never appropriately disciplined. The problems grew so out of control the following year with his next teacher, she told all of us she was retiring early from the stress of that child.

It was undeniable that I suddenly found myself as the recipient of a steep rise in discipline problems, more curse-outs from parents and even a middle finger in my face for daring to ask a parent to move her vehicle from the red zone. At first, I fell for the excuse that parents were the biggest problem, but I was very surprised to learn some additional information one morning while reading the newspaper. The writer made a statement that schools were under pressure to lower their numbers of suspensions. I didn't have enough context to fully understand the issue at the time, but a few months later an administrator in my district made a statement about our district "looking bad" if we had too many suspensions. I was totally confused, and even though I asked, no one could ever explain these comments to us teachers.

One year, I had so many severe discipline problems in my class, it was virtually impossible to teach. Each time I sent the struggling youngsters out for discipline, they returned far too quickly—sometimes within a few minutes—with punishments (like a note of apology to me) that were far too lenient for the ongoing disruptive behaviors, so they were emboldened to misbehave.

About this time, I was watching the evening news and sat captivated as fourth-grade teacher Aaron Benner shared with Bill O'Reilly his story of severe student discipline problems in Saint Paul Public Schools (SPPS) in Minnesota. He caught my attention because like me, discipline issues were needlessly growing out of control at his elementary school.

Aaron Benner said, "You are teaching your class and a student from another classroom just opens up your door, runs in, grabs a computer, and throws it down and runs out...you would see that student who came into your classroom and disrupted it still in the school. And that's mind-boggling. You're like, where are the consequences? What is going on around here?"

Aaron was passionate, and I stood in my living room cheering him on. Aaron and O'Reilly (a former high school teacher) discussed the vital need for strong disciplinary standards and parental involvement in our schools, and Aaron painted the picture of total chaos in his school district. Aaron shared, "I knew there must have been some sort of directive to keep these kids in school, in the classroom, no matter what. We are trying to close the achievement gap; however, the ways we are trying to close the achievement gap are making things worse."

I just had to meet Aaron, so my friend Kim Crockett (who fights for great teachers through Educated Teachers Minnesota)[55] introduced us, and we knew we had to band together for America's teachers and kids.

Aaron began teaching in 1994 and started a career-long habit of playing football with his students during lunch. A natural athlete, Aaron was a celebrated quarterback at a neighborhood inner city playground located near the community in which he taught, so he had star status among his students. He observed right away that the kids playing football during recess spent most of their play time fighting because the quarterbacks would throw only to their favorite friends, and a total lack of strictly enforced rules of the game was leading to constant disagreements and very real physical altercations.

Aaron decided to set up some new ground rules for recess football, and he gave up thirty minutes of his own break every day to lead the kids in their games. In order to increase the enjoyment and decrease the fighting, he became the "All Time Quarterback" for both teams, so no matter who was on offense, Aaron was their quarterback. He was teaching fourth grade and noticed most of the kids couldn't throw very far anyway, so this was a terrific solution on many levels.

Their motto was: "Win gracefully—Lose gracefully," and the rules were simple: One hand touch. Touch below the waist. Do not be vicious in any way.

Every play was a pass thrown by the All Time Quarterback and Aaron promised every student would receive at least one pass during the game. He realized he could differentiate football instruction this way too because some kids were only able to catch short passes and others could go very deep, so everyone learned at their level and made improvement throughout the year. Their final stated rule was that when the bell rang, one more play could be run, so the All Time Quarterback would scope out the scene and hurl the ball to someone he knew hadn't gotten much action that day.

Teachers like Aaron bring energy, passion, and skill to their daily lessons, and they intentionally seek to differentiate instruction to meet the individual needs of each student. Like the Master, Aaron saw a problem, thought up a proactive solution, and gave up his own personal time to implement the solution. I know loads of recess aides who would be thrilled to have Aaron on their playgrounds because his methods reduce friction, which is a very real problem on playgrounds these days.

He also brought imperative security to the learning environment. Aaron understands that students cannot learn (and teachers cannot teach) if they're afraid of individuals who are out of control or if their environment is littered with situations that make them fearful for their own physical space.

In December 2011, Aaron headed out to the playground to join his students for their morning recess football game just like he'd been doing every day for seventeen years. Clad in his business suit (like always), he took his place as the All Time Quarterback. Many of his inner city students didn't have fathers at home, so Aaron felt strongly that his personal example of professionalism and engagement in students' lives was vital. Aaron told me, "I couldn't bear to see students who looked like me failing."

On this particular day, the recess bell rang while the game was tied, so passions were high. Aaron threw a bomb to one of the most athletic kids on the field. He told me the boy was running so hard and gracefully he looked like a deer running down the field. The All Time Quarterback delivered a beautiful pass that landed right in the boy's arms inside of the goal line, but as so often happens in this game we call life, the boy dropped the ball before he could land it for a touchdown. Aaron's heart broke for the kid. As a former college wide receiver, he knew the devastating feeling connected to dropping a great pass—especially a touchdown pass to win the game.

The boy was totally dejected.

As his students lined up they all encouraged their friend and told him he could make up for the drop the next day. Aaron was proud of his kids for sticking to their "Win gracefully—Lose gracefully" motto, but he was disappointed when he overheard the boy cussing and saw him being rude to those who were trying to comfort him. Aaron walked over to the boy, put his arm around him and said, "Cheer up, great effort! You'll have another chance tomorrow," but instead of softening to the attractiveness of lose gracefully, the boy yanked away from Aaron and punched him in the chest as hard as he could. Aaron needed the help of another man to restrain the boy.

Aaron realized the boy was angry because he'd dropped the game-winning pass but punching a teacher and putting classmates in danger is not acceptable, so Aaron took him to the principal's office. As Aaron and his students approached the classroom door only ten minutes after the attack, the principal and the boy were standing at the door waiting for them. The principal understood the severity of the problem, but his discipline remedy was only to inform Aaron that the boy was sorry and ready to join his class. Absolutely nothing was done to provide consequences for the boy's behavior. Aaron could overhear the rest of his class whispering, "He gets to come back to class after punching Mr. Benner? That ain't right. That ain't right at all." Even the kids had the commonsense to know the boy should have been disciplined.

The principal gave Aaron a look and put his hands out as if to say he couldn't do anything more about the situation. When Aaron asked his administrators for an explanation on why students were not being disciplined even for violence against teachers, he received no explanation. In regard to the student who punched him, Aaron was glad the child was sorry; he was a good kid, but even this good kid needed an appropriate punishment. His principal's response was so strange, so out of character for school leadership, and so vague that Aaron got a sick sense there was something going on that was way beyond this kid. Something wasn't quite right, and everyone on campus—the principal, teachers, and students were being negatively impacted.

These unsettling feelings are not unusual for teachers working in public schools today. We constantly have weird senses that some unseen decisions are undermining our ability to do what's right for our students and school communities, and we often learn of strange policies being pushed onto our schools long after their initial implementations, and it's an uphill battle to try to terminate them. In addition, teachers are so doggone busy keeping our heads above water with all of the constantly new curriculum ideas, testing requirements, and growing discipline and family disintegration issues, we're way too busy to take on more work trying to wade through the maze of confusing education policies that are bringing even more stress to our jobs. Great teachers don't have the extra time to investigate what's at the root of our educational breakdown, but we're all aware something is desperately wrong.

It wasn't until Aaron happened to read an editorial in the *Minneapolis Star Tribune* that things started to come together for him. Similar to the article I'd read in my local paper, the editorial focused on racial disparities in suspension rates in America's schools and suggested educators were being unfair to children of color. Aaron felt compelled to respond with a letter to the editor.

> *Your recent article, "An Alarming Trend in School Discipline" is so full of misleading details that I don't even know where to begin. I am a Black male with 17 years of teaching experience in Saint Paul and have some of my own "data." First, Black students where I work are more disruptive than the other students. Secondly, some of these students have no respect for authority and appear to take pleasure in disrupting class. This article implies that teachers are disciplining/suspending these students too quickly because of their race. We are setting these students up for failure in the future when they will be held accountable for their behavior. It's time for my community to do some serious soul searching and have courageous discussions on this issue. My message for those who believe teachers are at fault: spend an entire day in an urban classroom then ask yourself if you could be an effective teacher with all of the "minor" distractions.*

His letter received a lot of positive support from the community, and many teachers and parents shared his concerns about the escalating violence, particularly involving students of color. Because of the response, and his position as a black teacher at a predominantly black campus, Aaron felt duty-bound to take action, so he addressed the Saint Paul School Board regarding the increase of student violence on campus.

His school district did nothing to attend to Aaron's complaints or suggestions, but his remarks inspired a healthy debate in his community and around the country. He discovered there were hordes of other educators who were also demoralized and concerned about the increase in discipline problems and violence in schools across the country. None of them (including me) had any idea why things were getting so out of control, but most of us knew instinctively some sort of new policy must have been driving the problem.

Aaron discovered that school district leaders across the country had received a directive from the Obama administration to lower suspension rates for students of color. Like me, Aaron and his colleagues had never even heard of the new policies that included some sort of school discipline guidance package.[56] I'm sure the leaders who imposed these new rules had the right intentions, but once again top-down requirements from experts far removed from the classroom were tying the hands of actual teachers, and instead of decreasing discipline problems, the policies were (and are) making them much worse.

Aaron soon discovered a new "racial equity" disciplinary approach had been bargained in the teachers' union contract in his district, which disturbed Aaron and other educators who were voiceless in the decision. Under the new approach, an outside group was hired to come into the district to help weed out "systemic racism." Instead of holding all students to high behavioral standards, the district was now focused on blaming teacher racism for student disciplinary issues and reducing suspensions for students of color even when their violent or disrespectful behaviors merited commonsense discipline.

Aaron was outraged. He told me, "You cannot tell me, as a black man, that this is right. You're setting black kids up for failure. They're going to have enough obstacles as it is. Now you're saying behavior doesn't matter? I've never heard anything like this."

As a twenty-eight year veteran classroom teacher, I can say with absolute authority that the most fundamental quality in a school and classroom atmosphere is safety—physical safety, safety to make mistakes, safety to try new and challenging tasks, safety to share personal creativity without fear of mockery or rejection from peers or teachers; in short, the safety to learn. The most vital ingredient in creating an atmosphere of safety is discipline. Aaron and other great teachers know this instinctively. In fact, running a structured and well-disciplined classroom is about ninety percent of a teacher's job, and without it, chaos and fear ensue and learning stops.

During a staff meeting in 2013, an unchecked comment by an administrator helped Aaron and his colleagues start to connect the dots. The administrator told the staff he would not be "receiving his bonus" because the suspensions were too high at the school. None of the faculty or staff had heard of any such bonuses, and they were alarmed that money could be at the root of the horrible decline in discipline standards. Aaron called an official at his union, Saint Paul Federation of Teachers, which is an affiliate of American Federation of Teachers (AFT) and reported what the administrator said. The official did some research and confirmed that the bonuses did indeed exist.

Aaron learned the Obama administration put pressure on school districts by investigating them if their suspension rates for children of color were above a certain threshold.[57] Districts received bonuses from the federal government if they lowered their suspension rates below certain criteria set for each district. If violence increased, the districts would obtain extra millions of dollars for "restorative justice implementation," which focused on counseling and therapy.

Aaron discovered the district, in agreement with the teachers' union, had hired Pacific Educational Group (PEG), a company based in San Francisco that believes "systemic racism" is the greatest problem in our schools. Aaron told me, "The goal of PEG is to train every employee in school districts—every employee must go to six mandated trainings so you can discover how your white privilege and your white biases are hampering black students' learning. It's the craziest thing I've ever heard of, and the union supports it. I don't support it. It's not working."

In November of 2013, Aaron wrote a letter, "The Elephant in the Room," to the editor of the *Saint Paul Pioneer Press* in response to an editorial backing PEG's practices and their attempt to close the achievement gap.

That elephant is that St. Paul Public Schools currently has a black agenda...

The agenda is to place blame on white teachers for low test scores and a high suspension rate among black boys...

So, we continue to make white people the scapegoat and set our kids up for failure with nonsense. We should be speaking with our black parents whose kids are doing well (and St. Paul has many that fit this criteria) and ask them what they do to ensure that their children succeed.

I'd bet my last dollar that we'd learn that education is valued in these homes and parents are involved with their children's education. This is not rocket science. Spending tons of money on this

consulting firm is a slap in the face to the taxpayers of St. Paul.
As a black man who currently teaches in St. Paul, PEG does not
represent my views on how to close the achievement gap.

Aaron knew exactly what he was talking about from personal experience. Three months after that student punched Aaron in the chest after their football game, Aaron sat with the boy and his mother during parent conferences.

Aaron loved being his teacher. The boy was bright and a gifted athlete. When Aaron brought up the day the young man punched him in the chest, his mother was shocked. She wasn't surprised her son had acted out in anger because she had been battling this at home too, but the principal had never even bothered to call her or make her aware of the incident. She was very upset with the principal. She was counting on the school to be in partnership with her in support of her son's education and growth as a man of character.

The education experts were so sure their policies were correct they crossed a sacred line and took over as parent in the life of this child without even considering getting the permission or blessing of the child's actual parent. This upright woman was mortified. She apologized to Aaron and insisted her son do the same. She told Aaron how much her son loved being in his class and that he was one of the boy's greatest male role models.

She also informed Aaron that because of divorce rules she had to send her son for mandatory visitations with his father all summer even though the father is a gang member and the environment is extraordinarily brutal and unsafe. She noticed her son was always more disrespectful and angry after visits with his dad, and his angry outbursts at home were increasing. She was thankful for the example set by Aaron because it helped solidify her efforts to train her son to be a well-behaved young man and to respect his mother.

With this understanding in place, Aaron and the mother set the young man straight and informed him they would be communicating regularly about his progress. Aaron and the mother were able to grow in mutual respect and appreciation too, and their growing parent/teacher relationship had an impact on the young man and the entire class. After this vital meeting, Aaron had no more problems with this young man, and his fantastic mom saw improvements too.

Because of the culture of fear intimidating public school educators, it's extraordinarily rare for teachers to speak out publicly about hotly contested issues in our schools, but the dangerous out-of-control behaviors dominating SPPS were so fierce that Aaron and four other teachers found the courage to put their jobs on the line and stand up to the education status quo.

In May 2014 Aaron and his four colleagues addressed the school board about the implementation of the racial equity policies promoted by PEG. To their dismay, while arguing for things like commonsense consequences for violence and disrespect, and safety for students and teachers, they were met with constant pressure and criticism by forces that should have been in line with them. Aaron told me, "The Saint Paul School Board tried to rally the community against us by painting us as five teachers who were anti-racial equity. They organized for several speakers—including the president of the Saint Paul chapter of the NAACP—to give statements at the meeting that were counter to our message."

The night before they were scheduled to speak to the school board, Aaron and his friends had another odd experience. "Our union had the NAACP show up and berate us and try to force us not to speak out about the discipline problems," Aaron told me. "The unions and NAACP were working together against teacher concerns and student and teacher safety."

The attacks that started against Aaron and his colleagues at the school board meeting soon became personal. Aaron read news reports in the *Pioneer Press*[58] of the NAACP president accusing his colleagues and him of bamboozling the district with "hyperbole" and "propaganda." He also claimed Aaron's group was "a small, vocal group," speaking against the district's racial equity policies.

Aaron told me the NAACP representatives were arguing that the PEG policies were needed to protect special needs and minority students, so if Aaron and his colleagues questioned the violence on campus they were labeled racist and uncaring toward the needy.

The spouse of a teacher in SPPS shared with Ruben Rosario in the *Twin Cities Pioneer Press*, that the racial equity discipline policies were ruining her husband's life.

He feels so beaten down, physically and emotionally, that sometimes he just goes straight to bed. He's exhausted, wiped out, depressed. Every day, he deals with students who threaten him physically, who swear at him, who disrupt his classes so profoundly that nobody else can learn. Every day, he sees classrooms where kids are out of control and face no consequences. Every day, he sees a complete lack of any sort of discipline. Meanwhile, I see the toll this takes on his health, on our marriage and on our family. It's constant, and it's crushing.[59]

Aaron's teacher's aide, Sean Kelly, told *The City Pages,* "I've been punched and kicked and spit on and called the n-word and every cuss word you could possibly think of." He also shared, "What keeps running through my head is these kids are being exploited by the district."[60]

When I asked Aaron why he thought the teachers' union, NAACP, and district officials stood against quality teachers in solidarity with policies bringing harm to children and the community, without hesitation he answered, "Money."

"A teacher almost got killed in one of our schools; the unions never protected him," Aaron told me. "We all could have marched against violence, but our union didn't care about the injured teacher. They used him as a bargaining chip. They used his injury to gain money; to bring in more school nurses and counselors; more workers who have to pay dues to the union."

Circumstances had reached such a critical mass that defenseless teachers quit their jobs; Aaron said white female teachers were the most traumatized because even though they were remarkable educators and loving to the kids, they were accused of being racist.

Aaron tried following up on a behavioral referral he wrote after witnessing a female teacher's aide being threatened by a student. The teachers' aide later reported to Aaron that the student was never disciplined, but the administrator bullied her because Aaron followed up on the issue.

In September of 2014, the systematic harassment of Aaron Benner began. Although Aaron had a stellar reputation and outstanding evaluations from his superiors for thirteen years in SPPS, suddenly he was hit with four separate "investigations" within a six-month period. "It was constant harassment, constant lies," Aaron told me. "Anything I did with discipline, they would turn it against me."

Aaron witnessed a boy punch a fourth-grade girl in the face, knocking her out cold. He called the mother two days later to check on the girl, but the mother was shocked—the school hadn't notified her. Aaron was accused of breeching confidentiality.

He was falsely accused of inappropriately handling a bullying incident in his class by questioning the student in front of the class. Thankfully, his teacher's aide was in the room and witnessed Aaron taking the child outside of the room.

Aaron was investigated when he brought a doctor's note as excuse for a sick day. The validity of the note was questioned, but it was valid.

A hurting girl who was traumatized and acting out in all sorts of disturbing ways hit Aaron. When the administration learned of the girl's attack on her teacher, they asked the girl if Aaron hit her first. Thank God the girl was honest and told them absolutely not. She loved Aaron because he had worked tirelessly to meet her overwhelming needs. She was safe with Aaron.

Throughout all of this stress, Aaron sought the counsel and support of his union leaders. He'd been told they were there to protect him from false accusations, and he paid them 750 dollars a year in dues, but they were totally incompetent, and it slowly dawned on him they were not his allies. "It took me a whole year to figure out my union was in on this," Aaron told me.

After the fourth investigation, Aaron met with union officials who were supposed to represent him against the harassment, but instead they recommended he plead guilty to one of the investigations to smooth things over. "Plead to what?" Aaron asked a union official. She said, "Just say you did something so I can plead down the other investigations." Aaron refused. His union representative told him if he agreed to say he did something wrong and took an anger management class, he would get two of his investigations pleaded down so those incidents would not be placed in his personnel file.

Realizing he was receiving no support or protection from his union, Aaron was feeling strong-armed to go along with union forces. He was so frightened he decided to take the plea in the office that day, but he immediately changed his mind while driving home because he was innocent.

Unbeknownst to him, the district went through his file immediately after the coerced plea and pulled out statements made by Aaron's teacher's aide, which supported Aaron's innocence. Since Mr. Kelly was supportive of Aaron, and Aaron had agreed to the pressured plea, Mr. Kelly was fired on the spot. "They twisted my coerced plea and said Sean Kelly was lying. He was a good man who spoke the truth, but they fired him in their desire to silence me." Mr. Kelly told *City Pages* that he felt the principal was trying to get him to "throw Benner under the bus," and that he believed "the district fired him in retaliation for backing Benner in his various investigations."[61]

Aaron complained to his union that an innocent man was hurt. "The union rep didn't even care he got fired!" Aaron told me. "She said he had his own union rep to look out for him." Aaron was devastated that his fear of no representation resulted in the job loss of a really hard working and honest man. "He was so great. He was phenomenal," Aaron told me.

Aaron told his union rep he was going to the press. She begged him not to and said it would "look bad." Aaron responded, "Look bad? I've got four investigations against me for things I never did, and you've done nothing for me! I've asked you to send letters to the superintendent; you won't do it. I'm wrongly accused, and you're worried about looking bad? What do I pay you union dues for?"

The harassment continued with all sorts of annoying accusations and questioning of the kids. Even when he was assaulted two days in a row by a student, the administration responded by asking the kids if Aaron hit the student first. Thankfully the children were honest and reported the truth, but if just one child had decided to bring harm to Aaron, he could have been falsely accused of a criminal offense.

So why would Aaron's union abandon him when he needed it most? Here are the NEA's amendments on the racial equity issue from the 2017 NEA RA.

> *Amendment 7: New I. Racial Justice—Amend by addition on page 24, line 15 of the yellow book:*

> *The National Education Association acknowledges the existence of, and will actively advocate for, the construction of social and educational strategies whose goal is the elimination of institutional racism.... Referred to the Resolutions Committee....*[62]

And Amendment 8: New I. Racial Justice—Amend by addition on page 24, line 18 of the yellow book:

The Association encourages its affiliates to educate members about the ways race privileges certain people. The Association also encourages its affiliates to work with family and student partners to develop, initiate, and promote programs that will lead us to repair, heal, organize, and advocate to achieve racial justice so that every student and educator may fulfill their full potential. …Adopted as modified.

Aaron resigned his position in SPPS in August 2015, and his inner-city students lost their greatest teacher and ally. He also filed a lawsuit against SPPS in May 2017. Aaron told me, "In fairness to NAACP, I'd like to mention they are now standing with me, but I heard some members of the NAACP are still upset with me for my appearance on O'Reilly."

Aaron accepted a position as a dean at a private high school and he loves his new job. Students at this school are held to high academic and behavioral standards and parents are intimately involved in the educational process, so no surprise the school runs smoothly, and students are respectful, well behaved, and thriving academically and otherwise. Teachers can instruct their students with excellence in a peaceful atmosphere conducive to learning.

The education experts would likely criticize this school as experiencing success because it's private and funded by high-earning parents. They would overlook the students on scholarships too. Instead of learning from the successes of these types of schools and asking themselves how we could mirror those accomplishments in our public schools, the education status quo criticizes and blames the wealthy and claims public schools are short on funds. Yet many private and charter schools do a much better job educating children with far less money.

What do charter and private schools, serving the same sorts of families in our urban neighborhoods, have on our traditional public schools? Well, actually it's what they *don't* have—government intrusion caused by teachers' unions. Charter and private schools are able to escape a lot of the top-down government overreach caused by union forces that hold our traditional public schools back. Parents (who are lucky enough to have access to charters or who can afford private schools) can choose schools full of innovation and passion, kids and teachers are protected from oppressive racial equity discipline policies and the warzones they create, so teachers are free to teach, and kids are free to learn.

In the spring of 2017, Aaron learned that the entire city of Saint Paul had adopted PEG too. In fact, the CourageousConversation.com website has a quote from the mayor of Saint Paul that reads: "The City's leadership has used Pacific Educational Group's training and the Courageous Conversation™ protocol effectively to launch our racial equity work. Sharing these concepts and approaches with our partners, Saint Paul Public Schools, has created a level of trust and understanding around racial equity we didn't have before."[63] According to Aaron, Mayor Coleman has ambitions to be governor of the state, and the NAACP leader who opposed Aaron and the other concerned teachers is now the director of the human rights department in the city of Saint Paul.

The leaders pushing these top-heavy policies may have the best of intentions, but there are two key things they do not have: a classroom full of students they have to control and educate, or the burden of placing their own children in violent, failing schools.

Experts shouldn't mandate others to survive in dangerous school environments unless they're willing to come live the nightmare with folks every day. I'm certain, like all parents, the NAACP's leader would want his child in a safe school and wouldn't want authorities imposing their "expert" parenting decisions on him and his children. In fact, when Aaron took his new position as a dean at the high performing and safe private school, he noted right away that NAACP leader's child was a student in the school.

CHAPTER 13

RACIAL WORKSHOPS
FOR KIDS

*"Supporters of the racial Seminar Day labeled the parents request-
ing balance as 'bigots,' 'haters,' 'against free speech' and even heckled and laughed at an African-American pastor from the South
Side of Chicago..."*

Throughout my teaching career, I've had more than my share of severe
discipline problems, but the troubles destroying SPPS were far more severe
than the issues I faced. We didn't have PEG, but like teachers all across
the country, ever since these racial-equity-discipline policies entered our
schools we've been exhausted and demoralized by the extreme change and
lax in discipline standards. Stress reigns, and many teachers are suffering
from physical and emotional illness. Things got so bad in my classroom
because of an almost total lack of any real consequences for severe discipline
issues, three different doctors told me, "Your job is killing you."

Our public schools and universities have become social and political
warzones, and as my teacher friend Chalone discovered at that CTA sponsored "Social Justice Forum" at which teachers were instructed in how to
make their students social justice warriors, the divisive battleground is once
again compliments of government unions.

An entire group of parents and kids at an upper middle-class suburban
public school told me they're being harassed because of identity politics
pushed by unions and union-loyal administrators.

I ran into several of the parents at an event in Chicago who told me their story about the "All School Seminar Day" their children were exposed to at New Trier High School in Winnetka, Illinois. Here is what one of those parents shared with me.

"New Trier is renowned for providing a top-notch education. But when the school required students to attend—for two consecutive years—a day of racial workshops, based in large part on the belief that 'white privilege' is to blame for social inequities, some parents took a stand and advocated for balance and inclusion of diverse ideas in the day's teaching." Peter Berkowitz even wrote about it in the *Wall Street Journal*.[64]

The parent continued, "Upon reading the course descriptions for this racial 'Seminar Day,' titled 'Today's Struggle for Racial Civil Rights,' it was clear the day's agenda was one-sided, lacked balance, and was insulting to minorities. It left out an entire school of thought—held by many African Americans—that minorities are far more affected by lack of economic and educational opportunities and other issues than by racism. Not to mention a growing body of evidence demonstrating that focusing exclusively on race often serves to inflame racial conflict, not reduce it."

This group of parents was deeply concerned because their children (just like white teachers in Aaron's district) were being taught that all white people (including them) have white privilege and are blinded by institutional racism. Though many teachers were loudly touting the Seminar Day as good, the parents at New Trier were not aware of NEA Resolutions when they and their kids were accused of institutional racism, but they went to work immediately to discover the root causes of the injustices and to protect their kids. Their story continues:

> In early December of 2016, a group of parents with concerns about the one-sided curriculum for the Seminar Day began connecting through a flurry of emails, texts, conference calls and kitchen table meetings. By January we had a website[65] to provide information to other parents and the community in an attempt to achieve balance in the Seminar Day's agenda. But what ensued was a hugely divisive controversy that resulted in 700 people attending a school board meeting in the school's theater and a campaign assisted by a professional group and the New Trier administration to oppose our efforts.

This campaign deceptively garnered more than 5,000 signatures on a petition, which they dramatically unfurled circus-style at the 700-person school board meeting.

Supporters of the racial Seminar Day labeled the parents requesting balance as "bigots," "haters," "against free speech" and even heckled and laughed at an African-American pastor from the South Side of Chicago who spoke at the school board meeting in opposition to the identity politics and white privilege themes of the racial Seminar Day.

These parents also told me that they learned how "white privilege" groups like the National SEED Project (Seeking Educational Equity and Diversity) and PEG have been training New Trier staff—and teachers across the country—for years to embed white privilege/grievance politics into classrooms without notice to parents or the public.

Their story continues:

Some students who attended the racial Seminar Day reported to their parents they did so solely because teachers pressured them. The troubling trends commonplace on today's university campuses have trickled down to K–12 education. New Trier is also currently working with one of the nearby local K–8 schools to provide "professional development" to elementary teachers in an effort to roll out these principles about race and privilege at the elementary level, thereby making this an even more troubling trend.

The New Trier school administration and board ultimately refused all requests to add balance, claiming the Seminar Day would proceed "as is." And while they decided not to hold a Seminar Day on race for the next school year, they have pledged to embed racial "conversations" into the curriculum, so parents must remain alert and be prepared to balance out the left-wing ideology being foisted upon their kids.

As an addition, one mom told me, "Some kids chose not to attend Seminar Day and instead joined some peers visiting a low-income neighborhood to learn firsthand about the history of the area and its current needs, as well as meeting with high school kids from the Woodlawn neighborhood and forging some new ties. After returning to school, my child was publicly humiliated by a teacher—in class—for not attending Seminar Day."

Imagine, a teacher humiliating a child. It's shocking. But we hear about it a lot these days. There's only one way great teachers, parents, and kids can escape the harassment and lack of excellence dominating many of our schools today: we have to stand together and hold to account the state and national teachers' unions, and work to remove their negative impact from our schools.

But too many parents, teachers, and citizens are standing on the sidelines—too confused, too divided, or too afraid to speak out—so when brave teachers, parents, and older students take a stand against abusive unions, they often get squashed.

CHAPTER 14

CHOICE: IT'S ABOUT FAMILY

"My personal email, my school email, my Facebook is filled every day with crying parents sharing stories about how heartbroken their kids are. They want to know why they cannot have their school."

Racial equity discipline policies, lessons on anal and oral sex, teachers like the Witch who manhandle kids, and so many other problems related to allowing teachers' unions to dominate our schools are all reasons many parents want school choice. You'll recall Nicole and her mother, Kim, are the ones who were traumatized by union-sponsored sex education curriculums but robbing her of her innocence isn't the only thing the unions have done to harm Nicole.

During Nicole's elementary school years, she was struggling greatly in almost every subject, so whenever our families would get together, I'd sit down with Nicole and work with her on her studies. Every single time she understood quickly and completed the work independently without mistake, so I couldn't figure out why she was earning D's and F's in school, and her parents were beside themselves with worry. In second grade, a medical diagnosis revealed the root cause of Nicole's struggles. She has epilepsy and suffers from "absence seizures," so she blanks out about twenty times a day, and most of her seizures occur in the early morning hours, so the seizures dominated most of her school day.

Her seizures and grades qualified her for an IEP (Individualized Education Plan), so a special resource teacher was assigned to support Nicole with her regular classroom work. Although she met with the resource teacher daily, Nicole was still earning D's and F's in every academic subject. Nicole's mother, Kim, told me, "I knew that special education teacher cared about Nicole. She was so sweet, but she was completely overwhelmed with behavior problems and a high degree of difficulty with many of her students, so Nicole did not get all the help she needed."

Kim noticed that behavior problems (that were rarely addressed by administration) were an issue in just about every classroom. The distractions were a huge challenge for Nicole, so she couldn't concentrate on learning. During fourth grade she was completely overwhelmed because after her teacher left for maternity leave, the district covered the classroom with four different substitutes, and the class was out of control. Nicole was totally lost. Her D's and F's continued in every subject (except drama), and her bright and happy personality became dark and depressed.

Nicole's parents were able to request her fifth-grade teacher, and he was so great Nicole grew in confidence, and she finally experienced success. Her mom told me, "That man was her saving grace. It takes that one teacher to turn the ship." But, when middle school started in sixth grade, everything fell apart again. Changing classrooms and teachers for every subject confused Nicole, and discipline problems reigned in her new school too. Her special education label embarrassed her because she was pulled out of class for tests, and she became so unorganized she couldn't keep her work straight, so she started withdrawing more.

Nicole became so despondent in sixth grade that her health worsened, and her anxiety level about school was so high she simply didn't want to be there. I asked her to share her experience.

"In sixth grade," she told me, "I missed two months of school altogether because I was so stressed out I had daily headaches." She was stressed because she didn't understand the work, she couldn't figure out how to make friends, and her teachers were requiring her to write essays almost every day. She explained that handwriting is especially difficult for her, but she's good on the computer, so I asked her why the school didn't simply include a laptop or typewriter as part of her IEP. She didn't know why, but she liked the idea.

Every year the parents of special education students have an annual IEP meeting with the school IEP team to discuss growth, new goals, and to allow parents to seek advice and information about their child. Kim told me, "I was very put off by the IEP meetings. They were just passing her along, and I didn't want that." Kim fought for what she felt was best for her daughter. She told the IEP team, "She failed math. I don't want you to move her on." Kim was disappointed with their response, and their power to make such serious decisions for her daughter.

"Oh no," they told her. "We don't hold kids back; it hurts their self-esteem."

"Self-esteem," without much regard to building responsibility or respectful behavior, seemed to dominate the school discipline plan. Ironically, Kim knew Nicole's struggles at school had landed her self-esteem in the toilet. She was depressed. As Kim reminisced on Nicole's sixth-grade year she told me through tears, "That was the year it hit me, and I thought, 'Oh, my God, my child may not graduate from high school.'"

It was about this time that Kim heard about a new charter school in town. She felt hopeful, but she'd heard the arguments used against charters, and was afraid Nicole would be rejected because of her special education label. Kim told me, "I called the school, and they had one seventh-grade opening." She told the woman on the phone. "But my daughter has an IEP; you probably don't want her." Kim said the woman sounded hurt that anyone would question their care of children with special needs, and she replied, "Of course we want her."

Kim told me, "On orientation day, Nicole was disrespectful to me in front of her new teacher." Kim choked up again as she recalled that teacher's comforting response of, "It's okay, I'm going to help her get through this. I will bond with her; she's going to be fine."

Kim told me, "That was the best year of Nicole's education."

During that school year Nicole's grades went from D's and F's to A's and B's—all of them. I talked to Nicole about her experience and asked her what made the charter school so much better for her than her traditional public school. She said, "My teachers had more time to work with me and if the class didn't understand something, they would slow down and teach it again."

Classes were smaller too. "I really liked the smaller size," she shared. "And at my old schools, I was always judged for not being outgoing." She shared that her teachers in the charter taught her some tricks on how to make friends and how to interact with others with more confidence. "I was really popular at the charter school because I learned communicating skills. I also liked wearing uniforms because I didn't feel judged all the time about my clothes," she told me. "And we started later in the morning, so I didn't have headaches, and my seizures happened less during class."

Kim appreciated the discipline policy too. "They had a no-tolerance policy," she told me. I asked Kim if the charter school was kicking out students who misbehaved because that's another talking point unions use to disparage charters. "No, they called the parents a lot when behavior issues were prevalent and made the parents take responsibility for their children. Kids were absolutely not permitted to disrupt the learning."

Kim shared her frustration with the way Nicole's former school leadership allowed discipline problems to grow so out of control that learning was compromised. She noted the positive impact effective discipline had on Nicole's new school community. She told me, "Teachers were empowered to teach because disruption wasn't permitted." (This comment alone made me feel like moving my home and getting a job at Nicole's charter school because I cannot imagine how much more effective I could be as a teacher if discipline problems were properly addressed by parents and the school administration.)

I asked Nicole if her overall health improved and if she missed any school while in the charter. "I missed two days because I had to go to the hospital for tests for my seizures," she told me. "But I didn't want to miss those two days." When I asked Kim about the overall impact of the charter school on Nicole, she told me through tears again, "She loved it. She finally belonged. She was a different kid."

Nicole's dad, Chuck, piped in, "She used to hate school and I had to fight her every morning, but when she was at the charter, she asked me every day all summer, 'When does school start, Dad?'"

Kim and Chuck were beyond grateful for the positive changes Nicole's charter school brought into their lives. Their daughter was thriving, and serenity returned to their home. Kim made it clear to me that Nicole had a few wonderful teachers during her traditional public school experience and they were especially thankful to her fifth-grade teacher, but the overall public school philosophy just didn't work for Nicole. "She was always left behind," Kim told me. "At the charter, every teacher was so motivated, and Nicole was a big star on campus."

Unions, and those they convince, have all sorts of arguments against school choice, and they may really believe them, but the truth is, parents desire school choice for myriad reasons. If you'll recall, when Ben was little, and I was single parenting, I just needed a school that was located closer to my job. The years of stress we endured and the vulnerable situations in which I had to leave Ben could have been avoided if we would have had school choice.

Most folks don't realize it, but charter schools in many states must obtain permission from local public school districts before they can open their doors to students. Since the unions fight against charter schools and union-funded politicians dominate most school boards, many charters are rejected and never even get the opportunity to open. Many that do open—and even thrive—are burdened with constant attacks against their charters by union-inspired forces that watch them like hawks hoping to find some way to threaten their existence.

Deanna Campagna served children in Chino Unified School District in Southern California for twenty years. She taught with a dynamic team of educators using proven methods with great results, but several of her colleagues were laid off due to budget constraints. Deanna and her team were demoralized because great teachers lost their jobs while those with more seniority, but less skill, kept theirs. Deanna told me, "In my experience, the union only protected those teachers that had no business being around children."

Deanna had tenure, so she had job security, but she gave it all up because she desired to teach with those great teachers in a school environment fully focused on the children. She said, "I feel so strongly: teachers make or break kids." She told me she and her teacher friends asked, "How can we keep this awesome team of teachers who really believe in the success of children together?" Their answer was birthing a charter school right in Deanna's living room. They taught all day and wrote their charter all night. "We wanted a perfect petition, so there were literally nights when we didn't even sleep," she told me. Chino Unified rejected their charter twice, but eventually these passionate teachers successfully launched their outstanding charter with full support of the superintendent.

At their charter Deanna told me, "It was all about the kids. It was the best teaching experience because we all had the same philosophy and parents were embraced." Their school grew rapidly, parents, teachers, and kids loved it, and they were the top-performing school in San Bernardino County. But then an administrator was accused of mishandling money. Deanna told me, "It was devastating. But we restructured everything and addressed every issue. We got rid of her right away, and anyone closely associated with her was let go." Even though the allegations against that administrator had not been proven but were under investigation, those who oppose charter schools used the alleged behavior of one school official to close the entire school.

Charters must be renewed every five years, and unfortunately, Deanna's charter was up for renewal. "It was a very, very stressful year," Deanna told me. "We went to the district. We went to the county, and it went all the way to the state. I don't know the whole story. Everything was so hidden. They wouldn't release the records because of the investigation."

In the end, 1,200 kids, their families, and teachers who were thriving and perfectly happy in their child and family-centered charter were forced to leave their hard-earned, award-winning school behind. When I asked her why education officials would shutter a high performing charter while parents, teachers, and kids were fighting to keep it open, Deanna told me, "Their concern was that many people were owed money, but nobody has come up to us and said, 'Hey, you owe me money.' You'd think that if somebody was owed a lot of money because of that leader, they'd be saying something. Nothing has been proven; the DA hasn't come back with any decisions. They haven't arrested anyone; they're just investigating, but they closed the school down."

Deanna and her friends put everything out in the open; they had no secret funds; they just wanted to move on with a new leader and serve the kids. She wonders, "Why can't the school continue to thrive?"

Deanna also made an astute comparison, "Someone in LA Unified was stealing money, and we thought, okay, are they going to close down all of the schools in LA Unified because of one person? No. But that's what happened at our school."

I had to agree with her. When Charles and I first moved into the Capistrano Unified School District, the district was reeling from accusations against the superintendent and assistant superintendent. They were accused of keeping an "enemies list" against parents who criticized the district. They faced felony charges and spent four years fighting in the courts before being vindicated and having their case dismissed in 2011. Not once during those four years or after did the education status quo threaten to close any of the schools in Capistrano Unified. The district simply brought in new temporary leadership.

But Deanna and her friends are aching from the loss of their school. She told me, "My former co-workers now cry as they drive to work. Monday is always the hardest day." The parents are grieving too, "My personal email, my school email, my Facebook is filled every day with crying parents sharing stories about how heartbroken their kids are. They want to know why they cannot have their school."

Because her colleagues are outstanding educators, they were able to find jobs, but they were not able to find a good match for their deep sense of commitment to making children's needs paramount in all school decisions. She told me, "When one of my friends asked his new grade-level team when they could meet to collaborate, they told him, 'No, no, it's not like that here. We respect each other's time.' It hurt my heart when he told me that. We've never abused each other's time. This is what you do. You work together as a team to do what's best for the kids."

She added that her friends are telling her that parents are not allowed on their public school campuses during the school day. She said, "At our charter school we embraced parents. They helped all of the time. You know that saying, 'It takes a village'? We really believe that. It wasn't 'your student,' it was 'our student.'"

Just like Deanna and her colleagues, the teachers and parents who started Nicole's charter spent years fighting to obtain approval for their school too. It was an independent study charter school, which was permitted to operate outside of its approving district. There are many of these independent study charters in California, which are ideal for kids like Nicole who are underserved in traditional settings. Though Nicole was finally thriving and loving school for the first time in her life, a tragic thing happened. During their first year in operation (the year Nicole started at the school), they were informed that their school was in danger of closing.

I talked with some folks familiar with Nicole's charter and was told there were two court cases in the state of California that threw a wrench into schools like Nicole's that were independent study charter schools not operating in their approving districts, so suddenly hundreds of schools operating all up and down the state were in jeopardy. Long story short, the education status quo found a loophole, and the home district had the right to start legal processes immediately to shut the charter down.

The parents fought hard and the community rallied behind them, but they would have to move their school one hundred miles away to comply with the new law—that's a brutal commute for a bunch of kids.

I was informed that Nicole's charter and independent charters all over the state were coerced to go to their home districts to receive approval for their existence. Many were denied for silly reasons, and not surprisingly, many that were approved were forced to give up their independent school boards and become dependent upon the local public school district just to keep their doors open. In other words, everyone's boss became the superintendent and the public school status quo, and all employees were forced to be part of the union.

Nicole attended her great charter for one school year—seventh grade—the only year she ever loved school and earned all A's and B's. The summer before eighth grade was that summer her father mentioned when she begged him every day, "When does school start, Dad?" Her parents hung onto hope all throughout the summer because it seemed so obvious the charter should be allowed to exist, but three days before school was scheduled to start, the families received notice that the school was forced to close.

Kim, Nicole, and her dad were completely devastated. I asked Kim what grounds the district had to close the charter. She explained it was two things: the school boundary issue and an attendance issue. "Our charter had an optional school day on Fridays," Kim told me. "Kids could come on Fridays for extra help, or they could work from home that day." Nicole piped in, "I always went to school on Fridays!" Imagine a child wanting to go to school! Isn't that our goal?

Kim continued, "Because so many children loved going to school on Fridays, we couldn't continue our charter." Huh? The children loved school so much they came when they didn't have to, but the status quo saw this as a bad thing? Kim told me, "They had a grievance against us. They closed us down because we went too many hours to school."

Why would the education status quo, using their grievance mentality, work so hard to shut down a safe and outstanding school effectively serving needy children like Nicole?

Money.

The teachers' unions are in self-preservation mode, and their lifesaver is their "a great public school for every child" campaign. That sounds nice, but it's really a campaign used to denigrate charters and school choice so teachers' unions can continue their lucrative control and power over our public schools. The real tragedy is by doing this they've turned what should be a family issue into a divisive political issue.

Unions spend hundreds of millions each year funding deceptive messaging to terrify teachers, parents, school boards, and taxpayers into rejecting school choice. Because people are unaware of the unions' self-serving motives, those clever talking points have a way of making it challenging for people to put empathy for families and children like Nicole above the hysterical claims of the unions.

Scripture says, "For out of the abundance of the heart, the mouth speaks," Matthew 12:34 (NKJV). With Nicole and Deanna in mind, let's hear from the union heart through Bob Chanin (NEA's top legal counsel for forty-one years) as he addressed the NEA Representative Assembly and they cheered over his words:

> *This is not to say that the concern of NEA and its affiliates with closing achievement gaps, reducing dropout rates, improving teacher quality and the like are unimportant or inappropriate. To the contrary, these are the goals that guide the work we do, BUT they need not and must not be achieved at the expense of due process, employee rights, and collective bargaining. That simply is too high a price to pay. When all is said and done, NEA and its affiliates must never lose sight of the fact that they are unions, and what unions do first and foremost is represent their members.*[66]

And that brings me to my final and most important point, which is why, at least in my opinion, NEA and its affiliates are such effective advocates. Despite what some among us would like to believe, it is not because of our creative ideas. It is not because of the merit of our positions. It is not because we care about children, and it is not because we have a vision of a great public school for every child. NEA and its affiliates are effective advocates because we have power, and we have power because there are more than 3.2 million people who are willing to pay us hundreds of millions of dollars in dues each year...[67]

I have to challenge his assertion that 3.2 million people are "willing to pay" them "hundreds of millions," because we've all been *forced* to fund them for decades or we'd lose our jobs, and now charters are being *forced* to close unless they give up independence and join unionized districts, but his words make clear that advancing the interests of *unions,* so they can achieve more power is the motivation and abundance of the union heart.

In July 2017, the NEA adopted New Business Item 47, which clearly states its objective:

NEA will develop and promote resolutions that local associations can introduce at school board meetings calling for county-wide and state-wide moratoria on new charter school authorizations in every state that has legislation authorizing the creation of charter schools.

They also have a committee considering NBI 133.

I move that NEA develop resources for the organization of existing charter schools in all states where there are laws allowing them. Resources should include...specific steps each state should make in order to reach a goal of full charter unionization.

And make no mistake, the reason Nicole's charter no longer exists has nothing to do with educational quality or outcomes. Actually, it has nothing to do with education at all. It's about cold hard cash and union domination.

As the NEA's Executive Director Don Cameron told us:

NEA's future is inextricably linked to the well-being of public education…. [O]ur job is to continue advocating for our members, and the surest way to protect their jobs is to protect public education.[68]

It's all about the money. Kids be damned.

The unions got their way against Nicole's charter. After positively impacting the lives of many families who were thrilled to be there, the school closed after only one year in operation. Kim told me, "I had already told my other three kids they would be going to the school the following year. I loved that school. It vanished as quickly as it popped up."

Nicole is now back to navigating switching classes and teachers all day in a large and intimidating school environment with too little discipline, and she's struggling to organize her supplies for each class. She's in tenth grade, and last time I talked to her, she was stressed out about an upcoming test and completing work she doesn't understand. Kim shared through tears, "Some of the parents from the charter decided to homeschool, but I don't have that option; I work full time."

Nicole has to arrive at school in the early mornings again, at the height of her many seizures. "My headaches are bad," she told me. Beginning in 2017, she started suffering from grand mal seizures as well, as I finished this chapter I received a message that she was sleeping in the arms of her mother after another massive seizure.

I guess the union-acquired board members in Nicole's home district are happy now—they get the money that follows Nicole and any other students who were forced to return to their schools. I know the teachers' unions are really happy about the wealth and power they've restored by hanging onto more coerced teacher fees and tax dollars after picking on a bunch of families and their kids. Must be nice for them, and I imagine those collective bargaining sessions led to some fine benefits for union members, so they got what they wanted. Meanwhile, Nicole suffers from increased health concerns and report cards full of D's and F's.

CHAPTER 15

Choice: It's About Family, Part 2

"Rebecca, if I didn't go to Sunburst, I'd be dead."

I could share multiple personal stories of children like Nicole whose lives have been dramatically changed simply by having access to a school system with a different educational or discipline philosophy. School environments matter and have the power to change lives for good or bad, and in the case of our son Kyle, having access to the right school saved his life.

Kyle's in his twenties now, and he and Ben have grown so close Charles and I sometimes get overwhelmed with gratitude for our good fortune, but shortly after we married, Kyle's behavior was so dangerous we had to protect Ben from him, and we had to take on a frightening fight for Kyle's life. The only reason we won the battle was because of God's grace and an interesting educational option.

Kyle was entering ninth grade when we became a family. His big dream in life is to become a major league baseball player, so the first thing he did when we moved to our new home was join the high school baseball team. He was their starting pitcher and made new friends immediately, so we felt things were going pretty well for him, but about six months into our marriage, we began having some serious problems with Kyle's attitude and behavior. He started lying to us, stealing from us, acting out toward Ben and me, and he was becoming downright entitled and very difficult to be around.

One day, as we sat in the bleachers cheering for Kyle, I felt a thick wall of disdain coming from numerous mothers in the crowd; they were giving me the cold shoulder in a big way. It continued at every game I attended thereafter.

Unbeknownst to us, a key individual in Kyle's life was filling his mind with hateful attacks against Ben and me—especially me. Kyle didn't share this information with us at the time because he believed it, but he was told lies that would make any child hate his family and particularly a stepparent. He was told that I was abusive; that I was trying to undermine his other relationships; that I broke up his family, and about a hundred other things that he still won't tell us to this day because he doesn't want my feelings to be hurt.

Because of the outright attack on my character, Kyle directed almost 100 percent of his anger toward me, and he started treating Ben with contempt too. Someone was emboldening him to criticize and condemn us, and since Charles and I didn't bend to his entitled and destructive outbursts, Kyle resented us with a passion.

Throughout the next two years, the behaviors increased to such a degree our parenting methods were stretched, our young marriage was taking a beating, and we discovered Kyle was abusing drugs. We supported him through twelve-step programs, spent multiple nights talking to him into the wee hours of the morning, took him to weekly counseling at over 100 dollars a pop, and felt like prisoners in our own home.

Ironically, things came to a head with Kyle's behavior the very weekend Charles and I attended that CTA leadership conference at which the three hundred teachers were bullied into silence. Ben was visiting his dad that weekend, so he was taken care of, but Kyle had a job at a local grocery store, so he had to stay with friends near home. We chose a trusted family, and they were happy to take Kyle for the weekend because, like most of the parents, they liked Kyle. We made it very clear that he was not to come to our home for any reason, and we gave them Kyle's work schedule so they would know when he was supposed to be at work. The plan seemed foolproof, but since we were still unaware of the lies being told to Kyle about us, and the lies he was repeating to his friends and their parents about me, we had no idea these parents were questioning us as parents and didn't fully understand the need for strict adherence to our plan.

When we returned home from our weekend of being abused by the teachers' unions, we walked into an uncanny scene: slippery floors, girl's sunglasses on a side table, and a nine-inch tall pile of marijuana ashes in our backyard. A very large party had occurred in our house while we were gone, and Kyle and his buddy had missed a few items when they cleaned up the mess.

Though Kyle lied for hours about what happened, we had already talked to our neighbors and uncovered a few details. In the end, we discovered Kyle had gone around his high school all week telling every kid in the school (even those he didn't know) that our house would be open all weekend and they could come and go as they pleased. He wasn't even home for most of the weekend bender, and our neighbors got suspicious when hordes of kids were all over our house and cars were driving up and down the street with loud music.

We were horrified and knew immediately that we not only had to protect ourselves as parents and homeowners, but we had to get some serious intervention for Kyle. It's one thing for a teenager to throw a secret party for friends when parents are away, it's quite another thing to allow hundreds of kids—many of them total strangers—to invade your family home.

It was at this point we found out why the mothers on the team hated me. When we went over to talk to the couple in charge of Kyle for the weekend, they felt horrible about being bamboozled by Kyle, and because *they* had been his victim this time, they were finally able to see there were some serious issues with Kyle. After a long and sincere talk, I asked the mother why so many of the other moms were snubbing me and glaring at me because I'd noticed her attitude toward me had cooled too.

She told me honestly that Kyle told his teammates and their parents that living with me was like living with Hitler, and that I had broken up his family. Charles was a single parent for nine years before we met, so reality told Kyle the truth, but psychological indoctrination is powerful, and Kyle was captivated by it. He and the person filling his mind with lies about us were so convincing that the players on the team were regularly greeting Kyle with, "Hey, Kyle, how's life in the gas chamber?"

Here I was pouring my heart out for this kid, tutoring on the side to pay for his counseling, and doing all I could to encourage him as a young man, yet I was seen by him, his teammates, and many of their mothers as Adolf Hitler.

This was when we realized it wasn't enough for us to go harder on Kyle; we'd already done that. It wasn't enough to have him in high-quality counseling and addiction recovery; we'd done that too. His high school teachers and administrators had worked with us as well, but that wasn't working. Kyle had spent some Saturdays helping the custodians do manual labor around the campus; he'd served detentions; he'd been benched from games and more. Nothing we did as Kyle's Education Triangle was working; we all cared deeply about him, but public high schools are designed to meet the needs of kids in the middle, and Kyle was *far* from the middle.

After the weekend free-for-all that took place in our home, Charles and I made an emergency appointment with Kyle's high school administrators, his baseball coach, and the campus police officer. We told them everything that happened and shared our tremendous concerns that some child could have been injured, and that we felt incredibly vulnerable because we could be held liable for problems caused by a party we never allowed or condoned. Thankfully, they appreciated our efforts and took our concerns seriously.

After taking our testimony, the police officer became one of the most valuable angles in our Education Triangle. He could see we were great parents, but we were trapped in a situation that seemed to have no remedy. He had just that day received a flyer about a special military boarding school for sixteen- to nineteen-year-olds who were getting into severe trouble. Sunburst Youth Academy was located at the Joint Forces Training Base in Los Alamitos (about an hour from our home), and the National Guard ran it in cooperation with the County Department of Education. Kids attending Sunburst received the military structure necessary to help them overcome their behavior problems and high school instruction from teachers.

Most kids that choose Sunburst do so because they've gotten into so much trouble a judge gives them a choice: "Jail or Sunburst Youth Academy?" Those kids are motivated to choose Sunburst. Kyle was not motivated, and we couldn't force him to attend because it's a voluntary program, but we could give him reason to be motivated to choose Sunburst, so we asked God for wisdom and offered Kyle three alternatives. Two of his choices included losing baseball altogether, and the third included attending Sunburst, restoring himself to an upright person, and then returning to baseball and our home with the promise we would support his dreams of making it to the big leagues. Kyle chose Sunburst.

The program required each cadet's family to provide a mentor who would commit to the student for the duration of the program and for at least two years after graduation. Kyle's high school baseball coach stepped up as his mentor, and to this day almost a decade later, he and Kyle are very close, and Kyle assists with coaching when he's in town. We're eternally grateful to Coach Dave Gellatly.

On an early morning in January of Kyle's junior year in high school, Charles, Ben, my dad, my stepmom, Kyle, and I all showed up before dawn for the orientation for Kyle's six-month stay at Sunburst.

We had been asked to write out details about the reasons Kyle was coming to Sunburst; we took the assignment to heart, and the cadres were remarkably supportive and grateful to us for being totally honest and forthright about our son's issues; they said most families shared very little, and details would help them to better help Kyle.

Kyle joined the group of cadets, bending his newly shaved head to gather his duffle bag. We stood at a distance wishing we could give him more hugs and encouragement. As Kyle looked up at us, my father said, "He looks just like a deer in the headlights."

While Kyle lived at Sunburst, we were permitted to see him only three times, and he was allowed to call us every other Sunday. This was the first time since Kyle's birth that Charles had ever been separated from him for more than a couple of days, so he was grieving deeply, but we were so beaten down from the over two years of battling for this kid's heart, mind, soul, and body that we rested in the comfort of knowing he was in good and capable hands and we prayed he would find healing.

Life at Sunburst was very structured. Days were full of morning and afternoon exercises, military style drills, frequent field trips to gain cultural experiences, and regular service projects designed to teach the cadets that it's better to give than to receive. It was just what Kyle needed.

God blessed Kyle with the most remarkable cadre, and two of them had specifically endured similar problems with adults in their young lives who had undermined them the way the key person in Kyle's life had been destabilizing him with lies and addiction, so they saw right through the abuse and knew exactly how to help Kyle find healing. They got Kyle journaling right away, and he tells us he wrote pages and pages about the ugly things he was told about me, and then his cadre helped him to work through the lies and expose them to the light of truth.

They immediately noticed Kyle's athleticism and started playing catch with him. One of the cadre started a drill team (the military type with rifles), and Kyle was chosen as the leader because he had natural leadership skills and experience marching in complicated formations from his years in marching band.

I made a commitment to myself that I would write Kyle two long letters every week while he was in Sunburst. *Lord of the Rings* is his favorite book, so I nicknamed him Frodo (the hero in the stories) and told him that like all human beings, he had a high calling and God had a heroic mission for him. Every letter started "Dear Frodo," and I used this unique time to remind Kyle of how much we love him; how much we believe in him; how much we missed him.

To my great surprise and delight, one of Kyle's cadres sought me out on Family Day to thank me for my letters. He said that he and Kyle were so encouraged by them that all of the cadets started reading them and finding encouragement for themselves too. This was the greatest blessing because it was the first time since Kyle and I became family that he was embracing my love and care for him, and that my true motives were being valued and trusted.

Kyle shined so much at Sunburst that the other cadets named him "Captain America." He was named "top cadet," he was given the honor of making the graduation speech, and he even got to be part of a video to help publicize their program. During his speech, he thanked his dad and me and apologized publicly to us for putting us through so much hell. It was a miracle.

Now Sunburst isn't the right school for everyone. In fact, our Ben and sweet Nicole would likely have crashed and burned in a setting like Sunburst, but it was the perfect school for Kyle because he had been getting away with things at his traditional high school. He's so charismatic no one (even his counselor) questioned his words, actions, or motives.

At Sunburst, the cadre fully understood addictive behaviors and the deceptions that go with them. They saw right through Kyle's lies, and when he tried to play one cadre off the other during his first week, they caught him red-handed and called him on the deception immediately. Kyle couldn't be a poser at Sunburst, and the exposure of his deceptive heart humbled him.

Our decision to encourage Kyle to attend Sunburst was not an attack on his teachers; Kyle just needed a *different* learning situation to overcome his major behavioral issues. Because of Kyle's inborn personality traits and need for lots of direction, we honestly feel he would have done better if he'd been able to benefit from schools run in a military fashion throughout most of his K–12 years. His high school, middle school, and elementary school were not abusive or underperforming, but they weren't right for Kyle, and he learned very little as a result. Kyle needed more structure. It's too bad he had to practically disintegrate before we were able to get him into the kind of school that was right for him.

I've met lots of kids like Kyle throughout my teaching career—kids who would have a chance to grow strong in character, self-control, and wholeness if they were given the opportunity to be instructed in a more structured school environment. Their parents and siblings would be spared the horrible nightmare we had to endure too. Kids are not carbon copies of each other, so we can't expect them all to thrive in a "one-school-fits-all" model that is designed to teach to the middle and thus under serves anyone who falls outside of that narrow group.

Kyle came home after his life-saving experience at Sunburst and became the starting pitcher for the varsity baseball team his senior year, and they had a fantastic winning season. Major League Baseball scouted him, and a scout for the Seattle Mariners spent a few hours in our home talking to us about their desire to draft Kyle, but because Kyle wanted more time to mature, he chose to join Long Beach State University's baseball program and received outstanding training as a pitcher from some top coaches in the system.

Kyle required Tommy John surgery (ulnar collateral ligament reconstruction), so he had to "red shirt" one year, and even that was a blessing because Kyle actually earned a degree while playing baseball at Long Beach—truly a miracle for a kid who seems to be allergic to books.

In June 2015, Kyle's greatest dream became a reality. He was drafted by the Oakland A's. As I write this, he's in their minor league system working up the ranks and having the time of his life.

On Wednesday, July 5, 2017, Mike Trout was down in the minors re-habbing from an injury and needed to face some live pitching before going back up to Angel Stadium. Our Kyle was the starting pitcher facing Trout that night. He was a nervous wreck facing one of the all-time greatest hitters in baseball history, but you know what?

Kyle struck him out!

As you can imagine, my family and I went wild in the stands. We were screaming, jumping, clapping, and saying "Way to go, Kyle! That-a boy!" What family wouldn't?

But the game was held in the Angels' minor league affiliate ballpark, so Mike Trout fans wearing shirts declaring their devotion to him—"Trout 27"—were very unhappy with our behavior. They gave us dirty looks and a few even got up and moved away from us to open seats.

We weren't meaning to be objectionable—I've been an Angels fan since I was a kid and was even in the park for Nolan Ryan's 1975 no-hitter—we weren't cheering *against* Trout, we were cheering *for* Kyle. There's a big difference.

Of course, those fans had no idea the depths of despair from which Kyle had climbed to reach that pitching mound. They didn't know about the childhood abandonment, the lies that hurt Kyle, the drug abuse, or his six months at Sunburst. They had no idea that Kyle's very presence on that mound, facing Mike Trout, was a miraculous picture of redemption.

There's one other thing they didn't know. Only one week before Kyle struck out Mike Trout, he had been moved down from Double-A to Single-A—a discouraging demotion for a man desiring to reach the Major Leagues. He'd been struggling to control his off-speed pitches, so instead of dominating on the mound, he was getting beat up. I thought Kyle was going to be discouraged about moving down to high A, but he told me it was the best thing that ever happened to him, because the pitching coach got back to fundamentals and quickly discovered Kyle's struggle was a simple fix—he'd adjusted his grip without realizing it, and it was messing up his pitches.

What the crowd and Mike Trout didn't know that night is our Kyle was once again fighting to overcome defeat. It wasn't the kind of life-threatening challenge he had to overcome at Sunburst, but it was life and death for his future career in Major League Baseball and failing could have meant the death of his lifelong dream. That's why I sat silently as Kyle threw the last pitch; praying hard for God's best. And that's when Kyle threw an off-speed pitch, and Mike Trout swung and missed.

I'm pretty sure if Mike Trout had known the story I just shared with you about our Kyle and discovered all he'd so valiantly battled to make it to Minor League Baseball, he may have cheered for Kyle too. I imagine he would have likely tipped his hat to Kyle and maybe even autographed the strikeout ball, because guys like Trout—who volunteer their time for "at-risk" kids like Kyle used to be—know the redemption of a life is far more important than another home run.

I think the word "awesome" is overused in our culture, and really should be reserved for things like God's creation, the birth of a newborn baby, the Grace of Christ, things like that, but you know what? When Kyle struck out Trout, it was *awesome!* The redemption of a life always is.

You know, when those Trout fans gave us the stink-eye and moved away from us, it hurt, and we felt shunned and isolated. In fact, it felt exactly the way it feels when some teachers reject me for daring to stand against unions in favor of childhood innocence, teacher freedom and school choice. But just like I'm convinced that if those Trout fans had known Kyle's backstory they would have stood up and cheered with us, I'm also convinced that good teachers would stand for kids and families and support school choice if they realized they've been indoctrinated by union rhetoric. Good teachers don't want kids trapped in dangerous or underperforming schools, they know families are the key to success, and they know students thrive in educational environments that meet their specific learning styles, so good teachers should be natural allies of school choice.

Every time I ask Kyle if he thinks he would be pitching in Minor League Baseball today if we had left him in his regular high school instead of taking advantage of the choice of Sunburst Youth Academy, he wrinkles up his face and tells me, "Rebecca, if I didn't go to Sunburst, I'd be dead."

If Kyle makes it big, he wants to become a spokesman for Sunburst Youth Academy in hopes of helping other kids who are stuck in anger or addiction. That's how redemption works—it uses the humility and grace gained from overcoming past pain to help others find healing and redemption too.

I realize Sunburst isn't a charter or private school, but Sunburst offered us choice when we were completely out of options for our son, just like

Nicole's charter offered her and her parents an outstanding option when her traditional public school couldn't meet her needs.

Two schools, two families, two kids…why is one child saved while the other is thrown to the wolves? Because the government and teachers' unions think they know best. Kids like Kyle who display borderline criminal behavior sometimes receive resources and options (and often only after it's too late), while a kid like Nicole, whose only crime is epilepsy, is often given no options and little hope. The same can be said for so many parents who are denied the authority to choose what's best for their children for the basest of reasons—money and power for government unions.

CHAPTER 16

———◆———◆———

BEATEN DOWN

"If you don't do what the MSEA wants, they make your life a living hell. I swear it's like a Mafia or something. They're just scary people."

I used to tell people that teaching is the most fulfilling profession in the world, and it was, but thanks to union domination of our schools and their influence on local, state and national elections, my precious profession is no longer attractive to many highly gifted teachers, and those who try to remedy the situation (like the woman bullied into a heap at the CTA leadership conference and the one they labeled Rotten Apple) are often punished for their efforts.

Kelly Stephenson, a special education high school teacher in Maryland, was always supportive of her union. She served as the building representative for ten years in her local, Wicomico County Education Association (WCEA)—including two years as the treasurer and two years as the president. Though Kelly honestly thought her union was there to support the needs of teachers, her eyes were opened when she became a union official.

When Kelly served as treasurer she said she wrote checks to the state teachers' union for 30,000 dollars a month. As you know, lots of money goes to the national level too. "It's disturbing," she told me. "They got about 500,000 dollars a year from us and did nothing for us."

The problems for Kelly and her colleagues grew from a total lack of services and representation from the state and national unions. When serving as president, Kelly received constant complaints from local members. She told me, "They were all dissatisfied with representation, especially in [teacher] disciplinary matters."

Local teachers serving within the union work with state level "UniServ" directors whenever we have a grievance or an issue to discuss with our school districts. UniServ directors are supposed to be liaisons that are paid to support teachers with local level issues, but many of us have experienced these UniServ folks as roadblocks to real solutions and honest discussions with administration. The teachers in Kelly's district were no exception. Kelly told me, "Our UniServ director was so bad, he would not show up for meetings or represent the needs of members. I've also watched good teachers lose their jobs. I've seen some harassed, and the UniServ did nothing to help."

When Kelly sent an email to the chief legal counsel of her state union asking for support and where she could direct complaints against the incompetent UniServ director, she received a shocking reply. "You need to refer them back to [UniServ director]. It is up to the member[s] to express their concerns; and [UniServ director] will decide how to proceed. We do not allow members to 'shop' for an opinion that they like."

Kelly had a whole folder full of complaints from many members, so this reply put her and her fellow officers over the top. She told me, "It prompted us to have a meeting with MSEA [Maryland State Education Association] officials to try to work out our concerns over the lack of good and proper services for our members."

Well, as you might guess, the meeting with MSEA didn't go very well. In fact, after Kelly met with the MSEA president, instead of addressing the incompetence of the UniServ director, the state union leadership sent Kelly and her colleagues a troubling letter. "They gave us a list of demands and said if we didn't comply, they would take us over."

Kelly told me the entire situation was twisted into ineffectiveness and insubordination of Kelly and the members in her local association. She shared, "The letter stated that we were now under a 'work plan.' We were scolded for not raising enough money in PAC funds in support of union politics. The letter had nothing to do with their total lack of representation—it had everything to do with funding union politics."

Kelly was flabbergasted, so she replied with, "I'm not stupid. You play off the ignorance of all of the people in Maryland who think you're this wonderful organization that goes to bat for people."

Indeed, not only are the citizens ignorant of union operations, but the teachers themselves are in the dark too. During this time while Kelly was president, the teachers' unions were considering which candidate they wanted to support for governor of Maryland. Kelly told me as union officials they were "allowed" to vote for the candidate they thought the union should support, but they were only permitted to choose from a pool of Democrats. Kelly is a Democrat, but she wanted to choose the Republican. "He had a better record," she told me. "But I was not allowed."

Another thing that really bothered Kelly was the way the unions had only union officers choose the favored candidate without input from the rank and file. Officer votes were manipulated too because instead of offering private ballots, officers were told to stand in the corner of the candidate they wanted to support. "We were put under all of this intimidation to choose certain candidates," Kelly told me. "I didn't want any of them. There was lots of peer pressure. It's not a democratic process at all."

Because of the intimidation and one-sided politics, activist teachers who represent the unions' minority viewpoint dominate the leadership and call the shots. You'll recall the NEA's own 2006 survey *Status of the American Public School Teacher*,[69] revealed only 13 percent of teachers consider themselves decisively "liberal," so these extremely liberal leaders are not at all representative of the majority of rank-and-file members.

Though Kelly leans liberal, she believes, like most teachers, that the union's job is to represent teachers in their profession, and it's totally inappropriate for them to push for a political and social agenda. Kelly noted, "They claim to be tolerant of all ideas, but they are the most intolerant groups in the country, and they force those who disagree with their agenda to fund it."

Kelly attended the MSEA state level leadership convention for many years, and just like me and the other teachers I've highlighted in this book, she tried to speak commonsense to union leadership. As president of her local group, she asked, "Why are we here discussing things like the unions' position on gay marriage or transgender bathrooms and things that have nothing to do with teachers and what we're trying to do to get kids to learn?" She received the exact same answer the rest of us have received when we ask those fair questions about the use of our hard-earned money.

"They answered that these issues are important, and it *does* affect all of the kids in the schools," Kelly shared.

Most teachers and parents I know believe these issues are negatively impacting children and invading our schools with the unions' political and social agenda is undermining learning.

Kelly was quick to point out, "I believe in diversity, but I don't understand how a stance on gay marriage improves the school system. I'm not against gay marriage, I just don't believe that we should be voting on positions about it in our teachers' union." Instead, Kelly and her colleagues would have preferred their union help them with the growing number of discipline problems on every campus. "We had teachers that were physically assaulted by students," Kelly told me. "And teachers have been attacked in other districts as well, but our state union wouldn't even address the issue. MSEA has never come out with any kind of campaign against teacher abuse." This is reminiscent of Aaron Benner's testimony isn't it?

The unions tell the public and the politicians they lobby that they are working hard for all teachers. As you can see, that's a falsehood. Instead, the union abandons many good teachers when we need reinforcement, badgers us into supporting their political causes, and punishes us for not wanting to support their agenda with our own time and money.

To give you a clear picture of the unions' negligence in abandoning those paying them dues and fees, here's a breakdown of the dues structure Kelly and her fellow teachers were forced to fork over to the state and national unions.

MSEA—state union = 50 percent

NEA—national union = 30 percent

WCEA—local union (teacher led and valued) = Less than 20 percent

And lest you think this is an anomaly, think again. Almost all teachers' unions operate on the same dues structure.

Currently in California, the numbers are very similar. Since dues vary by district, I'll round off dues at one-thousand dollars a year (some teachers pay much more). Once again, it's easy to see that the state union gets the lion's share, so their abuse and misrepresentation is both egregious and scandalous.

Average California Teacher's Annual Dues = 1,000 dollars

CTA—state union = 700 dollars

NEA—national union = 192 dollars

Local teacher's union = 108 dollars

Kelly and her colleagues worked hard to stage a decertification effort to sever ties from the state and national unions and amend their bylaws. "Our basic premise was, why should we have to be part of the MSEA and NEA when we didn't agree with their political ideas, we didn't agree with what they were doing to us like strong-arming us and trying to take us over, and basically bullying us to do what *they* wanted."

Throughout my long career in America's public schools, I've found that a huge percentage of teachers are very happy with their local union (the teachers who represent them in their district), but they are very *unhappy* with the state and national unions. Most teachers I've spoken with would love to sever ties from state and national unions, and most are frustrated that our dues are used to push one-sided social and sexual agendas, but they don't realize that we have the right to decertify, which means we can sever ties with state and national unions by completely breaking apart our current union structures and creating our own independent local associations. As Kelly's story will reveal, we do technically have the *right*, but the unions make it almost impossible to decertify them, so most teachers just keep on paying their massive dues in resentful submission to the culture of fear.

Kelly and the other officers created their own association proposal with terrific representation benefits including double the amount of professional liability insurance, and a dramatic reduction in dues to only 200 dollars a year. One of the best perks was even though they would pay a fraction of their union dues, they would have plenty of money left over to give back to their own school system because nothing would be wasted on union politics. Kelly shared, "We felt we could make it way more affordable for people in our county, and it would make us more powerful as a local education group."

When Kelly and friends started their drive to change their bylaws to be freed from the state and national unions, the unions responded with their typical marketing campaign including lies and slanderous personal attacks. Kelly told me, "They filed a bogus recall petition, and they got a bunch of people to sign it, but they lied to them about what they were signing—accusing us of malfeasance. We asked, 'Where is your proof?'"

Kelly and her fellow officers were served papers that said they were no longer officers in their local union. There was no vote to remove them; they were simply ousted. A few local members then asserted themselves as "the interim managers." No one voted for these interim managers, but they took over anyway. Kelly recalled, "I know the MSEA was behind it and coached the interim managers through this because we couldn't even get into our office because they broke in and changed the locks." Kelly said the union claimed they had nothing to do with changing the locks, but she and her friends had evidence the union was behind it. She told me, "The chief counsel of the MSEA paid for it, and we have a copy of her check."

Kelly and the real officers had to take the group to court to get the rights to their office back, and they won, but those interim manager teachers wreaked a lot of havoc. "They broke open the filing cabinet. My whole office was littered with papers," Kelly told me. "They actually went to the bank where we had all of our accounts, and they opened all new accounts. They cut us off from the office and the money." Kelly had to get a court order before the bank would change all the accounts back.

The attacks were so bad, and the unions fought so hard with their endless supply of teacher-coerced money, Kelly and her friends had to seek help from some non-profit groups that exist to protect workers abused by unions. Things were getting very frightening for Kelly too. "They followed me to my home," Kelly shared, "One day, someone followed me all day, and they used fear to try to sway people from not leaving them."

Kelly told me the MSEA distributed a chart in the schools slandering Kelly and two other officers as the leaders of the disaffiliation. The unions painted Kelly, her fellow officers, and the decent non-profit folks as villains. They pictured them all on charts including the Koch Brothers (whom the unions always portray as bogeymen) and claimed wealthy special interests were behind the disaffiliation.

Kelly told me, "They lied to people. They just made this stuff up. I mean it was like a campaign against me. It was like I was Donald Trump running for president of the United States or something. They called us 'union busters' too, and how can we be union busters when we're trying to make our union stronger?"

Kelly learned, like all independent-minded teachers who try to work from the inside of unions learn, "It's not about serving teachers," she told me. "It's all about unions. No one can propose an idea that's different than the union's."

Kelly reached out to every school in her district and scheduled dates to meet with the teaching staffs to explain the value of becoming an independent association, but as always, the unions undermined those efforts too. "They stole my schedule of schools I was going to address," Kelly shared. "They would go to visit those schools before my scheduled visit and fill them with nothing but hatred for me, so when I came to visit, teachers would not even listen."

The wealthy union machine once again defeated the best interests of kids and teachers. Kelly told me, "If you don't do what the MSEA wants, they make your life a living hell. I swear it's like a Mafia or something. They're just scary people."

State and national union forces are indeed scary. Two dear teachers in Washington, Barb Amidon and Cindy Omlin, were in fact sued by Washington Education Association (WEA) for speaking up on behalf of their colleagues.

Barb had a lot of unanswered questions about the unions' use of her forced agency fees. She told me, "I wasn't getting the truth, so I spent almost two years digging for information at the Public Disclosure Commission (PDC) where any PAC or candidate has to record and document every month all of their political spending."

Barb traveled to the public library a few times a week, after working all day, and scoured through PDC documents on microfiche. During her detailed searches, Barb uncovered that WEA loaned their PAC 192,000 dollars for political output. This is key because a union is not permitted to use fee payer monies on politics, but a PAC is created only for political spending. "Then about three months later," Barb explained, "I see an entry that shows WEA forgave the loan! I almost exploded! I took a picture of all the documents, and I said, 'See, there it is.' I knew that was illegal because I had informed myself and read the laws."

Once Barb found that evidence, the door was opened to try to force some accountability from the teachers' unions. "We knew there was more stuff," Barb shared. "Cindy and I started scouring the WEA newsletters, and we decided to start our own newsletter, *WEA Challenger Network News* to keep teachers informed. We thought if teachers knew their money was being used, without their permission, for political activities with which perhaps they disagreed, they would go ballistic and call for union accountability."

Well, lots of teachers got upset all right, and many even took part in a lawsuit, but the unions employed their typical deceptive public relations campaigns and accused Barb and Cindy of being against teachers. They didn't stop there.

When Barb and Cindy traveled to the legislature to ask legislators to create a law that would require school districts to inform teachers of their rights to be agency fee payers, a literal mob of union activists showed up to intimidate them and speak against the bill. Barb shared, "The superintendent of public instruction showed up. The labor public relations employment commission showed up. They all showed up and laughed at us and teased us under their breath." Then she added, "Here we were, two female teachers standing up for our colleagues, but the unions brought out plumbers, longshoreman; they brought out all of the big union guys, all the AFL-CIO guys—to pick on two little teachers."

Then sometime around 1996 or 1997, Barb and Cindy received shocking news. "A toothless guy shows up at our door with a subpoena," Barb shared, "We were sued by WEA. It was getting very real."

Barb told me. "We started praying and asking God to provide. Then National Right to Work Legal Defense Foundation's Milton Chappell provided us an attorney. His name was Harry Korrell—we fell in love with him, and he fell in love with teachers. It was very cool."

Their case, *WEA v. Amidon and Omlin*, took over a year to complete. The WEA sued them because Cindy and Barb's teacher newsletter *WEA Challenger Network News* included the letters "WEA." Barb told me, "The unions said they owned the letters WEA, so they sued for 'tortious interference with business expectancy,' which basically meant they were accusing us of trying to make money off of them and steal their business."

Cindy and Barb had to produce documents, give a deposition, and answer heaps of questions. Barb shared, "It was clear to me that they thought we had money and backing from someone way bigger than us. They couldn't believe that two schoolteachers forked money out of their own pockets and bought stamps."

The unions put pressure on the ladies to produce their mailing list under threat of going to jail. Barb told me, "Cindy and I both independent of each other said the same thing, 'I will sit in jail before I give up those names.' I would absolutely do that to this day. I will stand between the unions and those people that trusted us." Thankfully, the judge said the union's request wasn't valid, so he threw it out.

People were always asking Barb and Cindy if they were afraid, and Barb said the most common question people asked was "Aren't you afraid someone will put a bloody head on your car?" Barb told me that she and Cindy came to realize that the louder and the more out-front they were, the safer they were.

"People always called us courageous," Barb shared, "but I don't feel courageous. The courage didn't come from inside of me. It came from this burning desire to speak the truth and to shine the light of truth."

Barb and Cindy won their case, but teachers in Washington are still funding lots of politics and are still being abused by union leaders, as are many other teachers stuck with state and national unions.

Kelly Stephenson and her colleagues never did get to vote on their decertification process. "The union stole the democratic process from us," she told me. "They told teachers things like, 'If you leave us, then your contract will be null and void, and the board of education will go apes over all of you." Kelly said the union scared teachers to death, but none of the threats were true. She told me, "There's nothing in our negotiated agreements that say anything about an agreement involving the state and national unions. Our collective bargaining agreements are between the local teachers and our local school board."

The unions won (again) using their typical psychological warfare: fear, intimidation, isolation, and ignorance, and they used other favorite tactics too: lies, slander, and division. When teachers and the American people fall for these schemes, that's the most exasperating part of all. I asked Kelly her opinion on why so many of our colleagues fall for the unions' trickery and cruelty.

"I think our colleagues believe them because they don't think for themselves," Kelly shared. "And I don't mean this in a hurtful way, but they just hear what someone says, and they're like sheeple [sheep people]. And it's reflective of many Americans today. They just believe whatever is put out on social media or the news, and they don't take the time to investigate for themselves."

Have you noticed a repeating theme in almost every story in this book? Union-dominated leaders control by dividing us. They squash parents who stand alone without teacher support, and teachers who stand without parents are silenced and abused by the union-dominated leaders. But in one story, Stella led her teacher friends to work *with* parents in the Capistrano Unified community, and we were able to stop the abusive sex education curriculum—for now. We'll have to be vigilant and keep on standing together because union allies are attempting to force us to comply.

Over ninety percent of the thousands of teachers I've spoken to across America desire to keep their local association and reject state and national union politics and bullying. If we all stood together (and parents, faith leaders, mature students, and citizens stood with us), we could decertify union control, form our own local associations, and get our voices back. You know teachers, with a successful "Keep Your Local" campaign, we would have so much money left over, we could either use it for our own families, or fund some fantastic programs at our local level. Here's a creative idea. Teachers could pool their saved resources to fund things that would actually make our lives and jobs better—like our own on-site daycares for teachers with young children, so even breastfeeding moms could visit their babies during their lunch breaks. That sounds ideal to me, and we could do it in a heartbeat too—we just have to convince teachers to stop attacking one another, to stop standing with the "pissed off" abusers while our colleagues and kids get squashed.

Working together with other teachers, Cindy and Barb helped found Northwest Professional Educators (NWPE),[70] a non-union, nonpartisan association partnered with the Association of American Educators. NWPE has equipped teachers in several districts to decertify their NEA affiliate and form successful "local only" bargaining associations. The teachers are very happy with the results.

We can fight for kindness and "Keep Your Local," or kowtow to more union domination and abuse. Kelly's still taking hits from those manipulated by union control. She shared: "When I walk into school, people stare at me, and I've seen stuff people wrote about me on Facebook."

God help us teachers and parents to stop believing union lies and stop participating in divisive attacks on good, honest, and loving people who take serious lifelong beatings because others blindly buy into deceptive union messaging. Kelly is a twenty-two-year veteran educator who has served her high school kids with grace and excellence, and she's served her colleagues remarkably too, but today, like the woman branded "Rotten Apple," she's still aching from the abuse she received from her union and those who believe their lies.

"There's not a day that goes by that I don't feel something about what happened. I think about it every day," Kelly shared. "By the end of it, it really broke me down psychologically. They tarnished my whole entire reputation. It was the worst thing that I've ever been through in my life."

"Pissed off," or "Be kind?" The choice—and responsibility—is ours.

CHAPTER 17

NUDGED BY GOD

*"Maybe things were hopeless for teachers, families, and kids.
I started to feel that maybe the unions are just too good
at being bad..."*

Around 2011, I resigned my position as a union leader. I still believed that many educators were good; many cared about the kids; and most were in education for all of the right reasons. I believed these things because I worked with some tremendous educators and watched daily as they gave their all to their students. But I'd gained a new understanding of teachers too. The large majority was totally unwilling to face or expose the abuse within our union because the unions' psychological manipulations—fear, intimidation, ignorance, and isolation—worked. I also learned that a very loud minority of angry, union-controlled (often union-recruited) "pissed off" teachers was drowning out the voices of the terrified overwhelming kind majority, and most of the terrified were never going to stand against pissed off no matter how hard I fought for their rights.

I completely understand the response of the majority of teachers to go along to get along; after all, the unions make every problem seem so big, complicated, confusing, chaotic, and impossible. Their meddling in our schools has created negative issues that are overwhelming to address. Then they tell teachers things like, "Don't worry, we'll take care of everything. We'll deal with the dirty rotten administration and political scoundrels," so teachers often don't know who to trust.

Teachers don't want conflict; they just want to feed their families and teach kids. They're under so much stress and pressure it's just a lot easier to let someone else deal with issues. Trouble is, when teachers give up their autonomy and allow unions to rule, great administrators like Eileen Blagden lose their jobs while unethical ones keep theirs. Outstanding teachers like Aaron and Kelly who stick up for kids, colleagues, and community get harassed and often leave their jobs. Child focused school board members like Julie Williams and Karen Cuen are often lied about, shut down and chased off the board, and fantastic newer teachers like Nathan Strenge and the ones in my district often get laid off without apology. Then you'll recall the unions say things like, "We'll take care of those teachers. The union will provide them a seminar on how to obtain unemployment benefits," instead of doing the tough and selfless labor involved in truly working together, debating, and finding solutions that are best for everyone involved—especially the kids.

Even though I'd stepped down as a leader within the union, I tried a few more times to work with my union leadership to improve morale and fight for our profession and students, but those attempts fell on deaf ears too. I offered again to write a survey—this time to allow teachers to share from their hearts (with anonymity) the devastatingly low morale they were suffering, and I offered to present the findings to our school board, so they could help to improve our work environment. Although my fellow union members said they liked the idea, the UniServ director nixed those efforts too, and my follow up phone calls went unanswered.

I was feeling very alone, but I still believed there had to be more educators and parents willing to fight, and that's when the unions' psychological manipulations came very close to working on me.

It was February 2011. I sat in my living room watching the news, and many of my worst nightmares about union domination of teachers and our schools played out on the screen in front of me. You likely remember the news accounts. Thousands of Wisconsin teachers and protestors —led by union leaders—descended onto their state house in Madison to protest Governor Scott Walker's attempts to balance the state budget. Whether folks agree with Governor Walker's "Act 10" remedies or not, he was democratically elected by the people to repair a projected 3.6 billion dollar budget deficit and was conscientiously doing his best to represent the wishes of the people.

Because collective bargaining by public sector unions had led to the serious financial woes for the state, Governor Walker sought to limit collective bargaining (not end it), to give teachers freedom of choice to leave their union if they wished, and to reign in massive pension debt.

It's important we all understand some basics about why it's vital more leaders address teacher (and other public sector) pensions. The unions and their allies base our pension calculations on investment earnings that are often far higher than reality, so our pensions have been grossly underfunded throughout the nation for years. In fact, our pension system, as it's currently designed (a defined benefit plan), has contributed to the bankruptcy of cities, the inability of city, county, state, and national leaders to disperse funds for other community necessities, and it's one of the main reasons taxes continue to rise drastically.

Financially astute leaders have been trying to fix the problems for years (not by cheating teachers, but by using a more realistic pension design), but state and national unions keep on fighting for our defined benefit pension programs that have become a major burden on American citizens.

So, teachers; what if your hard-earned pension isn't there for you as promised? What if you grow old and end up financially vulnerable because our unions refused to heed the wise advice and warnings of seasoned financial experts across the country? I know the taxpayers guarantee our pensions (that's really nice of them, by the way), but just like your family budget, there comes a time when overspending takes its toll, the people become overtaxed, and no amount of finagling can fix the deficits. Then there's California Senate Bill 807 which is pushed by unions seeking to exempt teachers with more than five years of experience from paying state taxes for the next ten years. Overly generous teacher pensions in California burden the taxpayers greatly, but unions push for teachers' state taxes to decrease to nothing while their neighbor's taxes continue to rise. What about The Golden Rule that we teach our students—"Treat others the way you want to be treated?" Did you know many of the folks funding teacher pensions make much less than teachers and have pension plans that are far less generous than ours and will live on tighter budgets than us in retirement? That doesn't seem right to me—we should be willing to do our fair share to help lessen the burden on our neighbors. They're certainly doing a whole lot for us. These are some of the reasons Governor Walker championed Act 10.

The unions knew they could lose hundreds of millions in forced dues and much of the power they'd established through unrestrained collective bargaining, so public sector unions across the country came together to fight Governor Walker and his colleagues. They told school employees, parents, and students their lives would be ruined if Act 10 passed. The teachers who descended on the capitol—crazed by union hysteria—never gave Governor Walker the opportunity to work toward equitable solutions; they just slandered him, harassed him, and mirrored with perfection the bullying behavior taught to them through years of "pissed off" union indoctrination in mandatory staff meetings.

As usual, teachers across the country believed deceptive talking points created by the state and national teachers' unions and believed passage of Act 10 would lead to Armageddon-like destruction of teachers and public schools.

As I always do, I tried to understand both sides of the issue. I learned most teachers in Wisconsin were paying very little toward their healthcare coverage and their pensions, and the governor was trying to fully fund pensions for public sector workers like teachers so their promised pensions would be fulfilled when they reached retirement age. He had a common-sense approach to fix a massive shortfall created by unions who always promise lucrative arrangements for their members, which are often impossible for taxpayers to deliver.

I listened to interviews with small-business owners in Wisconsin who were frustrated with the teachers. One man, a deli owner, shared that he was paying almost five-thousand dollars a year for his family's medical coverage, and an additional twelve-thousand dollars a year in annual medical deductibles. His insurance included no wellness, no dental, and no eye coverage. He had no sympathy for the teachers who were receiving Cadillac healthcare and pensions and good salaries; in fact, he felt used because teachers were unwilling to work with taxpayers to create a more equitable situation for all.

I knew right then that my profession was losing respect in the eyes and hearts of many hard-working Americans. I'm sure many of the teachers had no idea they were enjoying far greater benefits than the taxpayers funding them because thanks to union hysteria, ignorance and fear ruled.

Night after night, I watched disheartened as teachers—claiming they represented the values and desires of *all* teachers—displayed behaviors, language, and attitudes we'd never permit in our classrooms, and they entirely degraded our profession. I was discouraged, but I could see through the tactics of the unions and noticed many of the protestors were non-teachers who were bused in to make it look like *all* teachers agreed with the hate.

I prayed that other Americans would be able to see through the deceptions too, but then one day, I watched in total disbelief as teachers arrogantly displayed (on camera) fake sick notes written so they could be paid for the days they chose to leave the classroom and rob their students of learning. Their massive sick-out closed several school districts for days, and the signs they carried were covered with hearts and declared, "Care about educators like they care for your child." The hypocrisy knocked me off my feet—their "care" for the kids led to abandonment of the children, yet the teachers were so entitled they felt they deserved to be paid (by the taxpayers) for standing with unions against the better interests of taxpayers and children.

I watched in dismay as the unions brought in drummers, cowbell ringers, blow horn yellers, and protest organizers to lead deafening chants inside the Wisconsin State House all day long. Teachers filled all levels of the rotunda, hung their tacky signs all over the beautiful architecture, and even hung their bodies over the balconies screaming, "This is what democracy looks like!" I'd been teaching my students about democracy for decades, which I understood as free, fair, and equal representation of all people. This scene looked nothing like democracy to me.

Then I learned the capitol rotunda had been converted into a commune so protestors could occupy twenty-four hours a day—they took turns sharing sleeping bags so they could protest continually. In addition to terrifying the workers employed in the capitol and making it impossible for them to do their jobs, the teachers disrupted the legislative session multiple times, and Republican lawmakers were so harassed and threatened they had to receive police escorts through secret tunnels to get to and from work.

I was witnessing a side of teachers that was ugly and uncharacteristic of the true heart of teachers, and I was feeling demoralized.

Then I read reports that among other destructive practices, protestors had been urinating on the walls inside of the historic building, the odor dominated the building, and damage estimates to the capitol were set around two million dollars. The teachers and the union didn't have to pay that bill; the taxpayers did.

I was dumbfounded and deeply embarrassed; the name teacher embodies kindness, safety, decency, and respect. These "teachers" were behaving more like animals and were totally undeserving of the honorable name. Then, inconceivably, I learned some even attacked the kids.

The worst story I heard was of a ninth-grade young man who was severely harassed at a Wisconsin middle school and high school—at the hands of teachers and students indoctrinated by union rhetoric. I reached out to him.

Benji Backer told me, "I had a geography teacher who would take me aside before or after class and call me dumb, stupid, and she would insult my opinion. She would just argue with me one-on-one about how ignorant I was to be conservative." That was when Benji was twelve. He was in eighth grade. "She would treat me so bad, that I had to change schools."

Hysteria over the passage of Governor Walker's Act 10 was dominating conversations on school campuses, and children were being brought into a political battle with skewed information controlled by one side's opinions—the unions'.

Benji told me, "My new US history teacher told the entire class that she wouldn't be able to have another child because of Scott Walker's Act 10. So all of these twelve and thirteen-year-olds are like 'Oh my gosh, that's horrible,' and then these kids have this pre-conceived idea that Scott Walker is Satan and that he is the worst thing that ever happened in Wisconsin's history."

A substitute teacher in Benji's class showed the movie *The Newsies*, which is a musical about unions in the early 1900s. After showing the movie the woman gave a lecture on the superiority of unions and slandered Governor Walker. Benji spoke out because he was disturbed by the outright propaganda foisted upon kids. "This was a really important case of indoctrination," Benji told me. "Because first she showed a historical video that isn't biased, but it's from long ago, and then she backed it up by saying 'Today, Scott Walker's ruining these great unions. He's gonna send people back to the days when people were making five cents an hour.' The video by itself wouldn't do that much harm, but when you start relating it to today in an inaccurate way to uneducated kids, it's indoctrination. It was the video paired with what she said afterwards that really made it brainwashing."

Another teacher led a class discussion about the recall. Benji shared, "He said, 'I signed the recall,' and then for the next forty-five minutes of that class he ranted on and on about how much he hated Scott Walker, how much Act 10 was killing him, how he wasn't able to support his family. He was swearing a lot, and it was disturbing."

The teacher apologized to Benji later, but Benji told me, "His apology was meaningless because a few days later he did it again. In front of the entire class he went on about Scott Walker—swearing again, but this time, he attacked *my family* and *me* personally."

At this point, Benji decided to talk to his principal about the attacks. "My principal was visibly shaken about it and very upset, so he talked to the teacher, and the teacher was supposed to apologize to me." Nothing could have prepared Benji for the "apology."

"I went up to see my teacher, and he said, 'You know what, Benji? You know how you went to the principal's office? Well, I don't give a shit.' Then he said, 'The principal and I are good friends so it doesn't really matter.'"

Benji realized he was on his own for protection. "It was obvious I wasn't gonna get help at all."

Benji told the principal about the "I don't give a shit" apology, requested to change teachers, and did his best to move on, but another teacher called him "weird" in front of the whole class for supporting the Tea Party, and another substitute teacher went into a lecture about how Republicans are racists.

Just like my fellow plaintiffs and I who had to take our message to the public because we were bullied and silenced by union abuse, Benji realized he needed to come forward and tell the public that unions were abusing kids too. Benji wrote an editorial for *Freedom Works*. *Drudge Report* and several other outlets picked it up. Word got around so thoroughly that soon this small town high school freshman from the Midwest found himself as a guest on FOX News.

For a while, Benji was thrilled to be getting the truth out to the American public because he'd hoped shining a light on the darkness would help bring an end to the abuse of kids, but miserably, after Benji's interviews, things at school got worse. A district official gave an interview on a local news outlet. Benji relayed the memory.

"He claimed I had never told anyone about the issues, that they had no prior knowledge, and that they were going to look into it. That was a complete lie because I had told the principal numerous times and laid out what happened. I even told him that the teacher said, 'I don't give a shit,' and they did nothing about that either." When I asked Benji if it was possible that the district leadership hadn't received the information from the school site administrator, Benji replied, "I even talked to the district leadership before I went public with my story. I even showed them a rough draft of my article so they knew what was going to be published."

Because of misleading messaging from the school district, and the ignorance and hysteria already dominating the narrative, thanks to unions, Benji was made out to be a Benedict Arnold. "They were basically telling my community that I was backstabbing them," Benji said. "The real reason I did all of this was because I had heard from numerous students across the country that they had experienced almost the exact same problems, and I'd also heard from kids in my own city having the same kinds of problems in the same school district, so I knew that something had to be done about this." Benji never expected his story to go viral either. "The reason my story took off is because what I experienced was absurd."

Benji didn't want to hurt anyone, so he never named the names of any of the teachers whenever he spoke out in the media, but because of union hype and a palpable hate for Benji among some of the heavily influenced teachers, Benji was placed in a dangerous situation. "After the attacks on social media, people would knock on my window late at night to terrorize me, my house was egged, and every time I went outside, kids from my school would flip me off or swear at me. I received threats on Twitter, and my bike was stolen when I parked it outside of an ice cream store." Benji added, "I was sitting in my room late one night and our house phone rang. I answered it and the anonymous caller threatened to kill me."

Benji also had to endure the sneaky harassment of the government union establishment. He told me, "Three government unions followed me on Twitter"—*a kid!*—"and it was definitely a tactic to make me afraid for sure."

Benji told me, "People would come up to me in and out of school— more violently out of school where they would just pass me by in a truck and scare me and flip me off while I was walking my dog and say, 'F___ you, Benji Backer.' I couldn't even walk outside."

Benji's entire high school career was negatively impacted by this traumatic freshman year experience. "For the next three years, it was really tough for me to go to school because I had all these people always giving me looks or I'd hear my name in the hallways being thrown around in a bad way. Kids would Tweet about me all the time—things like 'Saw Benji Backer in the hallway today and wanted to punch him.' I actually carried a knife in my pocket. I went to live up north with my grandparents for a while because I couldn't stay home anymore."

The teachers and administrators who harassed Benji did not get fired, but Benji found his voice. "I agreed to tell my story because I didn't want to be silenced by ignorance—no matter if it was unions, teachers, or students—I wanted to speak out about what I believe in, and I did."

In an occurrence all too familiar to me, Benji shared that a few of his teachers told him they supported him but did it quietly and out of sight. Benji was very grateful for their support, but not one adult in his school district stepped up *publicly* to protect Benji—not one.

Why would loving teachers turn a blind eye to the abuse of a child, and why would they allow a child in their care to be terrorized daily without stepping in to protect him? Because Benji stood for independence in opposition to union-think, and teachers who dare to protect those who oppose union-think get squashed.

Feeling upset with teachers? Try putting yourself in their shoes. Were you ever silenced by the horrible political correctness dominating our society for years? Still silenced? Ever afraid to say "Merry Christmas" or admit your true convictions on certain social issues? Teachers have been living under that political correctness for decades because the unions and their allies are the root of it.

I believe all teachers should stand up for the kids and should stand together against union oppressors no matter the cost, but teachers in Wisconsin, like most unionized teachers across the country, choose to toe the union line, so they don't find themselves in the shoes of educators like Tracie Happel, a twenty-five-year Wisconsin teacher whose career was destroyed for daring to speak out in support of Governor Walker's Act 10 efforts.

Tracie's entire life revolved around her classroom. She worked long hours, led her deaf, hard-of-hearing, and general education students in a very productive program, and although she worked with many challenging families, her students performed well on tests and enjoyed school. Tracie was elevated by her administration to several leadership positions on district- and school-wide committees, and she was celebrated as a trusted mentor to other teachers in her district for years.

At the twenty-two-year mark, Tracie's job record was spotless. She was going up through the ranks, the administration leaned on her heavily for support with teachers and curriculum decisions; in fact, there was not even one negative mark on her entire record. Tracie was the kind of teacher any parents would be thrilled to have caring for their child's educational and emotional needs every day. She was loved, and she loved her job.

But union opposition to her support of Governor Walker's reform ideas turned Tracie's dream job into a nightmare.

Tracie was deeply disturbed by the hateful attacks on Governor Walker—done in the name of teachers—and she agreed limiting collective bargaining for teachers was in the best interests of taxpayers, teachers, and kids alike. She believed it was the best way to bring fiscal solvency to the state.

Tracie didn't blast her message from a megaphone at work or try to impose her views on her colleagues; she simply exercised her First Amendment right to freedom of speech and offered the American people the other side of the teacher story. Though she knew it was risky to speak out on behalf of voiceless teachers, Tracie worked with Association of American Educators (AAE) and courageously shared her support for Governor Walker. Instantly after she dared to display independence from union-think, Tracie's twenty-two-year career was in jeopardy.

Immediately, Tracie was removed from multiple leadership positions, and she was told it was to give others a chance to step up into the roles. Tracie told me, "No one ever stepped up, and no one ever wanted to. Here I am, a language arts lead teacher in the middle of choosing a new language arts curriculum for the district, and they suddenly want to give someone else a chance? Nothing lined up. It was 100 percent because of my political views."

Tracie didn't back down, so the administration claimed that parents called and complained about her stance on Act 10 and wanted their children removed from her class. No evidence of this was ever presented to Tracie, and her personal experience was exactly the opposite. "Many parents called, emailed, texted, or came to my classroom saying, 'I am so proud of you! Thank you for standing up for my child.' I'm still friends with some of them because they were so supportive, and I'll never forget them."

Since union-controlled forces were unable to silence Tracie, they harassed her every day. She was treated with disdain, accused of harming children, her requests for assistance with severe discipline issues were ignored, and the school leadership even tried to make others believe Tracie was mentally unstable. The constant personal assaults were so severe that Tracie, a teacher who loved her job and excelled at it for twenty-two years, was now crying every morning before work, couldn't sleep, was suffering from daily panic attacks, and felt paranoid to be a dynamic teacher. "I became a hermit," she told me. "I was afraid to hug the kids or have fun in the learning process. I became robotic because of constant fear of harassment and punishment."

Tracie was so traumatized by the relentless assault on her character that she requested a two-week leave of absence in order to cope and escape the attacks. While on approved leave, she visited a fascinating historical cemetery in Charleston, South Carolina. Within this church's cemetery are the graves of actual Mayflower pilgrims and a signer of the US Constitution. I've visited this remarkable cemetery, and anyone interested in American history would find this historical landmark fascinating and noteworthy.

Tracie posted a picture of one of the historical graves and another one of her sister and her enjoying dinner. Her sister was holding a glass of wine. Somebody took a screenshot of those two pictures and delivered them to Tracie's school administration with a note saying Tracie was not emotionally or mentally stable enough to be working with children because she was "obsessed with death and drinking." The day she returned to work after her short leave of absence, she was accused of being mentally unstable.

The administration informed her that they weren't sure if she was prepared to be a teacher anymore. She was required to get a physical and a psychological evaluation within thirty days or she would lose her job.

Tracie didn't cave, instead she found an attorney. Tracie won her case; she was totally vindicated of all accusations, and she returned to her classroom. But the harassment didn't stop. Just like in Aaron Benner's case, almost immediately Tracie was accused of hurting a child, so the administration came into her classroom, asked Tracie to leave, and individually questioned every child asking them if their teacher had ever harmed them. Every child said no because they had a loving and outstanding teacher in Tracie.

When Tracie returned to the classroom, the children told her what happened and smothered her in hugs. They were all traumatized by the very idea that they would be asked such a question about their beloved teacher. Tracie told me, "I couldn't believe the frightening ideas these school officials were putting into the heads of precious children." Tracie feared the union and administration would continue to bring harm to the children because of their hatred for her, so she decided to resign for the emotional protection of her students and her own mental health.

Once again, just like in Nicole's school, Aaron's district, Kelly's local association, and the Witch's classroom, union forces got their way. Vulnerable deaf and hard-of-hearing students lost their beloved teacher, parents lost their greatest advocate, and their sweet and capable teacher lost her career. The abuse was so extreme, just like Benji had to leave town for emotional and physical protection, Tracie moved out of state in order to cope.

"They ousted me from my passion," Tracie told me. "They won. I'm out."

She was forced to find work as a cashier in a grocery store.

These stories of extreme abuse inspired by union forces dominating our schools left me physically ill and thoroughly disgusted. It's beyond my comprehension that American educators can be so degraded as to participate in the harassment and abuse of a precious teacher, and to chase her out of her job for daring to share well-researched, independent thoughts in defense of her community. It's equally impossible for me to understand that the teaching profession has become so degraded as to allow, and in some cases tacitly encourage, an American school child *in their care* to be threatened with violence and even death for the crime of having *an opinion*.

Then it hit me: thanks to union domination of our profession, this is the picture the American people are being presented of teachers, and they're being led to believe we all behave this way. No wonder our morale is so low and we're being blamed for society's ills.

My response to the Wisconsin teacher protests was painful and visceral, and my reaction was not petulance because the teachers' unions weren't doing things my way. My eyes were being opened to a devastating reality: I was witnessing a fundamental breakdown of values, conscience, and compassion in the profession to which I'd devoted my entire life. Unions had changed my profession so much I didn't recognize it, and the values I held dear and understood didn't seem to exist anymore. I was navigating an outright crisis in my soul, and I had to wonder, had the unions so degraded the teaching profession through their decades of divisive rhetoric and culture of fear that now *educators* were reduced to destroying outstanding teachers, abusing children, and peeing on a public state house?

I wasn't ready to give up though. I'd devoted two decades to standing up for my colleagues and the families we serve. I'd met regularly with school board members, served as a union leader, reached out to my administration, met with countless teachers, and supported disgruntled parents, but no matter what I tried, no matter how hard I prayed, no matter how often I attempted to fight for what's right for kids and teachers, problems were never addressed, and I was always left with the same sorts of dissatisfying answers. Things like, "There's nothing we can do," "I pick my battles," "The administration is the problem," "The union is the problem," "Go through the chain of command Rebecca," "No, No, No, No." No one wanted to address or fix the problems—no one wanted to stand up to the union—*no one.*

The unions and the school leaders they've manipulated had already emotionally beaten the heck out of me, and even though I was still standing, witnessing the Wisconsin teacher strikes put me at a crossroads. I still loved the kids, and I still believed in great teachers, but I was totally demoralized by what I was watching. I had to admit to myself; even though many Americans were shocked by teacher behaviors displayed during the Act 10 strikes, I wasn't. The hateful attacks committed against good people at the hands of teachers didn't shock me at all. They sickened me, but they didn't shock me.

It was the first time in over two decades of teaching, I felt ashamed to be called "teacher." The name "teacher" had defined me my entire adult life; I'd dreamed of being a teacher from age twelve, and I was immensely proud to be one, but my profession and the good name we'd earned through such noble practitioners as the Master, Ruth Finnegan, Aunt Julane, and the one unions labeled Rotten Apple were under assault.

And now, I was exhausted. For the first time in my long career, it hit me that maybe the unions were way too big for me to continue fighting them. Maybe things were hopeless for good teachers, families, and kids. I started to feel that maybe the unions are just too good at being bad —too organized, too powerful, too in control of our government and schools, too good at manipulating teachers and convincing them to push the union agenda. It was the first time I thought to myself: you know, maybe I'll put my head down, collect my paycheck, work toward my pension, and become a burnout—something I'd never be able to become—but there was no other option. Every single thing I'd ever tried had hit a brick wall, and now all of America, and the entire world, was presented a picture of teachers that was the exact opposite of the true heart of my profession.

One morning, several months after the Wisconsin teacher protests, I was doing my Bible study and talking to God about the degradation of our schools and my once-honorable profession. I told Him that someone needed to help expose the way state and national unions had co-opted the good name of teachers and left us broken and terrified. I told Him nothing short of a miracle would work because we were oppressed, and our voices had been hijacked. I begged Him to inspire someone to speak out and show this.

To my great surprise and disbelief, the answer He placed on my heart was, "How about you?"

I fully understand that God works through people to bring about change, but I was (and still am) woefully ill equipped to be His vessel on behalf of good teachers and kids. Didn't God remember, I'd been trying to do this for over two decades and had failed miserably? But He was insistent. I felt nudged by Him to try one last effort in my school district in hopes of helping to lift the extremely low morale. He led me to send a message to a high-level administrator in my district to ask if we could work together to bring healing to employee morale. I had high hopes because God had placed the idea in my heart, but to my great disappointment, the administrator sent an underling who dismissed my concerns and told me nothing was wrong. When she asked me why I hadn't gone through the chain of command with my concerns, I told her I'd done that dozens of times throughout the years and never got anywhere because my administrators always told me, "I pick my battles." She told me my only option was to try again, and she blocked me from having a conversation with the level above her.

Just like every time before, no solutions were sought or supported by those with the power to impact change, but unlike every time before, God made it clear to me that He'd never again ask me to work within my school district or union to attempt to bring about positive change. I felt completely released from the burden of fighting within my district, and though I can't explain the experience, I knew God was pleased with my efforts even though I'd failed again.

If it hadn't been for the grace of God, the unions would have completely defeated me, but thanks to Him, my crisis and years of defeat became a turning point—a first kind of clarion call—and God used the devastation I'd received from years of union abuse as preparation for my next assignment. Just like He promises, not one of my painful experiences was suffered in vain.

My new adventure started in the fall of 2012. God laid it on my heart to start writing editorials to educate folks in my community about union domination of our schools and abuse of our teachers. He made it clear He wanted me writing for publication, but I was petrified. I wasn't afraid of sharing my writing or even my personal story, but I didn't have any connections with media, and I was afraid of being rejected by publications. I also knew union forces would slander me and twist my pure motives with high-dollar attack campaigns full of deceptively clever talking points—all funded by my forced union dues.

I spent days talking to God about His nudging on my heart, and the passion inside of me grew. I started to fully understand that He wanted a teacher to shine the light of truth onto the darkness in the teachers' unions. A teacher needed to speak out in defense of teachers, parents, and kids; a teacher who had been personally bruised by union abuse and who had attempted to right the wrongs from inside of the union, and God was asking me to be that teacher.

I prayed specifically for days asking God for the courage to obey His request. I came up with every excuse to avoid His invitation, but you know what? He tenderly addressed my fears, and then He reminded me of a story I'd known since childhood. You probably know it.

There was a poor widow who placed two mites (about the same as two pennies) into the offering jar, and her sacrifice touched the heart of Jesus. He pointed her out to His disciples and told them the widow who had given only two mites, had given more than all of the wealthy people or anyone else because she'd given all she had—she'd given in faith from her nothingness.

God nudged me again and laid these words on my heart, "Just give me your two mites, Rebecca. I'll do the rest."

I was convinced God was right, but I was still terrified to take the first step. I never told Charles about the widow's mite, but I made the now-glorious mistake of telling Charles that God and I had been having this discussion about me writing editorials, so he joined God's side and I was quickly outnumbered. I told them I would obey the call if God asked me to write something specific for publication and figured I was off the hook for a while; after all, both God and Charles knew I didn't have any connections to any newspapers.

The very next morning I read an article in the *Orange County Register* about the wonderful benefits of teachers' unions. The unions and their rhetoric had become more emboldened since their display in Wisconsin the year before, and I was sickened by their deceptive claims. This writer had clearly never been forced to fund government unions against his will, nor did he understand how many children were being hurt by union rules and policies. I sat at the breakfast table reading the paper, complaining about the deceptive messaging, and uttering all kinds of grunts and groans, when Charles challenged me, "Write a rebuttal."

Well, you need to know that Charles had been saying those three words to me our entire marriage. I'm a passionate newspaper reader, so he's often the brunt of my gasps and groans while I'm reading infuriating stories, so this challenge was not new to me, but my response was a surprise to both of us, "Okay, I will," I said, and I got up from the table, went to my computer and typed out a rebuttal.

Now, writing the response was easy, but sending it was another story. I had no idea how to submit an editorial because the paper only offered instructions on how to submit a Letter to the Editor, and to be honest, this was almost enough of an excuse to save the rebuttal in my Word documents and leave it there for the rest of my life. But God kept nudging me. I decided in the end to send my editorial to Letters to the Editor with a note explaining I couldn't find any other instructions on how to submit an editorial and would they please forward my rebuttal to the proper department. I felt humiliated to send it that way, and no surprise, I never received a reply, and I told God, "See, I was right. You picked the wrong girl. They rejected me." But God just kept pointing to the widow's mite and urging me to keep on trying.

Two days later, I was reading the *OC Register* again, and there was a story written by former California State Senator Gloria Romero. She wrote about the extreme problems with teachers' unions, and she shared that teachers sought her out constantly to complain about the abuse within the union, but no matter how frustrated they were or how awful the situation, most requested to keep their identities anonymous, and told her things like, "I'm terrified of the unions."

As I read the story, I kept thinking to myself, "I'm not afraid. I'm *dying* to tell my story," and then God did it again. He nudged me to contact Senator Romero.

Well, now this idea was way beyond my comfort level. God had already embarrassed me by asking me to write that rebuttal and send it to Letters to the Editor with my lame note, and now He wanted me to cold-call a senator?

"She'll think I'm crazy," I told God.

He doesn't mess around with small talk. "Email her," was the answer He placed in my heart.

I was petrified and feeling insecure again, but God urged me three times, so I looked up Senator Romero's contact information on the Internet and sent her an email. I attached my rebuttal I'd written for the paper and wrote her a note introducing myself and told her I wasn't afraid to tell my story.

I was shaking with fear about reaching out to a senator with my vulnerable writing, so I sat in front of my computer with my email ready to go for several minutes too afraid to hit send. I finally prayed and asked God to give me favor, found two mites worth of courage, and forced myself to hit the send icon. I immediately wished I could take the message back after it *blinged* out of my outbox, but do you know what? Senator Romero contacted me within thirty minutes, and she said, "We've been looking for a teacher like you for six years."

She hooked me up with Larry Sand, who you may remember is a retired teacher and president of California Teachers' Empowerment Network (CTEN), and Larry connected me with a bunch of other fantastic teachers across the state. Senator Romero liked my rebuttal so much she sent it in to the *OC Register* editorial board and to Larry. Within a few days, Larry and I were writing another editorial together, and I was learning the ropes.

Thanks to support from Larry, I started getting some of my editorials placed in various California publications and I joined CTEN.[71] This was amazing to me because my original goal was just to educate folks through our local newspaper, but soon online sites all over the nation were picking up my editorials. I countered the unions' spiteful "free-rider" argument by proving we're really *forced* riders—forced to fund union politics against our wills and punished and shunned if we dare to question union-think. I shared my take on the tens of millions in teacher monies the unions give to one-sided political campaigns.

This was a very new world for me, and I was stretched way out of my comfort zone, but it was liberating. It stretched my Charles too. As each editorial was published, I asked him if he would post them on his personal Facebook page. This was a huge request because he was the director of a school at a major public university dominated by teachers' unions, and a lot of university faculty and staff members are his Facebook friends. According to the unions and their political allies, almost all university professors agree with union politics, so Charles was really nervous that he would offend his colleagues by posting my editorials. You see, university professors are silenced by fear, intimidation, isolation, and ignorance too. In fact, Charles was paying twelve hundred dollars a year in coerced agency fees to be silenced by unions—no voice, no vote—and no protection from the *union he funded* which filed grievances against him in his role as department chair. Since he was stuck in the culture of fear too, he assumed every single faculty member within his influence agreed with the unions; he thought he was alone in his concerns.

But he's a loving husband, so he posted my editorials with innocuous comments like, "I'm really proud of my wife for standing up for what she believes." We thought he'd take a lot of heat for posting my articles, especially since faculty members weren't "liking" the posts, but one by one, many faculty, staff, and even students took Charles into private locations and told him, "Tell your wife thank you for fighting for us!" "I'm behind your wife one-hundred percent!" and "Your wife is my hero!"

Charles and I discovered something when we found the courage to share my testimony with our colleagues: many people all around us were feeling just as isolated and scared as we were, and they shared our values but were just too afraid to speak out.

Thanks to Larry, Charles, and the example of a poor widow who lived two millennia ago, finally, after twenty-five years of being bound, gagged, and grossly misrepresented by a union I was forced to fund, I had a voice. It was a small voice to be sure, and not even a blip on the unions' radar.

But it renewed my hope.

CHAPTER 18

———⟨———⟩———

THE TEAM MOM

"Arise, for this matter is your responsibility.
We also are with you. Be of good courage, and do it."
Ezra 10:4 (NKJV)

On March 20, 2013, an email popped into my inbox that caught my attention immediately. A couple of national teacher support groups were asking if fee-payer teachers in California were interested in being part of a lawsuit against the CTA and the NEA. I knew immediately I wanted to join, but since this was a huge commitment and battling the unions is always risky, I knew my family had to be on board too. I asked Charles if he could support the idea, and before I even finished my question he said, "That's great! Do it!" Since he's a professor trapped in the unions' culture of fear, his support was nothing short of heroic.

Ben was in public high school, and Kyle was at Long Beach State University, and I knew union-friendly teachers might hassle them, so their support was necessary too. I'm proud of my sons. Even though I warned them of the intimidation tactics of unions and their supporters, and the very real possibility they could be bullied, they both said, "Go for it!" When I added that angry people might attack our home or our vehicles, they didn't back down at all, but Ben, who had just obtained his driver's license said, "If they touch my car, I'll take 'em out, Mom."

Like most people, when it comes to conflict I would prefer to work together with others and come to mutually acceptable agreements. I can assure you that all the years I dreamed of becoming a teacher, fighting political battles was never once on my radar. I never went into teaching thinking it would be a super keen idea to be a plaintiff in a US Supreme Court case. That idea never entered my mind. I'm a teacher; I just want to teach. Teachers like me want to do right by the kids and families placed in our classrooms; we're not interested in controlling schools or the culture with politically charged narratives and social justice; we just want to be supported in our efforts to teach kids how to read, write and master mathematics.

But since God was leading me on a new adventure and directing me to expose the darkness in teachers' unions, I emailed the lawyers and said, "Please pick me!" Two weeks later, they did.

Just five months after I'd written my first editorial, and six months after I thought things were hopeless, I already had a louder voice. God always keeps His promises; He had delivered my miracle.

Since I'd been writing editorials, and wasn't afraid to speak out, the lawyers asked me if I'd like to serve as the lead plaintiff. I responded that I was very happy to be the lead as long as the other plaintiffs wanted me to serve in that capacity. In fact, I was tickled right down to my toes that the lawyers even thought to choose someone to lead all of us in our grand adventure, so I had big plans.

I was excited and full of ideas because I thought "lead plaintiff" meant I would be sort of a "team mom" for all of the plaintiffs—you know, I'd bake cookies, wrap up cute little gifts of encouragement, get some pompoms and balloons and cheer on our team with some of my old softball chants. My big plans included sending the plaintiffs encouraging notes regularly so they wouldn't feel so beaten down after days of being harassed at school; planning gatherings so we could get to know one another better, and I even had an idea to purchase special music CDs for them so they could be inspired by some great tunes about standing firm for what's good and right. I had already started making a list of songs.

Oh, I had the plans all right, and Charles was 100 percent behind me, so I couldn't wait to receive the contact information for all of the other plaintiffs and get started as the team mom.

On April 30, 2013, our lawyer, Terry Pell, came to Orange County, California, we filed our case with the local California trial court, and our press release[72] was sent out to the media. I finished up my day of teaching, worked with kids after school, stuffed a stack of essays into my bag for grading in the evening, and headed to a meeting place with Terry so I could give interviews to local media. Terry taught me about the *Drudge Report*, I had a couple of enjoyable phone interviews, and then I took off for home.

When I arrived home, Charles and I logged onto our *OC Register* online account to see if they'd picked up the press release. They had and even though I'd pre-approved a draft of the release, the article had one key addition I hadn't seen before, the name of our case, and that detail would radically change our lives forever.

"*Friedrichs v. California Teachers Association.*"

Friedrichs? What was my name doing as the case name? Charles and I sat there in our home office completely baffled by our last name appearing as the case name, and we'd decided we would inform the lawyers that our local paper made a massive error in their reporting of the case. Pretty soon, our buddy Larry Sand called and said, "Hey, why didn't you tell me the case was named after you?" I assured him it was a typo, and Charles and I were on the job of fixing the misunderstanding. Even though we both know full well that cases brought to the courts are named after the people bringing them, we were honestly befuddled by the words *Friedrichs v. CTA* because we'd assumed our case might be named *"Teachers v. CTA,"* or something like that, I guess.

Truth be told, we'd never really thought about the name of the case; I suppose it was just one of those things that hung out in the cloudy area of our brains. I gave Terry a call and informed him of the "Friedrichs" error, and I can't recall if he laughed out loud, sat on the other end of the phone in a dead silence, or thought to himself that he never should have selected a natural blond as his lead plaintiff, but I do remember him saying, "You're the *lead* plaintiff. The case is named after *you*."

Have you ever had one of those "*aha* moments" when your brain finally catches up with the obvious? Charles and I were sitting in our home office when our "aha moment" hit. "Holy Toledo," I said to Charles. "Being lead plaintiff means the case is named after me." Charles got a big smile on his face; he was proud of me, and he really liked the idea, and even though he's never said this, I think he felt proud to have his family name out there fighting the good fight.

I, on the other hand, was speechless. I was super happy to be speaking out on behalf of teachers and kids, and I was thrilled to finally have a voice after almost three decades of being bullied and silenced, but I was deeply humbled by the idea that my name would be used as a symbol of the true heart of teachers. I didn't deserve the honor, and I couldn't believe God trusted me with the privilege.

Even though Charles thought it was cool that our name led the case, almost immediately he became very worried about my safety and the safety of our sons. We'd heard and read all sorts of horror stories about unions abusing people, and we'd read that unions in California (and some other states) were given special exemptions from stalking laws when engaged in labor disputes,[73] so Charles was rightfully preoccupied with protecting us. Concerns of scary men in dark suits following me as I traveled my hour-long drive to work in the dark each morning or angry mobs inspired by blind hatred picketing our home troubled Charles.

He knew about the plastic forks in Julie Collier's yard that were placed there because Julie had the audacity to stand for school choice. We knew a local city council member who'd been the victim of a corrupt detective hired by the law firm representing a union. The detective placed a tracking device on the councilman's car and reported he saw the councilman drunk driving even though he had consumed only a soda. After legal intervention, the detective pled guilty to felony charges of false imprisonment and conspiracy to file a false police report and was sentenced to a year in jail, so we wondered, if union-supported law firms did this sort of immoral and dangerous stuff to local city council members, what sorts of attacks would be waged on a family trying to end forced unionism across the entire country?

Besides, people kept asking me, "Are you afraid for your life?" so the thoughts of personal attacks on his wife and family haunted Charles.

Publicly, the first few months of the case were very quiet, but things at work were starting to get awkward. Most of the district union representatives were mad at me. I can't blame them, I can only imagine the Armageddon-like lies they were told about our case and about me, but it still hurt since they knew me personally and had experienced my good and caring heart for others for nearly three decades. It was uncomfortable to have so many people angry at me when my motives were to fight for *their* constitutional rights and union accountability—the unions' culture of fear is so powerful, and their rhetoric so deceptive, even people who had trusted me for years were giving me the silent treatment. Suddenly, people were looking at me differently, treating me like an outsider, and I felt like I was walking through a wall of animosity when passing some of the teachers in my district.

But my fellow plaintiffs and I had a voice, and teachers and workers from across the country began reaching out to me. Almost all of the messages I received were full of gratitude and very encouraging, but once in a while my heart would fall as I'd open a nasty message coming through my email at work. About 6:30 one morning this hateful message stared me in the face.

> Ms. Friedrichs,
>
> I just read a story about your lawsuit against the teachers union in California, and I have to say that I am impressed. Sadly, I am impressed with your laziness and malleability. If you are too lazy to fill out a form once a year to opt-out of the political donation, then you probably are far from responsible enough to work with children on a daily basis. If it is too big of a "significant burden" as your lawsuit purports, you need some real problems. You are being manipulated by a group of people who want the only voice in politics to be the voice of the wealthy, who have enough money to donate millions to politicians to represent their interests. What about the interests of the rest of us…and the children? Hopefully, the Supreme Court is more intelligent than you are.
> Sincerely,
> A Concerned Educator

I admit these hurtful messages could knock me off my pins for a few hours and cause distraction in my mind while I was trying to teach, but every single time the writers were spewing hate, they never wanted to have a discussion with me and were too cowardly to sign their own names, so I'd think of the advice my parents always gave me, "Be grateful when certain people don't like you; it means you're making a positive difference."

Even though judgmental messages popped into my inbox on occasion, for every hateful message, I received a thousand positive notes, letters, calls, and emails. After one of my articles ran in national outlets, I received this message from a worker named Colin.

Best of Luck with your Supreme Court suit! I work in a State government office, and the conditions described are identical to my workplace. I appreciate and support ya all the way!

And after a national magazine interviewed me, a kind teacher reached out to me with this message.

Dear Rebecca,

I was pleased to read that you were challenging forced dues by the teachers union. I can just imagine the stress you must be under… The diversionary tactics used by the union to capture money to perpetuate their power is astounding and may provide grounds for your lawsuit… Your lawyer's strategy sounds good, not attacking the union, although I bet you'd like to attack them. I wish you all the best and will try to follow your case.
Fran

Throughout my battle the worst thing was that I almost always felt alone—especially at school. The unions' culture of fear and chastisement through isolation makes teachers so terrified that even those who agreed with me remained silent most of the time, so receiving messages from strangers around the country was very powerful medicine for me.

About six months into the lawsuit, the public side of the battle got going, and I unexpectedly was invited to be on *The Huckabee Show* in New York City. When I told my friend Mary Sharpe (a super high-energy kindergarten teacher who is also very patriotic) she came out of her skin with excitement and immediately asked "Rebecca, what are you going to wear? You need to look great! You're going to be on national TV!" We decided together that I likely didn't own the right kind of outfit and was in desperate need of wardrobe intervention, but there was nothing I could do about it because it was parent–teacher conference week, so my days and evenings were booked solid. I had no time to shop for clothes before my trip to New York.

Mary knows my heart, and she's also disgusted by forced unionism, so she was an outspoken supporter of my case; in fact, she was one of only a few teachers in my district who defended me openly, so she responded to my need with one of the kindest acts anyone has ever done for me.

In addition to teaching, Mary has a little clothing business on the side. She teases herself about it because she dresses very casually, but when it comes to fashion for others, Mary has impeccable taste. Without my knowing it, she went home after long hours teaching and conferencing with parents, loaded up a bunch of cute clothes in her car, and headed two hours in heavy traffic to my house to bring me clothes for my interview.

(I'd be remiss if I didn't mention that my friends Dottie Magnuson and Connie Veldcamp also gave me clothes throughout the battle. They both sent me to interviews, talks, and the Supreme Court with professional clothing right out of their closets. I was, and still am, overwhelmed by their kindness.)

Mary's gesture was one of the most tender experiences I'd had in my life at that point, but as my lawsuit journey lengthened and word got out, these sorts of loving gestures from friends and strangers alike became regular occurrences, and since most teachers at work were either angry at me, supporting me in the closet, or too afraid to talk to me about the case (so I didn't know where they stood), I can't express how much it meant to discover that I had so much support from teachers like Mary. Their reinforcement made all the difference.

The next day, I headed out in a plane for my first trip ever to New York City. I was so nervous about my first national TV appearance that I lost two pounds during the trip east, but the interview went pretty well. Governor Huckabee was terrific, and his audience was sympathetic; he asked me to come back once we got to the Supreme Court, and I didn't trip over a wire or fall off my stool, so things went much better than I'd expected.

God knew I was going to need that positive first interview experience because I was in for some major screw-ups. Governor Huckabee's show gave my lawyers and me a glimmer of hope that I'd eventually be able to figure out how to hold my own in an interview situation.

When I returned to school on Monday, I placed a new little replica of the Statue of Liberty on my teaching table. The kids fell in love with her. I never told them about my adventure on TV; in fact, I never talked to them about the lawsuit at all, but I did tell them about my quick journey to New York City to gaze upon Lady Liberty and the new Freedom Towers. I added New York City to our geography lesson for the day, and we sang one of our favorite patriotic songs, "This Land is Your Land," because the kids thought it was funny that it has the line "From California to the New York Island," and their teacher had just made that trip. We spent a few minutes dreaming of how fun it would be to go on a field trip to New York City, to ride on a ferry together and see Lady Liberty for real. That's one of the great things about kids; they can dream big, and even though they didn't know about my lawsuit, their natural ability to believe in something bigger than themselves was always a source of strength for me.

When I opened my email after school that day, there was a nice message waiting in my inbox. The subject line said, "Saw U on Huck; U gave me hope. I'll pray 4 U!" and here's the message that followed.

Miss Rebecca,

I was so glad to hear a public school teacher speak the truth. I was so impressed with your courage and intellectual honesty and I hope that regardless of the outcome of the suit you will continue with this precious cause. You're going to be on my prayer list right under Michelle Rhee. God bless you!
Chad

P.S. Ezra 10:4 "Arise, for this matter is your responsibility. We also are with you. Be of good courage, and do it." (NKJV)

CHAPTER 19

————⟨————⟩————

CRIMINALS, CLASSROOMS, AND THE KELLY FILE CATASTROPHE

You read that correctly, the teachers' union took a stance for the criminals and against the safety of kids and teachers.

Chad's encouraging message was just one of many, so I was starting to realize that just like the teachers I'd known for decades in California, large numbers across the country agreed with me and were desperate for relief from union abuse. I really wanted to give them a voice, and although I was still overwhelmed with the task, thanks to the wonderful experience with Governor Huckabee and his incredible staff, this interview stuff didn't seem quite as frightening as before.

A few nights later, I was watching a news show called *The Kelly File*. Megyn Kelly, the anchor, reported the jaw-dropping news that the NEA had just come out against a bipartisan federal bill that sought to prohibit convicted sex-offenders, murderers, and kidnappers from working in America's schools. You read that correctly, the teachers' union took a stance *for* the criminals and *against* the safety of kids and teachers.

I was outraged. In what world is it in the best interests of children and educators to be used as guinea pigs in controversial human research projects focused on the recovery of violent criminals? Furthermore, this was another one of those crazy policies teachers never even know about, yet the American people are told we voted on "democratically." In fact, I would wager that most of the teachers reading this book just discovered that their dues supported the union to make this dangerous stance on their behalf.

I've never met one teacher in my entire career who would agree with the NEA's stance to place the recovery efforts of perilous criminals above the safety and rights of children, and when I mentioned it in the teachers' lounge the next day, my colleagues were aghast, but knowing they're powerless and voiceless in the union they're coerced to fund, they just grew further demoralized.

Now, I believe in grace and forgiveness. If hearts are humbled and criminals are truly contrite, I believe God can heal their hearts and lead them to productive and fulfilling lives of service, but I also believe in discernment. The recidivism rates for violent criminals are high, so it's extraordinarily foolish to place them onto campuses full of hundreds or thousands of vulnerable children and educators, while they try to overcome their tendencies toward kidnapping, murder, and sexual assault.

According to the government's Bureau of Justice Statistics study[74] on recidivism rates of prisoners released from state prisons in thirty states in 2005, within five years of release, 71.3 percent of violent offenders were rearrested for a new crime. That translates to over two-thirds of all violent offenders wreaking havoc on the lives of fresh, innocent victims. Parents, do you want to take this sort of risk with your children? I don't. Teachers, do you want to worry about potential dangers on campus every day and be forced to fund these shortsighted and reckless ideas? Me neither, but tragically, like millions of other teachers across this country, the unions speak for us without regard for our views or our safety.

In response to the Sandy Hook slaughter of innocence and other shocking school shootings across our country, schools have gone on the offensive. I'm strongly cautioned to keep my classroom door shut and locked at all times as a precaution. Our children are locked in behind tall gates and monitored every second by cameras to protect them from the slim chance a violent or mentally ill attacker will sneak onto campus and open fire. Even parents have to check in at the office to get onto school grounds and are locked out of the campus during the school day. Yet, our government unions, who claim to represent the best interests of teachers and students, want to invite violent offenders into our school communities. This is insane.

And by the way, the NEA's own Resolutions for 2016–2017 state within Resolution "F-55. Volunteers in Public Schools," that when parents or other volunteers work in our schools they should be, "appropriately screened and trained…. The screening should be for the sole purpose of eliminating volunteers who are convicted felons, child abusers, or sex offenders." Why, then, would NEA come out against a bipartisan federal effort aiming to protect kids from these very same abusers? This is mind blowing, and a good example of why so many teachers have no idea how their dues are really spent.

I'm not one to get physical when I'm mad, but my teeth clenched and my stomach knotted as I listened to Megyn's reporting. I had a profound and instinctive need to tell the American people that *real* teachers were horrified by this extreme stance. Since things had gone well on the *Huckabee Show*, my lawyers reached out to Megyn Kelly's producers and, thankfully, Megyn was excited to hear the teachers' side of the story.

I was excited, too, for getting another chance to give voice to millions of teachers, parents, and kids across the country who are fed up with union recklessness and abuse, but after the initial excitement, I was struck with the sobering reality that I had to appear on national television again, and I was terrified.

My attorneys encouraged me to alert viewers to our case, and they helped me to anticipate what sorts of questions I might be asked and to articulate my feelings into short answers media folks call "sound bites." Although it seems like guests know the questions ahead of time, on almost all occasions the guest has no idea what the host will ask.

I would speak to Megyn via satellite from a studio in Orange County, California, and she would be in New York City. I had never given a satellite interview and had no idea what to expect, so I was a nervous wreck.

After battling horrific traffic and arriving only ten minutes before my hit time, I was hurried to a stool in front of the camera. After a quick makeup and sound check, I was told to look into a blank black camera screen at no one and informed that my earpiece would have a three-second delay. I was told to focus on the little happy face sticker fixed directly above the lens, and I listened as the show was in progress. Suddenly, a voice in my earpiece told me to smile into the camera as I was introduced to the audience, and at that moment everything in me wished I'd never gotten myself into the situation.

Megyn started her interview by telling the audience I was a public school teacher who heard her announcement the night before about the NEA coming out against a bipartisan bill aimed at protecting children in schools from convicted sex offenders, kidnappers, and murderers. Although I've listened to her show many times before and understood every word she spoke, while trying to decipher her questions through one ear piece and without the aid of facial cues, I was horrified to realize she talked faster than I could listen!

She asked me if I'd thrown something at my TV screen when I heard the news about the NEA. That was a pretty funny and passionate start to the interview, but I was so dang nervous my answer came out flat and uninspiring. It got worse from there.

As Megyn set up the next question, nerves gripped so tightly my mind wandered and drifted to some other consciousness. When I came to, I heard the last part of her question and did my best to answer it. I wish I would have wiggled my earpiece and claimed I couldn't hear the question, but I was such a novice I blurted out the first thing that came to my mind. "What about the kids?" I don't think my answer had much to do with her question, but at least it was from the heart.

She asked me another pertinent question, and I gave the same basic answer, "What about the kids?" I was like a broken record quipping out the same line over and over as the needle skipped over the crack in my vinyl. Megyn was gracious. I remember clearly the change in her tone. She went from excited and fast-paced to empathetic and calm. I think she felt sorry for me. It's a good thing too because the change in her pace allowed me to finally catch up and comprehend her questions.

We ended on a somber note, and I left the studio feeling totally embarrassed and ill-equipped to be the voice of teachers desperate for liberty. But you know what? Even though I was lousy, God used my disastrous interview for good. Although I totally forgot to mention our case and completely blew my chance to educate the American people on the problems with forced unionism, I think God's grace showed up and saved the day. The interview wasn't pretty by any stretch of the imagination, but I accomplished my main goal. I gave the American people a true picture of how real teachers feel about the kids. In fact, thanks to my broken record, that's practically all they heard, but because my heart for kids was the dominating message, all of a sudden, all of these people (parents, teachers, workers, and students) from all across the country started reaching out to me—relieved that there was a teacher who put the needs of children ahead of the desires of state and national teachers' unions.

One of those parents was Gwen Samuel, a single mom and education reformer from Connecticut. After learning about our lawsuit, she wrote an editorial about it in *Dropout Nation*.[75] Here are some highlights.

> *Upon reading the lawsuit, as a parent of color, I chose to be in concert with these teachers because no one should be forced to pay for a service that infringes on their principles, and violates their freedoms of speech and association...*

> *Then Friedrichs made me think this: Now teachers can see, first-hand, how parents feel when they are forced to send their children to schools that are unsafe and chronically low-performing. That teachers can see how our children are denied access to high-quality education and safe learning environments....*

> *We hope those teachers, along with others, will join alongside us to fight for high-quality schools that are safe and fit for the wellbeing of our children.*

Thanks to the unions' protection of bad teachers, and their multi-million-dollar assault on school choice, Gwen and her friends were stuck with many teachers who quite frankly didn't care about their kids, so they were shocked to learn that there were public school teachers standing up against union forces in defense of kids and families. Gwen and I started working together to bridge the gap between parents and teachers. Here's her first message to me.

Rebecca, words cannot express how appreciative I am, as a parent, that you and the other nine teachers have the moral courage to file this lawsuit. You not only give a voice to all the GREAT teachers that get caught up in the politics of unions & education & politicians and huge campaign donations that might not be in the best interest of teachers or children…but you give a voice to parents that want to build solid relationships with effective teachers, outside of the politics, so that all can succeed—the teacher in the classroom, the child in the classroom and the parents who support both of you.

I traveled to Connecticut and met with Gwen and a roomful of passionate, hardworking low-income parents who've been striving for years to improve their schools. I'll be honest, when I walked into that room the anger was palpable. Those parents were brutally honest with me and America's teachers especially need to hear their pleas. Their children are trapped in dangerous, low-performing public schools with many teachers who have no business working with children, and they told me some kids were being shut into dark rooms, all alone, as means of punishment. They were furious at public school teachers for clinging to unions and standing with them against school choice. With exasperation, they shared their dire situation and their deep discouragement because no matter how hard they've worked to change the situation, the teachers' unions always get in the way. It's turf protection. And they think it's inexcusable that more teachers aren't speaking out to stop it.

Educators, I think a lot of us work in schools that are safe, our own kids are safe, we're doing our best in our classrooms, so we close our eyes to the abuse and chaos going on in many public schools across the country. And if we're honest, we have to admit that most teachers have no idea what state and national unions are *really* doing with our money. Most educators have never even read union Resolutions or studied their policies, and most fall for cleverly worded union hysteria.

The status quo tells us the problems in our schools are the fault of parents and poor neighborhoods—that reformers are wealthy bogeymen who blame teachers and want to profit off the kids. But Gwen and her friends *are* the poor parents, and they *are* the education reformers too. They're desperate to work with great teachers. They're not profiting off kids—they're fighting for safe and excellent schools for their *own* kids, and *our unions* are the wealthy boogeymen standing in the way.

Here's the reality; the unions have divided us. They've made us feel as if our interests are somehow different, yet all great teachers and parents desire to put the kids first. But putting kids first means union domination must end, and the voices of parents must be heard. Instead, state and national unions bully the PTA into submissive neutrality, oppose common sense bi-partisan bills meant to protect children, push for abusive sex education lessons against the rights of parents and innocence of children, stand against parental choice, and apply Phillip of Macedonia's tried, true, and ancient technique for maintaining power: divide and conquer.

Do you remember why? As Don Cameron, former NEA executive director, reminds us again, "NEA's future is inextricably linked to the well-being of public education…. [O]ur job is to continue advocating for our members, and the surest way to protect their jobs is to protect public education."[76]

It's all about the money. Kids be damned.

CHAPTER 20

———— ✣ ————

ROTTEN TO
THE ROOTS

*People pointed out we were just like David standing
against Goliath. I found a lot of peace in that because David won.*

After my interviews with Governor Huckabee and Megyn Kelly, my opportunities to spread our message of freedom for America's teachers grew
exponentially, but things were still pretty quiet at work. My stance against
forced unionism inspired a new level of antagonism from some union leaders, but most teachers still weren't saying much.

During union votes in the past, I would simply leave the room or sit
quietly while others participated, but now that I was the name on a case
seeking liberty for educators abused by unions, at every single meeting
some of our local union leaders would announce loudly, "Fee payers are
not permitted to vote!" And those same leaders created flyers they would
place in all of our mailboxes. They said things like, "Bargaining Update
Meeting FOR MEMBERS ONLY!" They never mentioned I was paying
one-hundred percent of the collective bargaining fees and had every right
to attend their meetings.

As teachers across Orange County became aware of the lawsuit, several
started asking me if I could teach them how to become fee payers. It takes
about two hours to teach someone the steps necessary to become a fee
payer, and the punishments associated with opting out of membership, so I
started offering "Teacher Freedom Workshops" to save time.

We met in private homes and passed on our information by word of mouth only because teachers were afraid that if union officials found out about our gatherings, they'd show up to harass us.

The culture of fear is intense, and without exception, every time I offered a workshop, less than half of those who sought me out for help would show up. Everyone who reached out was angry about the way our union supports abortion, is highly political, and attacks Judeo-Christian beliefs and traditional marriage using teacher dues, but even in their disgust with union abuses and misrepresentations, many who attended the meetings were too afraid to opt out. This made me more convinced that our battle against forced unionism was good and right.

People constantly asked me if I was afraid for my life, if the lawsuit had ruined my job, and it was obvious they thought I was crazy to take on the unions, but they were thankful I was doing it. I admit there was a sense of danger, and I always watched my back, but other than that, I was having the time of my life.

It's hard to express because I don't go around suing people, and I don't enjoy confrontation at all, but I knew God called me to the battle, and it was obvious He'd called Charles and our sons too because my struggle morphed into our family crusade, so I felt comforted and strengthened. After twenty-five years of being harassed and silenced, it was liberating to be able to finally share the truth about state and national union abuse.

Our attorneys had a brilliant strategy. We were attempting to overturn a Supreme Court precedent (the 1977 *Abood v. Detroit Board of Education* decision). Lower courts have no authority to rule against Supreme Court precedents, so they truly could do nothing to help us, but we still had to file our case in the local California federal court first, then work through the appeals process before we could ask for review at the Supreme Court. We could have easily been stuck in the system for five to seven years. Our lawyers approached the bench and basically said, "Look, you cannot rule against a Supreme Court precedent, and our clients are being harmed because of that precedent and seek immediate relief. You cannot give them relief, so please rule against them and let us move on to the next court."

Amazingly, the union's attorneys agreed, the court ruled against us, and we were out of the local California court within eight months and headed to the Ninth Circuit Court of Appeals. This really was miraculous.

It's strange to think back on it now, but we actually discussed the importance of getting to the Supreme Court quickly just in case a Justice retired or died before we arrived.

Almost immediately after we filed our lawsuit, the attorney general of California, Kamala Harris, and the Obama administration intervened in our case on the side of the unions, so the State of California and the United States stood in support of massively wealthy special interests against their victims, us teachers. I was absolutely disgusted and shocked by this because I had no idea that politicians could meddle in lawsuits brought by desperate people seeking relief from powerful organizations who'd gained unbridled power from corrupt politicians—it all seemed so wrong to me.

Now, instead of ten teachers suing the most powerful teachers' unions in the country, we were ten public school teachers standing against the NEA, the CTA, the State of California, and the United States of America. People pointed out we were just like David standing against Goliath. I found a lot of peace in that because David won.

In summer 2014, I was invited to sit on a panel discussion at Heritage Foundation in Washington DC. One of my fellow panelists was Robert Wiersema, a Michigan high school teacher who was a member of the Michigan Education Association (MEA) for sixteen years and had given the union his credit card number for forced dues collection. When Michigan became a "Right to Work" state, Robert was thrilled to learn he could be freed from the union at the end of the negotiated contract period. But when Robert chose to leave the union, the MEA ignored his request, and continued to extract monthly dues payments from his credit card. He was baffled and angry, and he discovered that although none of the teachers or local union leaders knew about it, their union voted for a new bylaw—supposedly democratically—and that bylaw created a secret and very short opt-out window in the middle of summer vacation. Since Robert didn't send his letter of intent to leave the union during that short secret opt-out window, he was stuck in the union another year, and they had a legal right to his money.

I was shocked by this story because I thought Right to Work gave employees the power to leave the union without repercussions, but I was wrong. Even after Robert successfully opted out the following year, because the union was still the exclusive representative of the teachers, he was shunned, became a target for some people, faced lots of resistance, and was even harassed with a disciplinary hearing. Since teachers who wanted freedom couldn't figure out how to opt out, they started calling him on the sly, and he taught them, and he was honest with them that they would suffer punishments for exercising their liberties.

Robert's story blew my mind because our lawsuit was designed to make the entire nation Right to Work in the public sector, so I thought a win in our case would give all government employees the freedom to truly decide for ourselves whether or not we wanted to join or fund a union—without fear of reprisal. Robert's story exposed my naiveté and proved that even with freedom to choose, teachers and workers are abused, lied to, manipulated, intimidated, and isolated for daring to exercise their rights, so the culture of fear wasn't destroyed at all.

I was starting to realize that a win in our case would just be the first step toward freedom, and we'd have to fight a lot longer for complete liberation from union abuse. It was at this point that the visions I'd been carrying for years of writing a book to educate teachers and the public about union abuses started to grow into an essential need that I couldn't put on the backburner any longer.

Jennifer Parrish was the other speaker on the panel. Jennifer is a private, home-based childcare provider. She shared a story about the day a creepy man walked into her home, without knocking, while she was making lunch for six preschoolers she cares for in her home. As if it was totally normal to trespass into the home of a vulnerable woman and six little children, the man immediately started urging Jennifer to sign a petition asking the state to provide healthcare for home-based childcare providers. Jennifer was terrified and tried to get the guy out of her house fast. The only way she could get rid of him was to promise she would read and consider his petition if he left it for her to examine. No surprise, even though the man never once mentioned unions, when Jennifer read the petition, it was a union membership card. If she would have signed the bogus "petition," she would have become a union member and the Service Employees International Union (SEIU) would have been permitted to force her to pay union dues.

Jennifer and other Minnesota home childcare providers were forced into unions when their union-controlled governor signed an executive order unionizing home childcare workers. Their union-friendly legislature and governor reclassified home childcare providers as state employees, but only for the purpose of unionization. They didn't get a pension, benefits, or even help with their working conditions; they just got to pay union dues for supposed "benefits" they didn't want. Jennifer and her friends were also forced to sue for freedom, but they couldn't get justice because the Eighth Circuit Court of Appeals dismissed their case. The excuse for rejecting the case was it was too "ripe," whatever that means.

As I listened to Jennifer's story, I was completely incensed, and my mind was troubled with thoughts like, "Why wasn't this guy arrested? It's a crime to trespass into someone's home. She and those six children could have been harmed. Why do the unions have so much power to abuse everyone and get away with behaviors that would land the rest of us in jail?" I sat there in shock, and it reminded me of watching the Witch almost thirty years before, as she manhandled little six-year-olds in her class without any repercussions, while the unions protected her, and the school district put its relationship with a union above the safety and educational needs of small children. Jennifer's story opened my eyes.

Just like I couldn't figure out why union workers could barge into the homes of vulnerable women and children without being arrested, I could never figure out why social services didn't step in to protect the kids in the Witch's class (or other classes run by abusive teachers in our country), especially since educators are mandated reporters of child abuse. Jennifer's story motivated me to do some more research. Although I already knew police officers were unionized, I discovered social service workers are coerced to fund government unions too, so I had to wonder if the voices of great workers who want to protect our communities and our kids are silenced in those professions as well. During this very time, the news was full of reports about an enormous IRS scandal in which conservative groups were being targeted, so I did some research, and just as I'd suspected, the IRS is run by government unions too.

Then I heard multiple news reports that the General Services Administration, or GSA (the leader in federal government for standards of architecture, engineering, and others), was caught spending over 800,000 in taxpayer dollars on an extravagant conference for its workers including in-room parties, gifts for all, and a session with a mind reader—you guessed it—unionized.

On the heels of this corruption, a massive scandal broke about veterans being placed on ridiculously long waiting lists and being allowed to die while awaiting care; all compassionate Americans were disgusted by this disgrace. I listened to the excuses, watched the behaviors of those in charge, and saw right through their self-serving agenda, so it was no surprise to discover that government unions run the Veterans Administration too.

In so many instances in which corruption, waste, fraud, and abuse were universal in a government-run facility, the government unions were representing employees. This made me even more frustrated with the government leaders in the state of California and the Obama administration that stood in support of corrupt government unions against ten teachers trying to protect our profession and our students.

These stories infuriated me, but they gave me more assurance in the battle because I became even more certain that my fellow plaintiffs and I were doing the right and moral thing. I had no idea when I entered the battle that winning our case was so important for the health and healing of America, and again, I felt the weight of a responsibility that was way beyond my capabilities. When loving moms just trying to eke out a sparse living in their own homes while protecting little children are subjected to strange men barging into their homes, garnished wages sent to unions, and no one with the authority to protect them seems to care, things are out of control, and the abusers need to be stopped. This reality brought me to my knees in prayer because I knew I wasn't up to the task.

CHAPTER 21

———⟶—⟵———

SPAWNS OF SATAN

Profiting off the sick and vulnerable is a new low, even for unions.

In June 2014, the US Supreme Court released their opinion on a case called *Harris v. Quinn*. We were watching the *Harris* case because if they won, the Court would almost certainly accept our case. Pam Harris and her fellow plaintiffs received a 5–4 decision in their favor, so we were celebrating. Shortly thereafter, we received word that the Ninth Circuit Court of Appeals ruled against us, so after only eight months at the appeals court, we were free to petition our case to the US Supreme Court—another miracle.

Though successful, Pam's case freed only home healthcare providers and home childcare providers like Jennifer. Our case sought to go a step further; we wanted to free all government employees from forced unionism by overturning the 1977 Supreme Court precedent-setting case *Abood*.

On January 26, 2015, we filed our petition with the Court. If four Justices agree to review a case, it's accepted to the Supreme Court. We would have to wait until June 30 to discover if the Court would accept our case, but as we waited, many others filed *amici curiae* (friend of the court) briefs in support of our case, so the unions started to take us seriously, and things started heating up.

The collective state and national unions started a campaign to compel teachers across the country to hear their hysterical messaging against us. My name suddenly became a four-letter word on public school campuses across the nation. They, of course, painted our case as a threat to children and a crisis that could dismantle their organization, but the upside of their campaign against me was that teachers across the country started to learn about our case, and many of them agreed with us, so my fellow plaintiffs and I gained prayer support and lots of new advocates.

Thanks to the union's culture of fear, I had practically no overt support from teachers on my campus or in my district. It was as if I were Hester Prynne, the woman caught in adultery in *The Scarlet Letter,* and I was marked. My life was instantly one-dimensional because people couldn't see me as Rebecca Friedrichs, the teacher they'd respected for almost thirty years; instead my only identity was *Friedrichs v. CTA,* and rather than being a multidimensional woman with many interests and talents to offer, I became the woman who makes everyone feel uncomfortable because she's fighting the union. I was the elephant in the room, the most avoidable person in the district. The air of animosity blown my way was thick.

The saddest part was that some teachers believed the frenzied and deceptive union rhetoric over the pure motives of a longtime friend. I couldn't help but think how similar the situation was to watching a friend in an abusive relationship. You know, the friend who constantly complains about her abusive spouse, asking for advice, and sobbing in your arms after he cheats on her or mistreats the kids. You offer support and prayers and watch for years as she continues to allow the man to wreak havoc. Even though you don't really want to get involved, she keeps bringing the issues to you, so one day you finally tell her, "You've gotta leave that bum. You have to protect your kids and your own sanity." She's terrified to leave him because she relies on him financially and he'll likely come after her and the kids and abuse them more, and he's so manipulative and sly the authorities never catch him in the act, so she feels trapped.

She finally makes the break, and you offer her and the kids a place to stay while she gets on her feet, but right when you stand up in protection of her and the vulnerable kids, the abuser shows up, manipulates her with his deceptive words, and your friend and the abuser turn on *you* and they blame *you* for their marital disaster. *You* become the focus of the problem, and you're attacked for coming to the aid of the defenseless. Then you remember why you didn't want to get involved in the first place.

It was like this with my teacher colleagues. They'd been complaining to me for years about low morale, lowering discipline standards making it almost impossible to teach, and their frustrations of feeling unheard by administration and blamed for every problem in education. They were miserable about our political climate, about being used to pass deceptive bond measures, felt voiceless in so many areas of education, and were terrified of the rumors we continued to hear about new inappropriate sex education lessons invading schools.

They were super grateful when I stood up for them at school board meetings or as a union representative and loved it when I took their complaints to school board members, but when I discovered the real problem was state and national teachers' unions and I stood up to defend my colleagues and expose our unions as the cheating spouse, I got pummeled by some teachers as they joined the abuser in making me the central issue and common enemy.

You know, even though some teachers treated me unfairly, my heart really goes out to them. Most teachers don't mean to be hurtful to their defenders. They just truly are ignorant of how the unions are hurting teachers and kids, and how they are using the teaching profession as a smokescreen and funding source for their political, sexual, and social agendas. Teachers are also trapped in a far more abusive situation than you can imagine, and they don't stand up to state and national union abuse because, like the abused woman, they're convinced they'll lose everything if they do.

On June 30, 2015, three days after my fiftieth birthday, and exactly two years and two months after we first filed our lawsuit, the US Supreme Court granted petition of our case! It was the best birthday present I'd ever received, and I prayed that my gift the following year would be a decision in our favor.

During the long battle to the Supreme Court, God sent me a ton of loving support from several fantastic organizations, and the Orange County Lincoln Club even embraced me with a membership. Once our case hit Washington DC, supporters from all fifty states stepped up to surround my fellow plaintiffs and me. Though we felt alone for decades, all at once, we had a national network of people who were fighting the exact same battle.

The kind folks at Illinois Policy Institute wanted to provide me with support from someone who could relate to my personal experience of being lead plaintiff in a Supreme Court case, so they arranged for me to meet Pam Harris. Pam's son Josh has a rare genetic syndrome that produces extreme intellectual and developmental disabilities, and Pam is devoted to his loving care, so we never dreamed we'd get to meet one another. While Josh slept, I visited with Pam, her husband and their grown daughter. Pam and I got to do a fun interview together, and we cracked up about all of the times we've been accused of being "pawns" or "whores" of the Koch Brothers. Pam told me, "The unions have accused me of being a pawn of the Koch Brothers so many times, I keep joking with my husband, 'Has that big check from the Kochs arrived yet?'"

Though we were having a great time, our conversation took a serious turn when Pam helped me to understand that her son Josh, as a significantly disabled adult citizen, qualifies for a Medicaid waiver program often referred to as Home Based funding, which provides the family caretaker a small subsidy equivalent to less than minimum wage for about twenty hours a week. These programs save the taxpayers money, and they give the families the ability to stay together and offer dignity to those suffering from serious health issues.

Pam and her fellow plaintiffs (all moms serving as home healthcare providers) sued the former governor of Illinois because when Governor Rod Blagojevich (who was run out of office on corruption charges and sentenced to fourteen years in prison), was in office, he did a big favor for government unions. He declared home healthcare workers as government workers for the purpose of unionization. Blagojevich's successor signed an executive order, which gave SEIU (Service Employees International Union) exclusive representation rights over home healthcare providers, so the unions were able to unionize these moms and take a chunk of their small assistance checks to cover unwanted union fees. Sound familiar?

Pam shared with me how she and her family had been Democrats their entire lives and the first thing they did whenever they moved into a new town was to sign up with their local Democratic headquarters as volunteers. After she discovered it was the Democrat party allowing union abuse of families and taking money from the severely ill, she and her family left the party. She told me, "When I think of how the unions and the Democrat politicians wrangled and twisted our laws to legally siphon these precious Medicaid dollars from our sons and daughters into their own pockets, I am sickened. How dare they!"

Pam asked me if I'd ever been harassed outright by the unions. Then she and her husband told me about the night the strange man in a large vehicle parked across their driveway blocking in their cars and came to their door pretending to deliver pizza. They hadn't ordered any pizza. The man was huge, frightening, angry, peculiar, and he would not leave their front porch until they called the police. The experience left them feeling exposed and targeted especially with a special needs young man in their home. The memory of the experience prompted Pam to say, "I'm glad to pass the mantle to you and slip quietly back into my life of service to Josh. The burden of *Harris v. Quinn* was heavy and at times the notoriety was unsettling. I'm grateful to you for continuing the fight, Rebecca. Watch your back."

My meeting with Pam stirred something in my spirit. I was already disgusted that unions were forcing families to fork over part of their meager Medicaid support, so unions could build up more power and wealth, but I have to say that after meeting Pam and her son and seeing the challenges they face, I get ill when I think about this offensive situation. I thought the unions were debased for ruining the education of millions of kids across the country without even feeling guilty about it but profiting off the sick and helpless is a new low, even for unions.

As if meeting Pam Harris wasn't enough, the Illinois Policy Institute friends drove me to Springfield to meet Mark Janus and Governor Rauner. They brought a case against the unions too, and Mark is the lead plaintiff. Mark's case, *Janus v. AFSCME*, was on the heels of our case, so if our case couldn't overturn *Abood*, his case was next in line to get the job done.

As our case heated up, some in the media attacked my fellow plaintiffs and me for being Christians. This was odd because our case had nothing to do with religion (although the unions use our forced dues for things that are morally offensive to most people of faith, and as you'll recall, at state and national union events they directly attack Christian teachers for our beliefs, so we could likely have sued for freedom of religion abuses too), but religion wasn't included in our petition to the Court. When I was on the phone with one reporter, he kept accusing me of being a bigot and of hating homosexuals because of my Christian faith. He asked me leading questions designed to trap me into saying things to make me sound judgmental. I was talking to a man who had never met me, knew nothing about me, and supposedly wanted to understand the details of our case to free teachers from forced unionism, yet all he wanted to do was condemn me because he had a warped idea of what it meant to be a follower of Christ. He was judgmental, but he tried to twist that label onto me, just like the unions have been doing to teachers for decades.

When I took on my role in the case, I knew I would be harassed, slandered, and isolated, and that the unions would drag my reputation through the mud, but it started to dawn on me after my faith was repeatedly attacked that my union is the reason Christian beliefs are continually criticized in our public school system and political landscape as well.

The attacks on my faith got me thinking back to one time when I was serving as a union representative at the CTA UniServ offices near my school. While talking to us about phone banking, a UniServ director made a very disparaging comment about Christians and conservatives. He said it so matter-of-factly, as if all teachers agreed with his way of thinking. Several of the teachers with me were Christians and conservatives, so I knew I wasn't the only one hurt by his narrow-minded remarks. Then I started thinking about the significant changes teachers have witnessed over the past forty years in the removal of wholesome values from our schools, and I understood more fully why God asked me to help expose the exploitation of teachers by government unions.

Ironically, though union leaders criticized us for our Christian faith, in the next breath, they called us "spawns of Satan." We were characterized as "free-riders," and "pawns of the wealthy one-percent," suggesting we cannot think for ourselves but were being used by corporate bogeymen. Then they labeled us "union busters," which gave me a laugh because unions have been busting hearts, minds, and the human spirit for decades.

So, we thanked God that on November 24, 2015, the Justices of the US Supreme Court placed *Friedrichs v CTA* on their docket. It read, "SET FOR ARGUMENT on January 11, 2016." My entire body reacted with anticipation when I saw the Court's schedule. The long wait for the opportunity to plead our case was difficult, but the tragic stories I'd learned during those two and a half years and the hateful attacks against good teachers and parents made me even more convinced our argument was not only right, but righteous.

CHAPTER 22

MRS. FRIEDRICHS GOES TO WASHINGTON

"I never trusted the justice system or the educational system after that. They are litigation gangsters. They get paid to be bullies."

On Sunday morning, January 10, 2016, Charles, Ben, and I awoke in our hotel room in Washington DC. We had a busy day ahead of us including multiple interviews, and an evening gathering for all of the people who would stand in solidarity with us on the steps of the Supreme Court the following day. Many friends, some fellow plaintiffs, and strangers traveled from several states across the country to get to DC in time to take part in our rally at the Court, and thousands of people from around the globe were praying for us.

We had a fun interview with Shannon Bream, FOX News Supreme Court reporter, but the best part of our conversation was off air. Shannon's mom was a teacher for forty years, and she loved her students the way I love mine, so she and her staff thanked me for being a teacher. This might seem like a small thing to mention, but it was a big thing to me. Since many in the media were joining the unions in slandering my fellow plaintiffs and me, it was nice to hear kind words from media folks who saw through those ugly tactics to see our hearts for America's teachers and kids.

Our day was extraordinary, but I had some worries on my mind. Believe it or not, even if you're a plaintiff in a Supreme Court case, you're not guaranteed to get into the Courtroom to hear your own oral arguments. Each side gets a small number of tickets to the Court and because there are so many people involved in bringing a case like ours, and our case was high profile, there was a real concern that all of us who wanted to attend might not get tickets into the Court. There's plenty of room in the Court, but apparently, people with political connections often get first dibs on tickets.

Fortunately, my fellow plaintiffs and I each secured a ticket ahead of time, but we still didn't have tickets for Charles and Ben. If they couldn't get tickets, they would have to stand in line at 5:00 in the morning, amongst angry union picketers, to secure one of a few tickets available to the public.

The rest of us were told we'd arrive in taxis and walk through the mob of protestors to enter the Court. We joked about the need for disguises and bodyguards—only we weren't really joking, and I was seriously thinking about buying a dark-colored wig.

Throughout the almost three years we battled to get to the US Supreme Court, I kept asking our lawyers how we were going to provide the American people with a true picture of our battle for worker freedom on our day at the Court. You see, the teachers' unions use our money to stage massive rallies, they hire people to add to their numbers, they coerce workers to picket, and they even bus people in for their events. This gives them the ability to set the tone and narrative in the media for every argument. Remember how they brought in mobs to take over the state capitol for weeks in Wisconsin during Governor Walker's battle for Act 10 while drowning out and abusing good teachers like Tracie Happel and kids like Benji Backer? Well, Act 10 gave some freedoms to teachers in Wisconsin, but our case would free every public sector worker in America, so I could not imagine how the unions would battle us in front of the Court.

Sometime in early December, I called my friend Lynn Harsh, one of the terrific people from across the country who had been giving me moral support. Lynn works for State Policy Network (SPN). I explained to her my worries that the unions would set the national narrative with their angry rally, and likely shout down and harass my fellow plaintiffs and me as we entered and exited the Courtroom. I didn't know if Lynn would be able to help, but she took my request to SPN and they ran with it.

They supported us with a social media campaign, anticipated every last detail of our day at the Court, and on Sunday evening they hosted us at the Heritage Foundation offices in DC and showered us with the most tremendous support. We munched on pizza, took photos in front of a terrific "Trust Teachers" banner, and organized our troops for our rally in front of the Court. It was remarkable.

Thankfully, just a day before this gathering, a young teacher at work (whom I had no idea supported our case) passed on an incredibly encouraging story to give us hope, so I shared it with our supporters. She said her mother overheard CTA folks planning their rally against our case. Some CTA member recommended they make posters declaring, "We're for the kids." Her mother said someone piped in, "It's too late for that; everyone knows it's not true."

Then her mother said, "They're terrified of Rebecca Friedrichs and they're scrambling for ideas and funds to fight her." Then the young teacher said, "Tell Rebecca I hope she goes all the way and wins!"

This picture of vulnerability inside the unions gave us extra energy, hope, and faith because when you're going up against Goliath, you never suspect the giant has any weak spots. But union leaders aren't really afraid of me, they're afraid of the truth I speak. Truth shines light on darkness. They'd been able to keep teachers in the dark for decades—using us as a front and a money stream. They knew truth could set us free. Besides, we were praying union efforts would be thwarted, so our prayers were being answered.

While I was giving my talk, Gwen Samuel, the mom who started Connecticut Parents' Union, walked in the room with Kelley Williams-Bolar. This surprise was a great encouragement, and I believe God sent them to give me a last-minute reminder of the magnitude and importance of our fight, because teachers aren't the only ones who need to be freed.

Kelley was prosecuted and put in jail for rescuing her two girls from dangerous, low-performing public schools. Yes, you read that right. Kelley was *jailed* for protecting her kids. I was shocked when I read her story in my local newspaper and was so honored Kelley was standing in front of me having pizza with us at our pre-rally. I couldn't wait to hear her whole story.

After ten years of marriage, Kelley became a single parent, so she was working and going to college to make a better life for her two daughters. She and her girls lived in an inner city, high-crime area in Akron, Ohio, with dangerous and low-performing schools. Kelley's parents lived in a rural area with some of the best schools around. At the suggestion of some friends, Kelley decided to enroll her girls in the school in her parent's neighborhood for their protection. "I was a little hesitant because I knew it wasn't completely lawful," Kelley told me, "But I was working as a substitute at different schools and there were so many kids who did not live in the district and no one had gotten in trouble. All I want is for my children to have a quality education, and I want them to be safe." Kelley's girls were in third grade and middle school at the time.

Kelley told me about how great everything went the first year her girls were in the high-performing school. She said they were getting a huge head start, and to this day they do better in school just from the short time they were there.

Around Christmas time during the second year her girls were in the great school, Kelley received a letter stating she needed to remove the girls immediately because she didn't live in the district. When she asked how the girls could remain, she was told about something called "Grandparent Power of Attorney," so she applied for it and the court granted it, but the school district rejected it, so Kelley's girls had to return to the dangerous and underperforming schools.

Kelley and her girls were devastated. They'd been back in their home district schools for eighteen months, and Kelley had obeyed all she was told to do, but that wasn't enough for the tyrannical leaders running our public schools. Kelley told me, "The next thing I knew I received a letter—a postcard from the state of Ohio. It was an indictment that said, '*State of Ohio v. Kelley Williams-Bolar*.' I didn't even know what an indictment was; I've never been in trouble. My father received one as well."

The Copley Fairlawn City Schools (the district in which Kelley's parents lived) was charging Kelley and her father with two felonies: "grand theft and tampering with documents." They said Kelley's family was stealing education. Kelley's father had not participated in enrolling the children, so his charges were dropped, but Kelley was found guilty.

At first blush, this story seems like it's from *The Twilight Zone*—a parent found guilty for keeping her children safe and trying to give them an outstanding education? It's insane. But Kelley's punishment was so harsh, her story morphed into something more like a nightmare out of a communist regime.

Kelley told me, "The judge sentenced me to ten days in the county jail, two years' probation, random drug testing, sixty hours of community service, forty hours of political counseling, and I had to write about my counseling."

When Charles heard this he said, "Political counseling? What is this, the Soviet Union?" His comparison was fair too; Kelley told us that the political counseling was definitely designed to indoctrinate her, and I wasn't surprised at all, because I've been watching the teachers' unions indoctrinate employees and students for decades in our schools and universities, and they're successfully pushing their negative propaganda into the culture and our courts as well.

Kelley's punishment was so over-the-top that people all over spoke out in her defense.

"The community was picketing," Kelley told me. "The sheriff in the building told me that things were crazy, and they had to unplug the phone out of the wall because people were blowing up the phones from across the country saying, 'Are you kidding me?'"

Kelley originally had three charges, but they dropped one charge because of the outcry of the community, and her ten-day jail sentence was reduced to nine days because of the pressure on the court. Governor John Kasich even got involved in support of Kelley, and state senators visited her while she was in jail. Many people thought the attack on Kelley was racially motivated because she's black, but Kelley told me, "I had more visitors than anyone when I was in jail including state senators. These were well-off white men who were coming to say, 'We are with you, and this is wrong.' It touched me so much that these people were saying, 'We got you.'"

I have to wonder when people will start to realize that the teachers' unions and their favored politicians and judicial leaders deny school choice, liberty, fairness, and an outstanding education to children, teachers, and families of *all* colors (like my family, Nicole's family, Eileen Blagden's family, and many others who come from all different racial backgrounds) because they don't care about kids and families; they care about collecting dues monies from educators trapped in union-run public schools.

I also wonder when we'll wake up to the fact that state and national teachers' unions and their allies are the ones pushing the destructive racial divide in this country. It benefits the unions when we blame their treatment of families and kids on racism because then no one focuses on the real problem—union greed.

Kelley and her girls were denied choice and great schools because union supported politicians, school leaders, and judges are motivated to push the unions' agenda onto everyone, and the whole team rallies together to achieve more power and control for themselves. Remember how the NAACP (an organization established to protect the civil rights of blacks) was involved in denying safe schools to black parents, teachers, and kids in Aaron Benner's district in Minnesota? Recall, they were working in conjunction with the teachers' unions. Don't forget that since then, the NAACP in cahoots with the teachers' unions declared a moratorium on charter schools across the country, and the Chicago Teachers' Union even imposed a suspension on charters as part of their contract; even though parents of all colors in Chicago want school choice. I stood there listening to Kelley's story hoping and praying that people would start to connect the dots between union domination of our schools and society and the tyrannical treatment of good and honest people—of all colors.

The most heartbreaking part of Kelley's story is what happened to her father. She told me, "The courts were mad because they're used to doing whatever they want without anyone questioning them," so even though her father's charges were dropped, Kelley said the court was angry about the negative attention from across the country, so they used a "Discovery Box" to dig up dirt on Kelley's family members going back all the way to the 1960s. Kelley told me her lawyer said he'd never seen anything like it in his entire career. Kelley's father had worked hard running his window washing business—working on skyscrapers—for his entire life, but he suffered a stroke near retirement age, struggled with some brain damage, and his health deteriorated, so he was unable to continue running his business. After that, he was on disability, and the courts caught him on a disability technicality. Since he had not reported his wife's income, they threw him into the penitentiary.

Before Kelley's father was sentenced and while she was in jail, her father would come to visit her. She shared, "He would put his finger on the glass, and then I would put my finger on the glass." She was dead silent for over a minute as her voice caught in her throat. When she regained her composure, she said, "Those were some of our last times together. My dad died in jail."

Kelley told me, "I've never been in trouble before, and I haven't been in trouble since. My parents were good citizens, and we've always strived to be good people. I've tried to be a good example to my girls and teach them to be good young ladies. I told my girls that what I did was not right. I just wanted them in a good and safe school."

No surprise, Kelley was diagnosed with PTSD after her horrific experience and she went through a deep depression; all the while her girls were negatively impacted by all of this and also back in their horrible schools. Her mother was unable to keep her home after her husband died. The judge also told Kelley that if she did anything while on probation, she would have to go back to jail for ten years. Kelley told me, "I never trusted the justice system or the educational system after that. They are litigation gangsters. They get paid to be bullies."

Rather than educating children in the safest and most outstanding schools possible, we put families in nightmarish situations and then punish them for trying to escape. Two little girls lost their grandpa and their best chance at a great education. A loving daughter lost her father and suffered a deep, dark depression; a devoted wife lost her husband and her home; and a man who likely had many more years of love to give his family died in jail. But the education status quo got what it wanted, and most of the precious little kids like Kelley's girls dreaming of a safe and excellent education, are still stuck in dangerous and underperforming schools unable to escape since unions spend millions against school choice. Since Kelley's daddy isn't alive to speak for himself, I'll offer up what my daddy would say in a situation like this:

"I'd be ashamed."

CHAPTER 23

TEAM FRIEDRICHS IN THE COURT

Like Moses begged the Pharaoh of Egypt, I felt the urgency to stand up and cry out to the Justices, "Let my people go!"

Some people think it's glamorous to take a case to the US Supreme Court, or that those of us who put our necks out there do so for attention, but that's a complete misunderstanding of the reasons people like my fellow plaintiffs and I are compelled to bring a lawsuit against a massive power like the teachers' unions. As you know, I've sacrificed the trusted reputation I had with my colleagues that was built over almost thirty years of faithful service to kids. My family has sacrificed thousands of dollars each year as I worked part-time so I'd be enabled to bring our case correctly. I've sacrificed thousands each year in my future pension disbursements too. My friends put a security system on my home and cameras around our house because they (and my husband) were so worried about the safety of our family. My husband lost many nights of sleep because of nightmares. I've been called spawn of Satan, free rider, and other hateful names, and I've lost some of my dearest friends because they've been captured by the fear created by deceptive union messaging which convinces them our case and my fight is an attack on their schools, their pensions, and their careers.

There's been nothing glamorous about this experience. My fellow plaintiffs and I brought the case of forced unionism to the US Supreme Court because America's teachers are being exploited by angry, abusive, and selfish individuals who falsely claim to represent all of us. And we'd do it all over again, if necessary, to protect our students, colleagues, and American liberties.

Our attorneys were unable to obtain extra tickets for Charles and Ben, but Terry Pell offered up his ticket to our family. Terry sat in a lawyers' room above the Courtroom and listened through speakers instead of being part of the action in the Court so that someone in our family could be with me for support. We'll never forget Terry's kindness. We had only one extra ticket though. If I had to use one phrase to describe Charles to you it would be "servant leader." Charles said, "Ben should be with his mother in the Courtroom." That was the end of the discussion.

Because of this, Charles would have to get up at 4:00 a.m. on argument day to stand in line outside the Court in the freezing winter cold to try to obtain a ticket with the rest of the public. We're from the West Coast, so his internal clock would read 1:00 a.m. but he was determined to get inside of that Courtroom.

Sleep evaded me the night before arguments. I wasn't worried; I was just extraordinarily excited and the encouragement from our supporters that night, the emails and texts I'd received, and the promises of prayers from thousands across the country dominated my thoughts so much my mind couldn't settle into sleep, and I was worried about Charles. Things at the Court are run in such a mysterious fashion; no one could tell us exactly how many tickets would be available to the public, as the number available is different for each case. I wouldn't know until we arrived at the Court if my husband would be allowed to support me inside, so prayers for his entrance also kept me awake all night.

Getting ready that morning was dreamlike. Charles headed out in the dark. Ben and I met Terry and the plaintiffs in the hotel lobby. Five other plaintiffs were able to come: Karen Cuen, Jelena Figueroa, Harlan Elrich, Peggy Searcy, and Finn Laursen. We had a fun-filled breakfast and were all surprised when Lynn Harsh and friends showed up and announced they'd secured two large vans to deliver us to and from the Courthouse. They'd located a special drop-off and pick-up zone away from the abusive union picketers too. I cannot even describe the relief we felt—especially because I'd never bought that dark wig.

We arrived at the Court without incident, and as we walked alongside the building we could see our many supporters gathered at the bottom of the steps. They set up a nice podium, had a DJ, threw their gold "Teachers Deserve Choice" t-shirts on over their coats, and were already brandishing their terrific signs. The unions' group outnumbered them, but somehow our supporters were louder, and their volume wasn't the result of screaming or ugliness either—it's unexplainable, but kindness drowned out "pissed off" on the steps of the Court that day.

To be honest with you, I was so mesmerized watching our brave picketers, I can't even remember how we got into the building, but once we got inside Lynn started directing us, and we were in line for our secured tickets. It was about this time I received a text from Charles that read, "I got a ticket! They gave out 50. I'm #35!" He also informed me that he happened to stand in line next to Mark Janus (lead plaintiff in *Janus v. AFSCME*), so they became friends. Mark had ticket number 34. Team Friedrichs was in the Court!

Charles had to go through security later than we did, so we were not permitted to be together, but I was relieved and thankful to know he would be in the Courtroom. Ben, the other plaintiffs, and I handed our personal belongings over to Lynn for safekeeping since no one can bring purses, coats, phones, or other items into the Courtroom. I think we were permitted to bring in a pen and notepad, but we went in empty-handed, and Lynn and the SPN friends took care of our stuff. For those who don't have an amazing friend like Lynn looking out for them, the Court rents little lockers to store things during Court proceedings.

As we went through security, we were far outnumbered by union supporters and leaders who had somehow obtained way more tickets than we were able to muster. They were everywhere, and if looks could kill, I would have been dead on the floor. Ben noticed the hateful stares aimed at his mother, so he whispered in my ear, "Hey, Mom. All these people are shooting really hateful looks at you. What do you want me to do about it?" Gosh, I love that young man. Here he was, twenty years old, and he was not only able to read the hurtful intentions of others, but he desired to stick up for his mom. What a great son. God has been good to me.

I whispered back to Ben, "You shouldn't do anything. I'll just smile and be kind to these folks, but you can pretend you're my Secret Service agent."

Ben got a wide grin on his face; he liked the idea. He was looking dapper and very official in his handsome suit, and his hair is cut short and he's super handsome, so he actually did look like a Secret Service agent.

At that point, I wished I'd bought him one of those fake curly wires that look like the ones the Secret Service agents wear on the backs of their ears, and I wished the Court would have allowed Ben to keep his sunglasses on. That would have been epic! But Ben didn't need any props; his protection came from a heart of love because he knows me better than anyone on this planet, and he knew those mean folks were misguided and wrong about me.

Immediately after our whispering session, Ben struck a new pose, and he maintained it throughout the day. He drew back his shoulders, flexed his biceps, puffed out his broad chest, stood up taller, and portrayed a withering look on his face. Anytime a union operative shot a hateful glare (and they were constant), Ben shot back a look that said, "Back off, Jack." I never dreamed I'd get such a terrific chance to be proud of my son on my day as the named plaintiff in the United States Supreme Court, and it only got better as the day went on.

After going through security, a Court assistant directed Ben and us plaintiffs to our seats. Our wooden bench was like a pew in a church, and it was exactly long enough for our group of seven. We were in the middle section of the room about four rows behind the special lawyer section of the Courtroom. Plaintiffs don't sit with their lawyers in the Supreme Court; we're seated with the general public, and our lawyers are in a partitioned off section at the front of the Courtroom.

Ben was seated directly to my right, and we were both immediately overcome by the history in the room. The first thing we noticed was the stunning artwork covering the highest parts of the walls around the entire perimeter of the room. Much of it was biblical and brought to mind God's hand on our country. All of it spoke to liberty, fairness, and blind justice.

I had seen photos of the inside of the Court, but the stories sculpted into the walls in relief form are awe-inspiring in person. I found instant comfort from Moses's position with the Ten Commandments smack above the center of the Justices' seats. Ben told me the Justices better rule fairly with Moses hanging over them like that. I prayed they could see the obvious correlation between thousands of years of stories of one group of people being oppressed by another, and our plea to be released from the oppression of forced unionism. Like Moses begged the Pharaoh of Egypt, I felt the urgency to stand up and cry out to the Justices, "Let my people go!"

A few minutes later I saw Charles and Mark Janus ushered into the room. They were seated about four rows behind us directly behind Ben and me. I really wanted Charles next to me, but it was nice to know he had my back, and I turned around and winked at him several times before the proceedings began. Union operatives filled the rows in front of us and behind us, and they dominated the sections to our left and right as well, so Ben was busy casting his withering look in all directions, and he was downright good at it. I felt safe with my son, the Secret Service agent, by my side and my devoted Charles a few rows behind.

I pinched myself at least ten times because being in that Courtroom was like an out-of-body experience. I had dreamed about it for years, and here I was, living a dream come true. But my mind and body were so overwhelmed they refused to acknowledge my reality.

A hush fell over the Court. We were told there's no talking during proceedings—that Court monitors were staged all around our seats to enforce the rules, and we would be removed if we chose to disobey. Then we heard, "All Rise," and the nine Justices of the United States Supreme Court came out from behind the bench and took their seats. After several minutes of the swearing in of lawyers who had recently earned their rights to argue at the nation's Highest Court, the Justices got to work on their only case of the day, and though my mind couldn't fully grasp the scene, this is what I heard Chief Justice Roberts say at 10:04 a.m. from his position in the center of the bench.

"We'll hear argument this morning in Case 14-915, *Friedrichs v. California Teachers' Association, et al.*"

Our lawyer Michael Carvin stood up, Ben squeezed my hand, my heart started to pound, and God comforted me with reminders that thousands were praying, and He was in control.

CHAPTER 24

JANUARY 11, 2016—ORAL ARGUMENTS: *FRIEDRICHS v. CALIFORNIA TEACHERS' ASSOCIATION*

The unions and their allies had just conceded to our argument, and everyone knew it.

Court was in session, and we all sat transfixed by the majesty involved in what was a novel, once-in-a-lifetime experience from our perspective. I looked forward from my spot about midway back in the Courtroom at the Justices seated at the bench and thought about how society places those who are normal human beings (no different from the rest of us) on pedestals simply because they hold positions of power, fanfare, and influence.

I could see the backs of the heads of our legal team seated left center of the bench, and the unions' legal team seated center right. Michael Carvin, our lead counsel, would do the arguing for us, and his associates, William Coglianese and James Burnham, would offer support.

The unions boasted a much larger team. The solicitor of California, Edward C. Dumont, would argue on behalf of the attorney general of California. David C. Frederick would argue for the unions, and General Donald B. Verilli, solicitor general at the Department of Justice, was lead counsel on behalf of the United States. Their legal teams surrounded them, so just like union operatives in the crowd of onlookers outnumbered us; high-ranking government officials outnumbered our attorneys.

We should have felt intimidated, but our thousands of praying supporters were asking God to thwart the collective efforts of our gigantic opponents, and you know what? He did.

When cases are argued at the US Supreme Court, each side is given thirty minutes for arguments, then Court is adjourned, and the Justices enter their private chambers to discuss and vote on the case. However, because California and the United States intervened, the Court allowed forty minutes for each side. Michael Carvin got forty minutes to plead our cause, and the Respondents split their forty minutes between their three attorneys representing the unions, California, and the United States.

US Supreme Court arguments are more like conversations than monologues; even though the attorneys plan their arguments and hope to make their key points, the Justices can interrupt with questions or comments at any time. Attorneys are lucky if they can utter even a few sentences before being interrupted by a Justice seeking information.

Goosebumps covered my body as Michael Carvin began. "Mr. Chief Justice, and may it please the Court, every year petitioners are required to provide significant support to a group that advocates an ideological viewpoint, which they oppose and do not wish to subsidize. *Abood's* authorization of this clear First Amendment violation should be overturned, both to end this ongoing deprivation of basic speech and association rights, and to restore consistency and predictability to the Court's First Amendment jurisprudence."[77]

That's as far as Mr. Carvin got before Justice Ginsberg interrupted him.

I was glad I'd read most of the briefs that were submitted to the Court because in reading them I'd learned about all of the cases to which the attorneys and Justices were referring throughout our arguments. As best as I can understand, the courts make their decisions based on past precedent, so the arguments and decisions related to past cases are of utmost importance—especially when trying to overturn a past precedent like *Abood*.

I was thinking about Mr. Abood a lot during our arguments. He was a teacher like me. He taught in Detroit and fought all the way to the US

Supreme Court to try to free teachers from forced unionism in 1977, so we had a lot in common. I tried to find him about a year into our case. I wanted to let him know ten teachers in California had picked up his baton and were trying to make things right on behalf of him and millions across the country, but I discovered he died shortly before we filed our case. He was heavy in my heart during arguments, and I empathized with how devastated he must have felt when the decision came down against him after fighting so hard for liberty. I thought about how he had to return to the classroom and continue paying those awful fees and watch helplessly as they were used to undermine his profession and his country. Mr. Abood's testimony gave me extra courage.

Mr. Carvin told the Court that collective bargaining in the public sector is political because everything for which the unions bargain has an impact on taxpayers and public policy. None of the Justices challenged him on our arguments that forcing us to fund collective bargaining was a constitutional violation, instead four of them focused on the need to keep things the way they are in order to promote labor peace and to keep workers from "free riding" off the efforts of the unions.

Those four Associate Justices—Sonia Sotomayor, Elena Kagan, Stephen Breyer, and Ruth Bader Ginsburg—focused a lot on "*stare decisis*," the idea that we don't overturn past Supreme Court decisions because they hold precedent (established practice) in other cases and in government contracts with employees. They said we had a heavy burden of proof to convince the Court that *Abood* was decided wrongly and needed to be overturned.

I was amazed at the energy that went into arguing for *stare decisis*—to keep *Abood* as law just because it was decided that way forty years earlier as if the courts could never get things wrong. Justice Breyer was worried that if they overruled *Abood*, the American people might feel the Court isn't so stable in a world with a lot of change. Justice Kagan was worried overturning *Abood* would result in a lot of labor unrest as thousands of contracts are based on *Abood*, and Justice Bader Ginsburg was worried that a bunch of workers would want their money back retroactively.

Mr. Carvin argued that the constitutional rights of millions of Americans should be given greater consideration than a poorly decided precedent, the government's need to run things smoothly, or a Court tradition of *stare decisis*.

One of the frustrating things about being a plaintiff was that attorneys and Justices had conversations *about* us, but we were never permitted to add pertinent information to their exchanges that really could have cleared up many topics of confusion or at least blown a hole in deceptive arguments dreamed up by union public relations teams.

The mom and teacher in me wanted to approach the bench and have a heart-to-heart. I wanted to tell the Justices about Aaron Benner, abandoned by his union for trying to protect kids and teachers; Sue Halvorson and her friends, harassed annually at the NEA RA for daring to suggest children should be protected from lessons promoting and normalizing anal and oral sex; and the Witch, protected by union grievance procedures while vulnerable kids were abused.

I thought if those four Justices clinging to Court precedent could hear the real-life stories of folks being hurt by the *Abood* decision, maybe in a stand for liberty and morality, they could break tradition and get beyond the practice of *stare decisis.*

When the Supreme Court Justices decided *Abood* forty years ago, they couldn't possibly have anticipated the unintended consequences. Surely, the Justices in 1977 didn't understand that permitting forced union fees would result in the abuse of workers and children, the downfall of our educational system, and that unions would become the poster child for the saying, "Absolute power corrupts absolutely." Had they foreseen those things, they likely would have ruled in favor of Mr. Abood, so wouldn't it be wise to overrule *Abood* now that we have more information and work posthaste to restore constitutional freedoms better late than never? It was particularly ironic to me that Justices who believe the Constitution is evolving with time, had trouble grasping the idea that perhaps our understanding of forced unionism has evolved.

Although those Justices posed many serious questions for Mr. Carvin, he continued dazzling everyone with his lawyering prowess, and things were looking good for our side. Since teachers and other employees really are being abused and used to fund all sorts of politics against our will (even through collective bargaining), Mr. Carvin's arguments were strengthened by the weight of constitutional rights, and truth. Things went on nicely for a while, and all of us plaintiffs were sharing smiles up and down our row until several minutes into the arguments when Justice Sotomayor made a statement that made my heart fall into my stomach and likely gave everyone else on our side a case of indigestion.

She intonated that if we were freed from forced unionism, the *government* may be able to impose the fees through taxpayer assessments. She said, "Because this union under California law is a State entity…would it be illegal for the government, as employer or government, to fund the union?" Mr. Carvin refuted the idea and explained that unions are not state actors but simply have an official position. Still, I was absolutely sickened at the very thought that unions could be considered a state entity. It was absurd, and it was the first time it even crossed my mind that, even if we won, we may never be freed from forced unionism.

I fully understand the ways unions use technicalities, the letter of the law, and their political heft to lord it over everyone with their tyrannical reign. I also knew what had been going on at home in California, and I was petrified that Justice Sotomayor's statement might be used as a loophole unions could use to their advantage giving them even more power and leverage.

Back in California, the unions were on the warpath and started something dubbed "The Friedrichs Fix." Those in "the know" in the California legislature told me about extreme union lobbying efforts to get "The Friedrichs Fix" passed before our case was decided, so this was heavy on my mind during the exchange with Justice Sotomayor.

From what I understood, the fix sought to provide unions with three things: continually updated personal contact information on all employees in union shops (and legally deny that information to all others), require all new employees to attend a thirty minute meeting on the benefits of joining the union (on the taxpayer's dime), and force the taxpayers to fund the dues of any unionized employees who objected to paying unions.

In other words, even if we won, the "fix" would ensure unions hung onto all of the money and power they desired without having to earn it. Since the unions have already stacked the California legislature with a two-thirds majority in their favor, and they run roughshod over legislative decisions and proceedings through their favored caucuses and devoted politicians, I was already very worried they would succeed with this disturbing plan in our state. But after hearing Justice Sotomayor's statement, I was concerned they might be able to push this horrifying abuse of power onto the entire nation.

Since I'd witnessed personally the unchecked power of unions and their political allies for decades, the butterflies in my stomach were unrelenting after Mr. Carvin's exchange with Justice Sotomayor. Thankfully, the moment Mr. Dumont began his arguments on behalf of the State of California, Justice Alito interrupted with a question that gave me hope.

He asked, "Could I just ask you a preliminary question that came up earlier in the argument? Do you think that the California Teachers Association is an agency of the State of California?"

Mr. Dumont replied, "No...a union that becomes an exclusive representative...it does not become an organ of the State." Justice Alito's question forced admission from the solicitor general of California that unions are not State entities, and do not possess special rights to taxpayer monies, and I hoped beyond hope it would help with "The Friedrichs Fix."

Thankfully, five of the Justices seemed to understand that teachers like me are forced against our will to fund politics and ideas with which we disagree, and Justice Anthony Kennedy articulated that he could see through the unions' free-rider argument. He said, "The union basically is making these teachers compelled riders for issues on which they strongly disagree." He was spot on, and he was just getting started. He continued, "Many teachers think that they are devoted to the future of America, to the future of our young people...agency fees require that employees and teachers who disagree with those positions must nevertheless subsidize the union on those very points."

Our entire row of plaintiffs and Ben expressed our approval with hands clenched in a "Yes!" position and collective head nods. Our expressions of joy were far from over though because Justice Kennedy was on a roll. He pointed out that the unions have public relations programs, which they use to push their agenda, yet teachers like us who disagree with the unions' speech are forced to fund those campaigns through our fees. His strong grasp of the issues placed Mr. Dumont in the unfortunate position of trying to defend the unions' use of teachers' forced fees for political speech.

Mr. Dumont did his best to argue on behalf of his boss, Kamala Harris, but their arguments were just plain weak. No matter how they twisted or manipulated forced unionism to be helpful to the state, the raw evidence proves forced unionism is a serious attack on First Amendment rights of American citizens, and an abuse of power.

Justice Kennedy asked Mr. Dumont outright if any of the things he mentioned that unions push as part of their public relations campaigns are chargeable expenses forced onto all teachers as part of mandatory fees. Mr. Dumont was forced to answer, "I believe under current law they are." Realizing his side was losing and sinking quickly, Mr. Dumont started to say, "And if there's a need to adjust the current law because the Court feels that some of those things are more in the political or legislative sphere than they are in the collective bargaining sphere…"

That's when Justice Antonin Scalia provided the greatest moment of the day.

Justice Scalia interrupted Mr. Dumont, and said, "The problem is that everything that is collectively bargained with the government is within the political sphere, almost by definition. Should the government pay higher wages or lesser wages? Should it promote teachers on the basis of seniority or on the basis of—all of those questions are necessarily political questions. That's—that's the major argument made by the other side."

"And, Your Honor, I don't disagree with that," Mr. Dumont replied.

The audience let out an uncontrollable, collective gasp. Though we had been threatened with removal if we made any noise, we simply couldn't help ourselves. The unions and their allies had just conceded to our argument, and everyone knew it. For years, I had stated hundreds of times that collective bargaining is just as political as anything else the union does, but the unions had denied that argument throughout the entire case. Mr. Dumont had just admitted we were right, and since collective bargaining in the public sector *is political*, the unions had no constitutional right to force any of us to pay them one red cent.

CHAPTER 25

⟩—————❦—————⟨

THE CASE
IS SUBMITTED

"None of us felt sorry for the union…they were losing; humility looked good on them, as it does on every human who wears it."

It's hard to describe the celebration that was going on inside of my heart after Mr. Dumont's admission that collective bargaining in the public sector is political. Part of me wanted to jump up and down, and another part of me wanted to get on my knees and thank God for His answer to our prayers because I was watching as He was thwarting the efforts and exposing the lies of the massive union giant right before our eyes. Ben and the plaintiffs were visibly excited too. I was dying to look back at Charles, but I didn't want to get kicked out of the Court, so I sat still in my personal celebration, and then believe it or not, things got even better.

As Mr. Dumont tried to backpedal out of his answer, Chief Justice Roberts interrupted him and asked, "You said you agree with that. You agree with that everything you're negotiating over is a public policy question?"

Mr. Dumont answered, "No," but Chief Justice Roberts challenged him. He said, "If you disagree with that…what is your best example of something that is negotiated over in a collective bargaining agreement with a public employer that does not present a public policy question?"

Mr. Dumont answered, "Mileage reimbursement rates or how you're going to have public safety."

Chief Justice Roberts replied, "It's all money. That's money…and the amount of money that's going to be allocated to public education as opposed to public housing, welfare benefits, that's always a public policy issue."

Bless Mr. Dumont, I did not envy him being in that situation, and he seemed like a nice and honorable man, so I felt bad for him being taken to task while doing his best to defend the indefensible. Though I was cheering for our case and hopeful we'd win freedom for millions—especially with this concession from our opposition—as a fellow human being who's been in many difficult situations in my life, my heart went out to Mr. Dumont.

While we were inside the Courtroom witnessing the most interesting and emotion-inducing oral arguments, things were dramatic outside the Courtroom as well. Teachers, parents, pastors, school principals, policy experts, and even some legislators were out at our rally speaking on behalf of teachers and our First Amendment rights to freedom of speech and association.

Jade Thompson, a Spanish teacher from Ohio, shared her story of when the Ohio Education Association (OEA) used her forced dues to fund a slanderous campaign against her husband when he ran for state representative. She told everyone OEA was running high-priced television and radio ads against him claiming he was dishonest and lacking integrity. She shared, "My mom received fourteen high-priced glossy flyers all aimed at my husband. They highlighted really ugly pictures of Andy. They placed a pig in the picture with him and showed him barbecuing and put an insulting little chef's hat on his head. It was mockery. They made him look like a buffoon."

Before we went inside the Court, Jade shared with me that she came all the way to Washington DC to support our case because she'd lost her voice thanks to union abuse. When she heard me speaking out about union abuse during an interview, she didn't feel alone anymore and found the courage to speak out too. She told me, "I'm sick of being the cow that's slaughtered. I'm finding my voice."

Our rally was so well organized, our DJ so fantastic, and our signs so compelling that union picketers continually came to our rally looking for signs. Most of them turned on their heels embarrassed when they realized their mistake, but a few of them stuck around and asked some questions.

I was later told one man had a conversation with some of our supporters. He told them that his boss instructed him to leave work (while on the clock) and run down to the Courthouse to help with picketing in support of the unions. He worked in a union shop, but he had no idea what all of the picketing was about, so he asked our teachers. They told him that ten teachers were standing up for the rights of workers across America to decide for ourselves without fear or coercion whether or not to join or fund a union. After he was informed, he not only said we were right, but that he agreed with us and hoped we'd win.

Back inside the Court, Mr. Dumont continued to fight for the State of California claiming, "There is no restriction on any individual employee's speech as a citizen, either in the workplace or out of the workplace." It was statements like this that made me want to stand up and add clear context to the claims of the union and their allies. It's true the union cannot force me to speak in support of their political agenda, but they sure are permitted to bully, slander, isolate, verbally attack, and harass those of us who refuse to stand with them and support their agenda. And there are thousands of teachers who dutifully show up for union rallies, strikes, and political efforts only because they're too terrified not to.

As you know by now, the unions also take our money and use it toward their agenda in myriad ways (like fighting against school choice and pushing for inappropriate sex education curriculums), and I could have easily ticked off a list of many ways my money was being used as compelled political speech for the union, but those truths were never heard in the Court that day, so I prayed.

After Mr. Dumont's argument, David C. Frederick approached the bench on behalf of the union. He started out by admitting that many of the collectively bargained topics are "hot-button issues," but then he claimed that the unions spend money "trying to ascertain what the positions of all members of the workforce are before the union presents a policy." Now this made me want to scream, and I thought to myself, maybe he's misinformed, but that's completely wrong. In my twenty-eight years as a teacher forced to fund unions, I have never once been asked my position or been given a vote upon any union policy issues—and when my teacher friends and I questioned them as local, state and national union representatives or delegates, we got squashed.

Many of the unions' policies have brought harm to my own children, and they've been used to silence my voice as a professional educator and a mother. I wish I could have said all of that to the Justices in that Courtroom, but at least I had the satisfaction of hearing Justice Kennedy retort, "Well, I suppose, if that's so convincing, the union can convince teachers to join the union." That was truth, but sadly, Mr. Frederick responded with another union deception. He said, "We're talking about a service fee for the State law that provides for the exclusive representative to be the union when that is voted for by the majority of the workers."

Oh boy, another doozy. I wanted to stand up and assert, "My union was voted in when I was a small child, and we've never had a recertification vote!" All of us have been forced, and many of us are offended, but Mr. Frederick claimed we all had a vote, and none of us got to refute his claim, so my fellow plaintiffs and I were happy it appeared at least five Justices could see through the union charade.

Now up until this point, everything was argued in general and professional terms, but Mr. Frederick, in his desperate attempt to save union arguments, used a typical union tactic and took a personal shot at me. Mr. Frederick said, "Ms. Friedrichs has said publicly she's happy with the positions the union is taking on pay. It would be anomalous to suppose that we're going to decide a case of this kind of constitutional import with a lead plaintiff who has said publicly she agrees with the union's positions on pay."

Even though I had endured over three years of union lies about me, slander of my good name, and attacks painting my fellow plaintiffs and me as the devil, this falsehood made me mad. I don't know what statement he was planning on twisting, but I had said multiple times on television, radio, and in print interviews that I thought it was immoral to put the financial desires of adults above the educational needs of children. I never once stated that I agreed with the union's positions on pay (or anything else for that matter).

My body reacted instinctively as a look of complete disapproval covered my face, and I shook my head in disagreement with his misrepresentation of me. I had publicly stated that I would prefer to make less in order to provide funding to hire teacher's aides for every classroom, specialized teachers to run things like science labs and music, and more teachers to support the special education children who do not receive the services they deserve. I had publicly told the story of trying to save the jobs of multiple teachers in my district by offering a pay *cut* for myself, but the unions would not even consider my offer, and several outstanding teachers lost their jobs.

I've seen students devastated because unions refuse to consider the needs of others before pushing for more money for teachers, and I'm disgusted by it, yet this man was telling the Court that I agreed with the unions' positions on pay.

Ben was shaking his head too—hurt by misleading lies about his mom because he watched me fight against my own union for the jobs of teachers in my district, and he'd been personally impacted when the unions refused to work with our local school district and Ben lost the two best teachers he'd ever had while his two worst teachers kept their jobs.

Though I couldn't say a word, Mr. Frederick's mischaracterizations of me made me wish we could get the unions out of our schools completely because they constantly use deception to divide us. As I sat there witnessing the dishonorable behavior of the unions who claim to represent the best interests of teachers who are dedicated to training children in good character, the golden rule, and honesty, my dad's words came back to me again and I thought to myself, "I'd be ashamed."

Mr. Frederick's argument didn't work, and he got taken to task too, but unlike Mr. Dumont, I didn't have empathy for him.

At the end of the arguments, Michael Carvin stood up for his final rebuttal, and he was not only brilliant, he made me feel vindicated too. Though he did not directly address the lie about me, the first thing out of his mouth was regarding it, and he made clear that the unions were avoiding answering real questions, building a real factual record, and providing true data to form allegations against our pleas because they had none. Mr. Carvin said, "They can't make such an allegation in the real world."

Mr. Carvin and a couple of Justices talked back and forth for a few minutes, and then as if ending arguments in the most important battle of my life was as common as saying "Good morning" to a co-worker, Chief Justice Roberts said, "Thank you, counsel. The case is submitted."

Oral arguments were over at 11:26 a.m. I think we all had to stand as the Justices walked out of the room, but I don't remember exactly. My mind was still disoriented by the enormity of the situation.

Our group was the first out the doors. Supporters engulfed us offering hugs and heaps of congratulations. We didn't hear anything from the picketers as we exited the Courtroom, which was a welcome relief. To our great surprise, the union rally was dead silent, and their picketers looked forlorn and sort of lost.

Then the minute we appeared at the top of the steps, I heard, "There she is!" and every single person rallying for our side started chanting, "Stand with Rebecca! Stand with Rebecca!" After three years of being shunned, slandered by loud and prolific union operatives through the media, and treated like an outsider at work, I could hardly believe our rally for good had overcome the rally of deception—God came through again.

We descended the steps as a group of plaintiffs and attorneys with my Charles right behind me and my Ben by my side. We were all overwhelmed by the incredible support. In a show of gratitude to our fantastic supporters, I stopped on the steps and blew some kisses, waved, and offered thumbs up as a way of communicating that I thought we won the arguments. Lynn led us all to an area toward the bottom of the steps that was loaded with microphones and camera-laden reporters.

As we got situated in front of the reporters, our supporters became silent, and that's when the unions' rally started its chant. It was soft and slow, and to my surprise even felt humbled. Quietly and in an almost imperceptible voice, the union rally chanted, "Let's work together. Let's work together."

Without saying a word, every single one of us plaintiffs turned and looked at each other. We all rolled our eyes, shrugged our shoulders, and wrinkled up our faces with expressions of complete bewilderment, and said to each other at the same time, "Are they kidding? We've been trying to work together for *fifty years and all they've done is bully us!*"

None of us felt sorry for the union, and our puzzled expressions stayed with us for a while too because the only thing we'd ever experienced from state and national union leaders and their allies up until that very moment was hate-filled rhetoric and divisive attacks inspired by massive amounts of arrogance and pride. But now they were losing; humility looked good on them, as it does on every human who wears it.

Nina Totenberg, Supreme Court reporter for National Public Radio, seemed to be the leader of the gathering of reporters. I was glad she was in charge because she'd interviewed me a few weeks before, and even though

I knew she didn't agree with me, and her radio show heavily edited the taped interview we had, I still liked her. As the union rally continued its quiet chant, Nina stuck a microphone in front of Michael Carvin and me, several other microphones quickly surrounded hers, and the group started peppering us with questions.

We were all in high spirits because the arguments undeniably went in our favor, and Carvin was in a particularly good mood after giving likely the greatest legal performance of his career. Throughout our case, the unions kept trying to make us out as a bunch of pawns of politically motivated rich people. They were determined to drown out our true testimonies by playing politics.

We'd been battling their ugly lies for three years and responding with grace, but now arguments were over and heightened tensions were lessened, so when one of the reporters asked Carvin something like, "Isn't this case political?" Carvin answered with pure sarcasm and boyish charm, "You bet it's political." And went on to say if the unions were forcing everyone to fund the Republican Party the ACLU would be the ones here defending the plaintiffs! He was correct, and the double standard against people with more traditional American values is breathtaking.

Remember how I worried that the unions would paint their deceptive picture for the American people by staging a huge rally and shouting us down? Well, immediately after our press conference and early the next morning as news agencies across the country carried the story of our day in Court, almost every single news agency used pictures of *our* rally.

Even *The New York Times* printed pictures of *Friedrichs* supporters, and one of our plaintiffs received word from a family member living in Israel that our team had made the papers in Israel too. God came through in the Court, on the steps, and in the media.

You know, I have to be honest here. As great as we were all feeling, the sweetest experience I had on the steps of the Court was so personal that only Ben and I knew about it. As we were descending the steps to the cheers of "Stand with Rebecca!" Ben grabbed my arm and stopped me for a few seconds. With the sweetest look on his face, he leaned over in all of the commotion and whispered in my ear, "Mom, all of these people are cheering for you. They're all chanting your name. Mom, I'm so proud of you!"

I get the chills all over and a gush of love in my heart just recalling the moment. As I'm sure any mother or father can understand, it's extraordinarily rare to receive words of praise and pride from a twenty-year-old son or daughter. I didn't expect Ben would ever feel genuinely proud of me in his entire life, and if he did, I never thought it would happen until maybe he hit fifty or sixty years old and I was wrinkled and gray.

So, you know what? I really owe a debt of gratitude to state and national teachers' unions. If it hadn't been for their abuse of teachers and their negative impact on our schools and society, I never would have had the opportunity to do something that would inspire my young adult son to feel proud of me. Though I detest the way they abuse teachers, what they do with our money, and how they use our profession and students for their political gain, I'm grateful to the unions for giving me the chance to teach my sons how to stand up for what they believe. And thanks to this battle that's taken over our lives, Ben and Kyle are now more prepared to fight for good during their lifetimes too. That was a gift I never saw coming and a blessing our family will enjoy for generations to come.

CHAPTER 26

◆————◆————◆

THE BROOM TREE

At 5:46 a.m., on the morning after what appeared to be our complete victory, I received the following email from Lynn Harsh.

Good Morning Rebecca,

I've been deeply impressed to send these thoughts since standing on the sidewalk yesterday after lunch. Is this encouragement for you, or perhaps someone else in your circle of love or influence? Is a fellow plaintiff or associate in quiet trouble? Nothing in me thinks this impression is meant to prepare us for a loss in this court case. It's more likely related to the human experience when God calls us to step out of a quiet life into a more public battlefield. But I'll stop speculating, because I don't know. Just obeying here.

After a day of miracles where Elijah defeated the prophets of Baal and outran Ahab's chariots, we find him sitting under a broom tree in despair. He had personally experienced some of the greatest recorded miracles, yet Jezebel's threat on his life seemed to tip him over.

Was he discouraged? After all the public miracles God performed through Elijah that day, Jezebel was un-persuaded and determined to kill him. No doubt he was discouraged to the core.

He was hungry and physically exhausted. Jezebel's palace was about 17 miles from the action of the day. He had run there to give her the news. After she threatened his life, he ran another 100 miles. Think about what that much adrenalin did to his body.

It doesn't take bad news, or a threat on our life, or a 100-mile run for us to go looking for a broom tree. It's human norm after protracted focus on an object of desire, when the adrenalin produced to get that object subsides. The rest of our real-life challenges reassert themselves in our vision, often resulting in an unpleasant jolt. Sometimes we crawl for the solitude and protection we imagine exists under the broom tree. Or we may refuse to slow our pace, and what was temporarily necessary to get the job done turns into frenetic activity. Of course, we don't see this in ourselves.

T his little missive is not coming from me to you as "a word from the Lord." It's obedience on my part, and you and He can decide what to do with it. You and Charles touch the lives of many people, so who knows.

May Charles, Ben, and you have a blessed day and week. You'll need this time just as a family. I'll see you at lunch.

Affectionately,
Lynn

As I read the email, I got this uncomfortable feeling that it was inappropriate the day after our arguments, since we should have been celebrating our apparent victory. Its message was so out in left field, and yet, since I know, trust, and love Lynn, I knew there was something to it. That's why, even though I questioned the message, I marked it, and placed it into my "encouragement file" in case I needed it later. I felt unsettled about the message for days, but I figured God wouldn't have impressed upon her to share it with me unless He wanted me to get the message.

CHAPTER 27

THE RUTH EFFECT

"Some of their parents are in jail; some of them have no parents anymore; most of them have troubled lives. I always try to inculcate their minds that there's hope in life."

It was two weeks before Christmas in 2016, and I stood in the multipurpose room at Manhattan Christian Academy (MCA) in New York City.[78] Although poverty and danger dominated the neighborhood (it has twice the poverty rate of New York City's average), this little school felt so safe I left my purse and cell phone unattended on a bench surrounded by the parents and visitors in the room. I never would have done that at my own school.

I'd been invited to visit MCA, and they gave me the great honor of leading their daily devotions at their school-wide morning assembly. I was assigned a passage out of the book of Ruth—the story of Naomi's deep depression after the deaths of her husband and her sons in a foreign land, and Ruth's tender devotion to her mother-in-law as she journeyed to Naomi's homeland with her and stayed by her side in Bethlehem for life. Naomi told her friends to call her Mara, which means bitter. I explained the meaning of bitterness to the first graders in the assembly in hopes of ensuring that all of the kids through grade eight would comprehend the deeper lessons in the story, and I asked the kids to raise their hands if they'd ever felt bitter. Every child raised a hand, and so did many of the adults.

I did too.

It had been ten months since Justice Scalia's sudden death changed everything for our case; nine months since the remaining eight Justices handed down their 4–4 deadlocked judgment leaving the Ninth Circuit

Court of Appeals decision against us in place; eight months since we'd filed a petition for a rehearing once a ninth Justice was added to the Court, and six months since they'd rejected our petition. Our case ended in defeat on my fifty-first birthday.

The unions won by default. It was a bitter loss.

You'll recall that Charles and I grieved heavily for a few days, but like Ruth in her quest to bring relief to Naomi, we couldn't get caught up in bitterness. Too much was at stake; way too many kids were still in dangerous and underperforming schools; teachers were still forced to fund abusive sexual ideas invading our schools, and God made evident our battle wasn't over—it was just taking an unforeseen turn—unforeseen to us, but no surprise to Him.

In fact, God had sent me that message from Lynn. Moments after I learned of Justice Scalia's death, Lynn's email came to mind. For weeks I had ruminated about its possible meaning and significance, and now it suddenly became apparent. God sent it to protect and encourage me because He knew the defeat of our case was coming, but He didn't want me to become demoralized, degraded, or ultimately destroyed—wallowing under a broom tree—by the "Jezebel" that is the teachers' unions.

I shared the story of Naomi and Ruth with the kids at MCA and explained that God sends people like Ruth into our lives to take action with us when our circumstances are overwhelming, so our bitterness can be redeemed into something beautiful and sweet. Lynn was my Ruth. She helped me to see our circumstance through God's eyes. Reminding me that it was His battle and that God doesn't ask a girl to put her neck on the line and take a case to the greatest Court in the world just to abandon her.

I actually said these words to supporters across the country who were demoralized by Scalia's death, our case's defeat, and what seemed like the certain doom of our cause: sadly, to little effect. You see, incredibly, I'd become the elephant in the room again, but this time to the people who loved and supported me. I was a reminder of our bitter defeat.

So, I told the kids at MCA that God loves working through all of us—even little children—to sweeten the lives of those around us, and that in fact, He was using them to sweeten my bitterness that very moment. At that time, I was on a leave of absence from the classroom to continue the battle and write this book, so the visit to MCA was the highlight of my trip to New York City because I hadn't seen my students in months. I missed them so much it hurt.

It filled my heart to be surrounded by hundreds of kids loaded with energy, big dreams, and love even for a stranger. They looked exactly like my cute students too—same sort of mix of ages, nationalities, and personalities, but the overall mood and school-wide love were far greater than anything I'd ever experienced in my career because the Ruth Effect had brought so much redemption in the lives of these families.

The kids were poverty stricken, and many had faced all sorts of tragedies, but I observed stellar behavior, respect for authority, superior knowledge, well-reasoned answers, a lack of entitlement behaviors, strong character development, and lots of joy. MCA couldn't remove the harsh realities from the lives of the kids and their families, but like Ruth, their devotion, actions, and genuine love provided the grace needed to bring about hope and sweet redemption.

I saw it in the eyes of parents as they walked their children into a school community full of warmth, kindness, and safety. It flowed from the hearts of teachers and administrators as they welcomed the families to school. I saw it in the faces of wiggly little boys who would have been labeled "deficit" at most schools but were permitted to be their gifted selves at MCA. They were all gas and no brake and distracted by their bowties and ruby red dress-up clothes as they prepared for their Christmas presentation to their parents, but they were well-behaved. After they told me about their school, they sent me on my way with big fat hugs and filled me with even more hope for redemption of all school children in America.

That's when I journeyed to the school library and sat riveted by the personal testimony of MCA graduate Justin Diaz. When Justin was only nine months old, his father died in a drowning accident. His dad was a teacher in a military school for kids trying to overcome severe discipline problems (similar to the school our Kyle attended); he had been a blessing to his family. Justin's mother, Judy, was devastated. In addition to becoming a single mother, she suffers from Lupus, and her illness often left her hospitalized. When Justin was in elementary school, Judy felt so desperate to provide a father for Justin that she married again. She had two more children, but her husband started abusing alcohol, then Judy, and then Justin and his siblings. She was forced to move on and raise three children alone while battling Lupus.

Judy always dreamed of having her kids in a private Christian school because her family values were undermined in public schools, and she was concerned about the poor discipline standards. Judy told me, "When I used to go to public school, I remember being bullied by the same person from the second grade all the way to the eighth grade, and it was horrible. I told the teachers, but they would brush it aside."

I could relate to Judy because I was bullied ruthlessly by female upper classmen as an elementary student and also received no help, and as a teacher who really tries to intervene in bullying situations, I've been frustrated my entire career by public schools' administrators who rarely provide enough discipline to stop the problems. They seem to reward bad behavior, often cave to parents who are discipline problems themselves and abuse the system, and frequently leave victims, their families, and teachers vulnerable day after day.

Justin told me he was full of anger because he couldn't understand why he didn't have a dad to love him. His mom had to work a lot to put food on the table, so he was looking for attention by acting out at school. During his years in public schools, he was in trouble a lot. His grades were poor, his attitude was bad, he was disruptive, and because discipline standards were lax, his talkative nature got him into trouble instead of into educational debates on topics of high interest.

Judy tried to get involved with Justin's education and work as a team with his teachers, but her experience at the public school was what she called "impersonal." She told me, "My problem was that the parents were never allowed past the glass door during school hours, and I couldn't get to know the teachers." As if that wasn't humiliating enough, she further offered, "I wasn't even able to go in and use the bathroom."

Being part of the Education Triangle is of utmost importance to Judy, and teachers like me are dying for parents to get involved, but because of the culture in their neighborhood public schools, she was locked out of the educational team.

There's no school choice in their neighborhood either, so Judy and her kids had no options. Thankfully she learned of MCA, and generous donors provided scholarships for all three of her children to attend, and suddenly their bitterness was sweetened.

"The thing I loved the most about MCA," Judy shared, "and it was really weird to me because I was raised in the public school, but at MCA, I could walk in any time of the day and no one would say, 'What are you doing here? or 'You're not allowed here.' I could walk in and feel comfortable and stay all day." And because of the culture of acceptance of parents as equal partners, the Judeo–Christian values, and the strict standards for personal conduct, Justin's behavior improved dramatically, and so did the conduct of his younger siblings.

The teachers at MCA took the time to understand why Justin was acting out, learned about the tragedies in his life, and got to know Judy on an intimate level too. They didn't label Justin or get frustrated with his behavior, but they did hold him to high standards of conduct. He lied so much they suspended him at one point. Justin told me, "If I didn't go through that, I never would have turned out the way I am today. They told me, we don't want you to lie anymore or be lazy in your work. The discipline was stern and unwavering, but it was also coupled with love because they showed and explained how much they cared."

Justin spent five years in public schools too. He said there were some good teachers, but their positive influences were overshadowed by the lack of values and the stress in the school culture. "I had to deal with a lot," he told me, "especially one teacher who was protected by the union. He was very lazy; he helped the class cheat on tests to make himself look good." Justin had another teacher who was sarcastic and cutting toward him, and many who simply did not live up to the high standards of ethical behavior those leading children should possess. Justin shared, "When someone cursed or said something inappropriate, most of the teachers just condoned it and never did anything about it. Then, all of a sudden, they're surprised when kids get in fights and are disrespectful to one another. They were allowing the things that added to the drama and stirred up the flames."

Because of the devotion and action, the MCA community breathed into Justin's life for six years, Justin had the skills and confidence necessary to overcome his negative surroundings in public high school. He's now studying criminal justice at John Jay University, and he has dreams of becoming an NYPD officer and hopes to advance to Commissioner someday. I hope he achieves those dreams; we need him leading in his community.

My heart broke though when he shared the fate of his friends who didn't receive the blessing of a scholarship to MCA.

"A majority of my friends in the public high school did not graduate," Justin told me. "A lot of my friends are not in college, they're not working; some are pregnant and didn't finish school—big things really changed the direction of their lives. If my friends had been given the values I received at MCA, they would have made better decisions; they would have been better off."

Justin told me his story while sitting next to one of his favorite MCA teachers, and I was drawn to their relationship. He told me she was the strictest of all, but the playful grin on her face let me in on the secret that she was also the most fun, and she was passionately dedicated to helping Justin become all he was meant to be. The look on her face while her former student shared his testimony revealed her pride in him. They held each other in high regard, and his respect for her was profound. "She wouldn't let me go," Justin shared. "None of my MCA teachers would; they saw potential in me and in all children."

Every kid should be blessed with a school like MCA—*every single kid.* That's what my fellow plaintiffs and I were hoping to inspire by winning our case against the teachers' unions, but as you know, Justice Scalia died exactly one month after oral arguments. Then the unions that were finally humbled a bit and saying, "Let's work together," on the steps of the Court, started their gleeful and ghoulish celebrations mere hours after Scalia's death.

You'll recall the number one question I received during the case was "Are you afraid for your life?" Now, with Justice Scalia gone, the most common question became, "Do you think the unions killed him?" I don't, but the fact so many people do exposes the extreme abuse inflicted on cowering victims exploited and controlled by unions.

Lots of folks were distraught when Justice Scalia died. I was tempted to be devastated too, but I looked to Ruth and Naomi, David and Goliath, and other biblical exemplars American schools used to teach our kids before the unions came in and removed our values, and I found the determination to keep on fighting. Just like Ruth, I didn't have time to wallow in grief because only two weeks after Justice Scalia's death I read about Joseph Ocol, another teacher being brutalized by unions as he battled for the good of his students.

In 2005, Joseph Ocol learned that one of his elementary-aged students had been shot dead in the streets of Chicago. Ninety percent of his students live below the poverty line, and some of their parents are drug dependent or pushing drugs. Shocked and full of unspeakable grief, Joseph sought for answers. He discovered kids in Chicago are most vulnerable between 3:00 and 6:00 p.m., so Joseph started an afterschool chess club and opened it to any kids who wanted to participate.

At first, only a few kids came. Chess isn't as cool as basketball or hanging out doing nothing, but when kids heard they could win a slice of pizza for playing three games, a piece of candy for winning one, or even a dollar bill for best out of three, they started showing up, and soon, they were competing in nationwide chess competitions and winning. Joseph told me, "It was never in my mind to help them win medals or trophies; I just wanted to keep them safe after school, but these African American kids who belong to the most depressed areas in Chicago are able to shine when given the opportunity to excel."

Excel is an understatement when it comes to Joseph and his chess-playing kids. Part of Joseph's personal income goes to food, snacks, bus fare, prizes, and even chess sets for tournament winners. Their club doesn't have money to hire a Grand Master to mentor them, so Joseph taught them to mentor each other. Joseph encourages friends, parents, and teachers to get involved by letting the kids teach them how to play chess. He told me, "I know as a teacher that you can master a skill if you teach the skill." His players—second- through eighth-grade boys and girls—are mastering life through playing and teaching chess.

They travel with Joseph on weekends to chess tournaments. They've won such high honors as tournament champions they were invited to the White House, met President Obama, and even received a visit from Phiona Mutesi, the girl who became a chess master while living in the slums of Uganda and whose life inspired the Disney film *Queen of Katwe*.

When I read about Joseph in the news two weeks after Justice Scalia's death, he inspired me, but sadly I wasn't reading about his amazing chess program or the lives of kids redeemed by it. Instead, I was reading about how Joseph was expelled from Chicago Teachers Union, an affiliate of American Federation of Teachers (AFT) because he dared to cross their picket line—he was ejected from union membership, but they still forced him to pay full union dues. They called him a "scab," and slandered him mercilessly because he went inside of the school to teach his students and keep his promise to his chess club—the kids were counting on the extra practice for a big tournament.

Joseph is my kind of teacher, and every child should have the blessing of a teacher like Joseph. He was worried for his students because when teachers strike, many kids are unattended, and some don't eat for the day. His student had been shot dead in the street because he was unattended, and Joseph wasn't willing to take that risk for a pay raise.

He told union leaders, "I will join your strike if you will do something for the kids. If you put up a classroom in the picket line, I'm willing to teach the kids to play chess in the picket line. You have plenty of food for teachers on the picket line. As long as there's food and something for the kids, I'll join you."

The union leaders didn't understand or respect Joseph's request, and they never will because as you know by now, their values are power and money. Joseph told me, "It hurts to know that this is all about money and greed for more money."

I could tell Joseph was a Ruth. His story shook me out of my grief and lit a new fire in me. I knew he was standing alone too, so I felt compelled to find a way to offer support for great teachers like Joseph so we can win back our profession and protect the kids we love.

Joseph shared that he's seen the depression and sadness in the eyes of his students. He told me, "Some of their parents are in jail; some of them have no parents anymore; most of them have troubled lives. I always try to inculcate their minds that there's hope in life." He does this through devoting his time to them and teaching them chess—helping them use their minds to grow in brainpower, confidence, and good character. He told me, "What the world needs now are thinkers. We need to develop more thinkers, and these kids need to see value in themselves."

This is why Joseph invites people to learn from the kids. He told me, "Once you give them the chance to speak all about chess, they see value in themselves. It's how you empower them. Kids who could barely talk before become confident and empowered. It's all about life."

Joseph is a natural teacher. His mother and father were both teachers in the Philippines, and his dad cashed in his pension to build a school for poor kids. Even though his parents have both died, Joseph still sends monthly support to that school and spends his summers in the Philippines serving the kids. Over eight thousand scholars have graduated so far. Joseph even started a charitable foundation to raise money for the scholars and the Chicago chess kids; he named it after his parents: Gaudy and Joy.[79]

Joseph should be awarded teacher of the century, but instead the teachers' union sent out a press release slandering him and set a hearing date. They told him they would reinstate his membership if he would give the union the pay he earned while protecting the kids on the day of the strike—pay he uses to personally fund poor kids in his family's school and in his chess club.

The union leaders never once showed any concern about the kids; they just continued hassling Joseph for teaching instead of picketing. Joseph didn't cave; he fought back, and he's still fighting. The only problem is, even though many teachers told him quietly that they agree with him, all of them hold picket signs, and Joseph stands alone.

Why aren't more teachers standing with Joseph? You can probably answer the question yourself by now, but by way of review: fear, intimidation, isolation, and ignorance. The unions have so successfully isolated teachers and beaten them down so dramatically with low morale and blame, teachers are hanging onto the unions for dear life. They're hanging on for all of the reasons you've read in this book: fear of union abuse, fear of isolation, fear of lost jobs, fear of being unappreciated, fear of losing their pensions, fear no one will respect them, fear wages will be lowered if unions leave, fear their students will be hurt, fear, fear, fear.

But state and national unions are the root cause of those fears. The only way we'll help teachers rebuild respect and our profession, protect the kids from things like lessons on anal and oral sex and condom relay races, and restore parental authority in our schools is to help teachers conquer the fear.

The most common question teachers across the country ask me is, "Can I keep my local association and get rid of the state and national unions?" The answer is *yes*, but most teachers don't know it. We've started a *Keep Your Local* campaign to educate teachers on their rights and to help restore our schools but getting information to teachers trapped in the unions' culture of fear is tricky, so you are the hope for our message. You're the Ruth we need, standing together with parents, pastors, mature students and community members in solidarity with teachers who want to reject union control and start their own local associations.

Teachers feel like Naomi: bitter, overwhelmed, and hopeless. A massive army of Ruths is vital to come alongside, shine truth and offer support. So, we've started a nation-wide *Adopt a Teacher* campaign too. All you have to do is find a teacher or two, reach out personally, and stand with them—*Embracing, Empathizing, Educating, and Enlightening* them using the stories you read in this book, and *Encouraging* and *Empowering* them with moral, prayerful, and hands on support so they can stand together for independence from state and national union bullies. The details are on our website. All we need is unity and like Ruth and Naomi we must move forward.

Joseph is moving forward *alone* on behalf of his students. Can you even imagine the impact if a Ruth—or a hundred Ruths—crossed that picket line with Joseph? Do you have any idea the encouragement he would receive, and how many teachers would suddenly find it safe to drop their pickets and join Joseph doing what's right for the kids? Do you have any idea how much impact it would make on society and how much light would shine on the love of great teachers and the darkness of the unions if Ruths all around the country joined together to stage counter protests, to educate their legislators on union abuse, to write editorials or letters to the editor, to speak out at their churches, and say enough is enough?

We don't have to guess. We have thousands of examples in history of Ruths who came alongside others and said, "I'm standing in the gap for my neighbor. I'm standing so he won't fall." Peaceful protests staged by Dr. Martin Luther King Jr., a Christian minister along with average church folks across our country, remain some of the most inspiring and redemptive actions of our time. Men and women saw their neighbors harmed and would stop at nothing to defend and free them.

Yet, Dr. King wasn't the first to use peaceful protests; he got the idea from the many Ruths who blazed the trail before him. In the late 1700s, a young Member of Parliament, William Wilberforce, led a small band of Christian brothers and sisters who staged their protests with so much determination, they successfully ended the slave trade in Britain while those in power fought brutally against them—slandering them in the same way the unions slander freedom fighters today. William Wilberforce and his cohorts acted to end the horror of the slave trade at the very time our American Founders were following the same moral truths to launch the freest nation known to mankind. They all knew from studying truth and history that if they stood by idly, men would continue to enslave each other and call it good.

My friend Virginia Walden-Ford is a modern-day Ruth who's been shining her light for decades. Since the 1990s, Virginia's led the fight for parents, teachers, and kids in Washington DC through an organization called "DC Parents for School Choice." Her group formed to support an effort by Congress to start a voucher program for 2,500 needy kids in DC. Some legislators initiated the idea, but the teachers' unions fought it tooth and nail, so Virginia and her friends organized over 3,000 parents to stand up for the good of children trapped in failing public schools.

Virginia and her friends started out like most of us. They'd never staged protests or spoken to Congress, but they learned. Just like William Wilberforce and Joseph Ocol, they came out of their normal lives and found ways to do what needed to be done. Virginia and her friends took a beating for sure, but they're on the right side of history, and they've made a massive difference for families.

You know what I love about Virginia? She doesn't let the abusive unions get in her way. Each time she testified before Congress, union supporters tried to shout her down. They said, "You're a stupid parent," "You've been brainwashed by Republicans," and "You need to learn to keep your mouth shut."

Virginia told me, "I talked about how important it would be for kids to have scholarships, and that's why the teachers' unions started hating me. They nearly threw me, but I remember thinking, *how dare somebody speak to me that way!*"

Instead of letting the nasty words of union supporters shut her down, Virginia responded by taking more parents to speak on Capitol Hill. The unions continued attacking them, saying cruel and ugly things and started an undercurrent of fear in parents at the schools too. Parents were told, "You have no right to speak against the traditional public school system," and union forces implied that if they continued to do so, their children would somehow be negatively impacted in school. Virginia lost some parents to fear. She told me, "These were really, really low-income black and white parents, and it scared them off; they were really frightened, but it *pissed* me off. Excuse me, but it made me really mad and more determined that I wasn't going to stop talking about it because *nobody* was going to tell me what I could and could not say."

Don't you love her? She and her band of parents stayed loyal to the cause too, and even though President Clinton vetoed the first piece of legislation they were able to pass, they kept on fighting, and eventually their efforts paid off so handsomely the DC Opportunity Scholarship Program was launched in 2004. And even though it's been threatened by many union-funded Democrats, it's still serving over 1,100 children at forty-two different schools in DC and provides an outstanding example of the positive effects of America's only private school choice program created by the collective efforts of parents and Congress.

The unions keep on trying to interfere—telling parents they're brainwashed or that the government will get into their business if they use the scholarships—but many parents see through the lies, so Virginia keeps on directing them to fight for what's right for their kids. Virginia admits the unions are obnoxious and the battle isn't easy, but she urges parents and teachers to stand together because we have strength in numbers.

Virginia's story is a picture of my dream for the entire country. She and her friends never attacked teachers. They saw through the deception of unions who use teachers against our will to push their agenda, and they stood together—united for the good of families, teachers, and kids.

The union's angry rhetoric and control of teachers has created that great divide between parents and teachers, but Virginia saw through the falsehoods because Virginia knows the true heart of great teachers. She shared, "I'm from a house of teachers. My mother and father were teachers; my uncles and aunts were teachers, three of my sisters taught, and one still teaches." Her father was the first black assistant superintendent of Little Rock School District appointed in 1967 amidst great controversy. She told me, "There were five girls in our family; we were taught to be careful of people who might want to hurt us because they didn't like that a black man was appointed to that position. We grew up very sheltered, but instead of scaring us, it made us all stronger."

You know, Virginia and all of the others who allowed me to share their stories in this book had to face fear. We were all scared when we first started speaking truth in the face of powerful deception. Virginia's life was threatened, and black cars drove past her house all hours of the night blowing their horns and shining their lights to intimidate her and her kids, and she was a single parent of three. She told me, "They couldn't intimidate me, but they could scare the hell out of me."

Yeah, they scared the hell out of her, and they've scared the hell out of Benji Backer, Jeralee Smith, Sue Halvorson, Aaron Benner, Ruth Finnegan, Charles, and me too. But you know what? Every single one of us grew immensely from the experience, and every last person highlighted in this book would tell you that because of facing the hate of the unions, because of standing up for good in the face of evil, they are stronger, wiser, more hopeful, more joyful, and their lives are far more fulfilled because they did what was right instead of surrendering to oppression.

Virginia told me, "People actually called my house and told me that if I didn't back off and get out of this voucher stuff, I might find myself not here and then they implied that things could happen to my children."

You know what she did? She sat down with her kids—they were eight, thirteen, and college-aged at the time. She told them, "If this scares y'all and y'all want me to stop doing this, I will."

You know what her kids said? "Don't stop, Mom. We know why you're doing this, and we want you to continue." Can you even imagine the legacy Virginia has left her kids? They won't be beaten down by tyranny, and they'll stand up for what's good and right because their mother stood up when others sat in silence.

Kelley Williams-Bolar was scared when she started speaking out. She'd already been jailed, abused, and harassed by our courts and educational leaders. You know what she did? She started fighting against zip-code laws to protect other families from the hell her family experienced. She could have caved to the bullying and given up, but instead she fought for the good of others, and her journey has led her all over the country fighting with others who refuse to be abused, and they're making a difference.

When Kelley sat inside the Courtroom offering Ruth support to us, she got more out of the experience than she gave because that's the way love works. She told me, "We were sitting in the highest Court in the land.... That was amazing to me.... I looked around as a woman of color. Slavery was in that Courtroom—those laws had changed there. *Brown v. Board of*

Education brought change there. That was just so uplifting, and it gave me extra energy. One day, all of this will come to pass, and I will be able to hold my head up higher and feel gratification and justification because this fight we're fighting is not in vain."

CHAPTER 28

THE NECKLACE

"Just give Me your two mites Rebecca. I'll do the rest."

I know the heart of the true teacher. If those serving who honestly belong in the classroom read this book and discover what's really going on within our state and national unions and in thousands of schools across our country, they'll join the fight too *if we stand with them in solidarity.* If their eyes are opened to the truth, they'll desire to do what's right for the kids and hold unions accountable. That's what real teachers do—we put the kids first.

One thing I learned during our battle is that courts are important, but they're not nearly as important as the voices of American citizens. Passionate parents, teachers and mature students standing together are the ones who will bring down the giants damaging our schools and country.

So how do we fight Goliath? We stand together and keep moving forward. We refuse to get stuck in the pain and anger of the past. Bullies always want to terrorize and destroy us, but when we stand on the side of truth and fight for the weak, we get strength we never knew existed, and darkness gets overpowered by our light.

Virginia told me, "God whispered to me that I needed to be doing something, and for a long time I tried not to listen. I'd be going, 'God, come on, give me a break.'" But Virginia finally obeyed, and some days she said, "Lord, this is hard," but she told me, "He'd tell my heart, 'You can do it. Don't give up. Get up and start over tomorrow.'"

Virginia went through that many times throughout her fight and she said God always placed her exactly where she was gifted to help the most.

She also told me, "The end result is that I became a different person and I became a better person for having listened to Him."

I discovered this in my life and family too. When we said yes to the lawsuit against the teachers' unions, we thought only horrible and negative things would happen to us, and that we would be ostracized and hated, and you know what? We were. But we also discovered several deep sources of love and support that not only bolstered us up but made our adventure one of the most enriching and flat-out joyful experiences of our lives.

Charles, Kyle, Ben and I are all growing—profoundly. Our family unit is stronger, our faith is deeper, our joy is fuller, and we're more courageous.

Ben's always complained about the constant attacks on his free speech and Christian values on his high school and college campuses, but he never did anything about it until after our lawsuit adventure.

During his first semester in the welding program at his new college, a union activist teacher harassed students during class. Regarding President Trump's victory, she said, we have a "president who is a white supremacist, and a vice president that is one of the most anti-gay humans in this country.... Our nation is divided. We have been assaulted. It's an act of terrorism.... The people committing the assault are among us..." Later she called out students who voted for President Trump, and they not only felt harassed, but were afraid she would fail them. One of those students started recording the teacher in hopes of protecting his grade and exposing the outright harassment of students in class. He showed the video to the administration, who refused to do anything about the problem, so the young man's friends posted it on social media. Because the teacher's behavior was so out of line, the video went viral. The school responded by punishing the young man. He was required to write an essay of apology, and he was suspended from school (and his championship crew team) for the summer and fall semesters.

Our community was outraged, and the Orange County Register ran stories on the issue every single day to put pressure on the college to do the right thing. Because our community stood together, the young man was finally released from the unjust punishments and allowed to attend school. The teacher was never reprimanded though. Instead, the teachers' union voted her "Teacher of the Year."

Witnessing this outright attack on his classmates changed my Ben forever. He immediately started a Young Americans for Freedom (YAF) chapter on campus and has been working ever since to restore civility, freedom of speech, and respect for all values and political views on campuses and in our community.

State and national teachers' unions are behind the large-scale student protests in schools across our country, but union messaging claims students are leading the charge, so mass quantities of students get silenced. Take the nationwide student walkouts in which children were inspired to abandon learning to be social justice warriors demanding stronger gun control laws—without parental consent and often against parental will. Ben's YAF chapter staged a counter-protest that day. Students approached them by the dozens sharing their support for the Second Amendment and disgust with the political ideology dominating their campuses and robbing them of learning. Many students had no idea why they were marching—some participated because their professors offered extra credit.

For years, state and national teachers' unions have been involved with all manner of angry protests across our nation including Occupy Wall Street, Black Lives Matter, The Women's March and more. Teachers who are troubled by these "pissed off" protests have been funding union websites, magazines, mailing lists, and media outreach advertising support for these politically-driven protests for decades. Unions encouraged PTA parents to take small children out of class to protest against President Trump the very day he was placed into office, and they're behind the hateful attacks on Betsy DeVos too. Huge numbers of union households, including teachers, voted for President Trump and appreciate his return to American values and support of Israel, but the teachers' unions continue their unspeakable campaign to undermine his presidency and to impeach him keeping Americans in a constant state of disruption and stress.

I'm thankful our battle gave Ben the courage to step up and speak out. We know it's scary to stand up to union bullies, but we can attest to you we've discovered a huge support system of people we never knew before, and we've made friends across the country who are far grander than any we lost.

Virginia tells me, "As you do this, Rebecca, know that there are many people behind you. More than you can imagine." We have people all over this country—brushfires of people—who are standing up. We just need to rise up together and organize our brushfires into an inferno of redemption. Will you join us?

Virginia and I discovered something kind of funny during our battles. One time an angry reporter supporting the unions wrote a hit piece about me, cutting me down for being "photogenic" and "outspoken." That just cracked me up, and it gave me an understanding of the psychology of the unions and their apologists.

We all have people in our lives who are difficult, and every time we spend time with them, we feel worse for it—almost dirty—and we get dragged down. Well, that's the union and their "pissed off" mentality. The union wants to drag you down into the mud because that's where they operate with expertise. It drives them crazy when we refuse to get into the muck with them and instead counter them with God's truth in love and a genuine concern for others—especially children. They don't like it when we look nice or when we speak out, exposing their ugliness and misery.

So, I'm going to keep on doing it. And keep on smiling.

Virginia had an experience like this too. She told me, "I remember a reporter wrote about me once. He said, 'You know, Virginia Walden-Ford is just annoyingly persistent. She just won't go away.'" Isn't that great?

Virginia and I, we come from large families, and we know how to be annoyingly persistent, so we're just going to keep on doing it. Joseph, Aaron, Kelley, Judy Bruns, Ben, Barb Amidon, and all the other terrific folks you met in this book are annoyingly persistent too, and we just keep doing the same things.

We show up. We speak up. And we support each other. That's all anyone has to do.

During the 1960s, before the NEA was taken over by unions, teachers spoke out a lot, because NEA was a positive association formed by teachers to support their profession and the children in their care. A sweet retired teacher reached out to my friend Larry Sand one day and said, "In the '60s NEA was not like it is today! I still have the booklets given to us in Teacher's Ed for memorization in the classroom. All of them are Bible verses." She sent me copies.[80]

The booklets, *Selections for Memorizing: Growth Booklets*, are full of Scriptures from the Holy Bible, prayers, writings, and poems about kindness, moral character, and even the vital importance of the Education Tri-angle. They were printed *en masse* by the NEA so that every child in schools across the country could have one every year.

Here's the quote from the back cover of *Selections for Memorizing: Growth Leaflet Number 284*, which says on its front cover: "Arranged by the NEA Journal staff in cooperation with many teachers including the public schools of Birmingham, Alabama; Chanute, Kansas; Cincinnati, Ohio; and Washington DC."

> It is important that people who are to live and work together shall have a common mind—a like heritage of purpose, religious ideals, love of country, beauty, and wisdom to guide and inspire them. The aim of Selections for Memorizing is to make such a heritage available in a form so inexpensive that copies can be placed in the hands of every student in our American schools. Think what it would mean to the future of America and the world if every young person were presented each year the PGL appropriate to his school grade, and were taught to understand, love and remember the great expressions of truth and beauty, which fill these pages! The torch of civilization is not passed on by accident, but by the sustained efforts of parents, pastors, teachers, and friends. Will you do your part? (Joy Elmer Morgan, editor, The Journal of the National Education Association [Eighteenth printing 20,000. Total copies 555,000])[81]

You see? There's a lot of reason to hope. This is how America's *great* teachers really think. It's how they instructed our children in our *public* schools (in unity with pastors and parents) until the unions barged in and all hell broke loose.

You may recall the words of Bob Chanin, longtime NEA counsel, as he bragged to union leadership at the Representative Assembly (as they cheered him on) about the pride they feel for destroying our wholesome values.

> When I first came to NEA in the early '60s, it had few enemies and was almost never criticized, attacked, or even mentioned in the media. This was because no one really gave a damn about what NEA did or what NEA said. It was the proverbial sleeping giant. A conservative, apolitical, do nothing organization. But then NEA began to change.

It embraced collective bargaining. It supported teacher strikes…What
NEA said and did began to matter. And the more we said and did, the
more we pissed people off, and in turn, the more enemies we made.[82]

Mr. Chanin is half-right; NEA was "conservative and apolitical," but it wasn't a "do nothing" organization. It was an "others first" organization; specifically, "Kids and Country First." It was an association created by loving teachers who sought to pass on "the torch of civilization, a like heritage of purpose, religious ideals, love of country, beauty, and wisdom to guide and inspire" children and young adults in our universities. It sought to teach them "to understand, love and remember the great expressions of truth and beauty." Oh, those teachers were doing a ton of work all right, and I can think of no higher purpose for an organization.

Unions have worked hard to undermine those loving teachers by promoting the "separation of church and state" deception too. Those words are not in our Constitution; they were part of a letter written by Thomas Jefferson to the Danbury Baptist ministers. Jefferson was assuring them that the state could not impose itself into their religion; he was not suggesting that Judeo-Christian values be removed from our schools or government. In fact, our founders insisted that Judeo-Christian values, including the teachings of the Holy Bible, dominate our educational and government systems because moral and well-educated people are essential to the survival of a free Republic.

Theodore Roosevelt articulated the incomparable importance of the values and high calling of those great teachers when he said, "To educate a man in mind and not in morals is to educate a menace to society." But the "love your neighbor," "Golden Rule" values America's great teachers taught for two hundred years with the support of great parents and pastors have been supplanted with an angry, self-focused grievance mentality, and a constant arrogance promoting "pissed off." No wonder our schools are failing, and we have so many menaces wreaking havoc in our culture today.

Unions have supplanted our values: they push theories as facts, undermine the scientific method, divide us by race and envy, and mock our faith as a fairy-tale. We must take action.

In 2014, parents in Huntington Beach, California, freaked out over an asbestos scare in their schools. It led to several schools being emptied for much of the school year, and kids and teachers relocated their classrooms to empty spots in schools across Orange County. Half of an entire school ended up on my campus. So, I must point out, parents and educators reacted with intense concern. They didn't sit back and say, "We'll get to that asbestos problem in ten or twenty years." They rescued the kids from possible danger *immediately*, and it was dramatic.

Our kids are in *far* more imminent danger with state and national teachers' unions, their political allies and obscene sex education lessons dominating our schools than they are sitting in asbestos-filled classrooms, so we cannot spend one more day complaining about the latest horror—the time is *now*. The key is *action*.

I found a terrific poem in *Growth Leaflet 284*. Kids and teachers across America used to memorize this and live by it before the teachers' unions took over and removed our values. It's an absolutely perfect encouragement for all of us today.

> *I am only one;*
> *But, I am one.*
> *I cannot do everything*
> *But I can do something.*
> *What I can do, I ought to do:*
> *And what I ought to do,*
> *By the grace of God,*
> *I will do.*

Will you do your part?

My annoyingly persistent friend, Mark Janus did his part. After Justice Scalia's death led to the death of our case, Mark's case, *Janus v AFSCME*, moved forward. Things looked impossible, but Mark stood strong. I asked God if He could give Mark a win on my birthday, and true to God's grace, Mark's positive decision came down on my fifty-third birthday—two years after our devastating loss. I've learned that God's timing is never my timing—it's better. Now the entire United States of America is "Right to Work" in the public sector, so all unionized government employees, including teachers, have the right to opt out of their unions and them pay nothing.

The unions still have monopoly control and exclusive bargaining power over unionized workers. They constantly complain that they're legally required to represent those "free riders" who opt out, but conveniently forget to mention unions demanded the legal right to represent everyone so they could mandate agency fees. Now that they'll pay nothing, those who opt out will be harassed more than ever, so we have to stand with them like never before.

In fact, during *Janus* oral arguments, that same union lawyer, Mr. Frederick, who made mischaracterizations of me, made the following statement to the Justices: "…the key thing that has been bargained for in this contract for agency fees is a – a limitation on striking. And that is true in many collective bargaining agreements. The fees are the tradeoff. Union security is the tradeoff for no strikes. And so, if you were to overrule *Abood*, you can raise an untold specter of labor unrest throughout the country."

Sounds like a threat to me.

So now you know. Those massive teacher demonstrations across the country claiming teachers are angry and labor peace is threatened, it's not really the teachers or the workers leading the "pissed off" charge; it's the unions. They're still bullying teachers and using us as a front, just like they use PTA families because union values—power and money—are at stake.

I know it's scary to stand in opposition to union tactics, but we must stand together, adopt our teachers and educate them about "Keep Your Local," because teachers have been trapped and terrorized for decades—ever since men in black suits intimidated sweet teachers like Ruth Finnegan and the one they labeled Rotten Apple.

You may recall, in October 2012 when I started writing editorials to educate the public on the truth about teachers' unions, I was terrified before I got started. I was doing that morning Bible study I mentioned earlier, and a question stared me in the face that I couldn't ignore. The writer of the study, Beth Moore, asked if I knew God could do anything and if I was seeking His purposes in my life. She asked if there was something I knew I was supposed to be doing, something that had been hanging out in my heart for a while; a deep desire I knew God might be stirring in me, but I'd let fear keep me from trusting Him and doing it. I knew immediately I was supposed to be writing for publication—I was supposed to be telling my story.

Then Beth took the question to another level. She asked if I'd trust God and do it. I was petrified. I'll be honest with you, I struggled with that question for three days before I answered it because I was not going to make some promise to God and then break it the moment the ink dried.

As you'll recall, I wasn't afraid to write or to tell my story, but I was scared of being rejected by publications. At that time, I didn't have even one connection to any sort of publication—not even my little complimentary city newspaper. Beth's question inspired me to take my fears to God, so I told Him I didn't have any connections; I told Him I was afraid of being rejected, and I also told Him my fears that hurtful people would attack my family and me and that those who gain power by slandering good people would twist my motives or bring pain to those I love. God listened to my concerns, and He empathized with me, showed me the truth that *He's* more powerful than the mean people who would definitely pick on me, and He gave me peace and a tiny bit of faith, so I could trust Him to direct me in the battle.

You know, I didn't write this book for sympathy, and I certainly didn't write it to paint myself as some kind of hero or superwoman, because I'm not. I wrote it because I firmly believe that state and national unions are not only destroying our schools, but our country too—the very nature and temperament of our country. I wrote it because I believe passionately about protecting children. But I also wrote it because I want you to know that I am one of the most ordinary and flawed people you'll ever meet. As you know, I've made dumb choices, I've been a coward, done things I'm embarrassed by, and even lost my faith in God for a time, and I hope this book has shown that. But I also hope it shows that even someone as ordinary as me can be raised up by God—and countless loving, supportive hands—to move *forward*.

I hope this book shows you that *you* can do great things too—that people *together* can do even greater things, and the only way Goliaths like the unions can have power over us is if we hand it to them by submitting to their fear, intimidation, isolation, and ignorance.

Believe me, I know what it's like to be scared. In the early days of writing those editorials, I wondered if I was wasting my time or just making a fool out of myself, but it was in those early days that I first heard the song "Brave" by Moriah Peters. The song contains this lyric that inspired me to keep on going. It's a simple line, but maybe that's what makes it so true: "Fear kills more dreams than failure." Then I thought about it. The Scripture teaches that God is not the author of fear, so if fear is dominating, God is not there.

The journey that I've described to you has taught me that once you take up His call, love and support are everywhere: whether in a Scripture, a song lyric, an email sent at 5:46 in the morning, or through the son who says, "I'm proud of you, Mom."

It has also confirmed to me that our collective greatest strength—and the unions' missing piece—is love. In fact, you'll likely recognize this Scripture in what's become known as "The Love Chapter." In it, St. Paul not only describes what makes us strong, but exactly what makes Goliaths like the unions vulnerable and weak.

> *"Love is patient, love is kind. It does not envy, it does not boast, it is not proud. It does not dishonor others, it is not self-seeking, it is not easily angered; it keeps no record of wrongs. Love does not delight in evil but rejoices with the truth." —1 Corinthians 13: 4–6 (NIV)*

Every step of the way: every "spawn of Satan," every "pawn of the wealthy one-percent," every outrageous hit piece against me, every weeping teacher, every "Rotten Apple," every "whore of the Koch Brothers," every frosty look and lost friend, every "union buster," every "free rider," every "Are you afraid for your life?", God has patiently calmed my fears and reminded me of the story He used to give me the courage to obey Him and completely change my perspective. Do you remember it? I shared it with you earlier.

There was this widow who placed two mites into the offering jar, and her sacrifice touched the heart of Jesus. He pointed her out to His disciples and told them the widow, who had given only two mites, had given more than all the other wealthy people because she'd given all she had—she'd given in faith from her nothingness.

As I read the story afresh, after praying those three days over Beth Moore's call to action in my Bible study, Christ's voice in my heart spoke to me. He told me He understood my worries and agreed the task He was asking of me was far too big for me; He gave me some clever ideas for dealing with the unions' slanderous attacks, and then He told me not to worry about publishers and connections—that was His job. He made it clear that all I had to do was show up and give what I already possessed—which was close to nothing.

You'll recall He told me, "Just give Me your two mites, Rebecca. I'll do the rest."

You know, I thought to myself, "That's a deal I can make," so I went back to the question in my Bible study and filled in the blank, "Lord, if you're willing, you can use my writing for Your glory." Two days later, I was submitting an editorial to the *Orange County Register*, and soon my editorials were being picked up by online sites across the country. Within six months I was the lead plaintiff in a federal lawsuit seeking to free teachers and other public sector workers from forced unionism, and after twenty-five years of being silenced, I finally had a voice for myself, teachers, and kids across the country.

I can attest to you that two mites go a long way in God's economy.

I never told anyone about the way God used that story of the widow's mite to give me the courage to step out in faith—not even Charles—it was my personal experience, so I never thought to share it with anyone. That Christmas, my sister Jody gave me a beautiful necklace. As I opened it and noted its unique design, I asked her if it was an antique. Jody answered, "The woman who made it finds something antique and then builds a piece of jewelry around it. See that little item inside of the glass pendant? That's the antique; it's an ancient coin from Israel." Then she added,

"It's a widow's mite."

Stunned, I sat silently staring at the necklace for a while. I knew immediately though Jody bought and delivered the widow's mite necklace, it was really a gift from God—a constant reminder that if I continued offering my next to nothing, He would continue showing up and doing the impossible.

Jody asked me, "Do you know the story of the widow's mite?"

Know it? That story had changed the trajectory of my entire life.

As we sat surrounded by Christmas packages, I told my family how God used my measly widow's mite faith to grow a single editorial, embarrassingly submitted to "Letters to the Editor," to put me in position to become the face of our national lawsuit against the very oppressors I had asked Him to expose.

I placed Jody's gift around my neck and told her, "This is my lawsuit necklace." It reminded me to keep on giving my two mites and not to worry about the big stuff—God could handle the big stuff. I wore the necklace throughout the lawsuit journey, I was wearing it in the Courtroom during oral arguments, I was wearing it the day Justice Scalia died, and it was around my neck when I received the news that our certain victory against the Goliath unions had ended in defeat.

God sent me the story of the widow's mite to give me the courage to step out in faith and fight, but I believe He sent me the necklace to give me the will to keep on moving forward, because He knew I was going to face some serious hurdles and my faith was going to take a beating. He didn't want me to get discouraged and give up—hiding under a broom tree.

I wear the necklace every day now—even when it doesn't go with my outfit—because it reminds me it's not my battle I'm fighting; it's God's. All I have to do is offer up my mites, and He'll take care of the rest.

So, I guess I'm letting you in on my little secret—standing up to Goliath isn't as scary as it looks. You just have to show up and give your two mites. God will do the rest.

Love requires action, and when we move forward, the Maker of love steps in and creates something beautiful and sweet out of our nothingness and bitterness.

Love has compelled me to encourage great teachers, parents, faith leaders, and students to come back together, and to provide a place where we can learn the truth from each other and make our voices heard. You can join us in our online community: *For Kids and Country*.[83] You don't have to solve all of the problems by yourself, and you don't have to know a lot either. Just show up, give your two mites, and brace yourself for adventure and redemption you never dreamed possible.

ACKNOWLEDGMENTS

There are literally hundreds of people who've supported my family and me throughout the thirty-year journey that led to this completed work, and I cannot possibly list only a few without mentioning every one of you. So, if you stood with me in the battle as my family, friend, fellow plaintiff, colleague, student, student's parent, pastor, lawyer, teacher, publishing crew, writing buddy, policy pal, fellow warrior, book previewer, prayer support, small group member, Bible study leader, supportive neighbor, or as a total stranger who supports our cause *For Kids and Country*, your encouragement was and still is used by God to give me strength and perseverance every single day. I've wanted to give up many times, but you were always there urging me to keep on going. Since I will never be able to thank you adequately, I'm asking God to pour out His grace on you to bless you the way you have blessed me, and I pray that this book will be a gift to you and will lead to positive changes for our kids and culture.

Thank you, Charles, Kyle, and Ben. I have no idea how you find the patience to live with and support a passionate wife and mom like me, but I'm grateful that you do. You are the only ones who know how many times I was grouchy or said, "I'm going to throw my manuscript in the trash, give up this battle, and crawl under a rock!" I said it a lot, but you never let me do it. I'm astonished and amazed at how God put a passion in my heart and then gave you the faith I needed to keep moving forward.

For all of these things and more, I thank Jesus Christ, my Sweet Savior Who brought all of you alongside to support me and graciously allowed me the honor of standing up for teachers, parents, and kids. His Word contains the answers to every problem presented in this book because He is the Author of Liberty and The Golden Rule.

Discover engaging book club questions for every chapter in Standing Up to Goliath *at* https://forkidsandcountry.org/book/

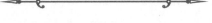

ENDNOTES

1   NEA General Counsel Bob Chanin Says Farewell, 2009. https://www.youtube.com/watch?v=bqn1rvv7Fis.

2   Ibid.

3   "Doctors, Military Officers, Firefighters, and Scientists Seen as Among America's Most Prestigious Occupations." The Harris Report, September 10, 2014. https://theharrispoll.com/when-shown-a-list-of-occupations-and-asked-how-much-prestige-each-job-possesses-doctors-top-the-harris-polls-list-with-88-of-u-s-adults-considering-it-to-have-either-a-great-deal-of-prestige-45-2/.

4   Bhakta, Bhavini. "California's Pink-Slip Shuffle." *Los Angeles Times*, December 16, 2012, sec. Collections. http://articles.latimes.com/2012/dec/16/opinion/la-oe-bhakta-teaching-20121216.

5   "California Teachers Empowerment Network." Non-Profit. California Teachers Empowerment Network, 2014. http://www.ctenhome.org.

6   Deposition. Dr. Mary Sieu, Deputy Superintendent ABC Unified School District #1, 2012. https://www.youtube.com/watch?v=Bq6CCjKNqdY&t=3s.

7   Sand, Larry. "Silencing the Whistle Blower." *City Journal*, January 11, 2013. https://www.city-journal.org/html/silencing-whistleblower-11150.html.

8   Haar, Charlene. *The Politics of the PTA*. New Brunswick: Transaction Publishers, 2002.

9   Ibid.

10   "Awarded Grants: Common Core." Bill & Melinda Gates Foundation, n.d. https://www.gatesfoundation.org/How-We-Work/Quick-Links/Grants-Database#q/k=Common%20Core.

11   Bullying 101, A Lesson in Civics, 2014. https://www.youtube.com/watch?v=vnHnBdaBKYQ.

12   "California Proposition 174, School Vouchers." Online Encyclopedia. Ballotpedia, 1993. https://ballotpedia.org/California_Proposition_174,_School_Vouchers_(1993).

7Num

13 "Big Money Talks: California's Billion Dollar Club." Sacramento, California: California Fair Political Practices Commission, March 2010. http://www.fppc.ca.gov/content/dam/fppc/documents/Education-External-Division/Big_Money_Talks.pdf.

14 Ibid.

15 Push Back Now - PBN. NEA Counsel Bob Chanin - Money & Power, Not Education, 2011. https://www.youtube.com/watch?v=RdgzBNh6kEM.

16 "California Teachers Association, Combined Financial Statements for the Year Ended August 31, 2015, Supplemental Summary and Detail Schedules of Non-chargeable and Chargeable Expenditures of Agency Fees for 2014-2015, and Independent Auditors' Report." California Teachers Empowerment Network, n.d. http://www.ctenhome.org/teachers-legal-rights-unions.html.

17 Haar, Charlene. 2002. *The Politics of the PTA*. New Brunswick: Transaction Publishers.

18 "New Business Items." National Education Association, 2017. https://ra.nea.org/business-items/?yr=2017&type=nbi&pg=5.

19 National Education Association of the United States. "NEA Form 990, Part VII—Compensation of Officers, Directors, Trustees, Key Employees, Highest Compensated Employees, and Independent Contractors." Guidestar, 2013. https://www.guidestar.org/profile/53-0115260.

20 "Average Starting Teacher Salaries by State." National Education Association, 2013 2012. http://www.nea.org/home/2012-2013-average-starting-teacher-salary.html.

21 "Digest of Education Statistics." Data Inventory. National Center for Education Statistics, 2013 2012. https://nces.ed.gov/programs/digest/d13/tables/dt13_211.60.asp.

22 Rosemond, John K. *Ending the Homework Hassle*. Kansas City: Andrews and McMeel, 1990.

23 "Attention-Deficit / Hyperactivity Disorder (ADHD)." Data and Statistics. Centers for Disease Control and Prevention, March 20, 2018. https://www.cdc.gov/ncbddd/adhd/data.html.

24 Haar, Charlene. *The Politics of the PTA*.

25 NEA Research. "Status of the American Public School Teacher 2005–2006." National Education Association, March 2010. http://files.eric.ed.gov/fulltext/ED521866.pdf.

26 Appleman, Eric M. "American Federation of Teachers Solidarity (527)." Campaign Communications. National Education Association, April 22, 2016. http://www.p2016.org/ads1/aftad042216r.html.

27 "Teachers Unions: Top Contributors to Federal Candidates, Parties, and Outside Groups." Interest Groups. OpenSecrets.org, November 2017. https://www.opensecrets.org/industries/contrib.php?cycle=2016&ind=L1300.

28   NEA General Counsel Bob Chanin Says Farewell, 2009. https://www.youtube. com/watch?v=bqn1rvv7Fis.

29   "CUSD Watch: Representing the Interests of Students and Taxpayers in the Capistrano Unified School District." CUSDWatch, July 11, 2018. https://cusd-watch.com/.

30   "New Business Items." National Education Association, 2017. https://ra.nea. org/business-items/?yr=2017&type=nbi&pg=3.

31   "Hate Groups: State Totals." Intelligence Report. Southern Poverty Law Center, 2017. https://www.splcenter.org/hate-map.

32   "About: The World's Largest Democratic Deliberative Assembly," 2018. http:// ra.nea.org/about.

33   "New Business Items." National Education Association, 2017. https://ra.nea. org/business-items/?yr=2017&type=nbi&pg=8.

34   "New Business Items." National Education Association, 2017. https://ra.nea. org/business-items/?yr=2017&type=nbi&pg=1.

35   Ibid.

36   "New Business Items." National Education Association, 2017. https://ra.nea. org/business-items/?yr=2017&type=nbi&pg=2.

37   "AB-329 Pupil Instruction: Sexual Health Education." Bill Information. California Legislative Information, 2016 2015. https://leginfo.legislature.ca.gov/ faces/billNavClient.xhtml?bill_id=201520160AB329.

38   "California Sexual Health Education Roundtable: California Healthy Youth Act (CA Education Code Sections 51930-51939)." 2016. https://www.aclunc. org/docs/frequently_asked_questions-california_healthy_youth_act-ca_sexual_ health_education_roundtable.pdf.

39   "AB-329 Pupil Instruction: Sexual Health Education."

40   "AB 329: CA Healthy Youth Act." Legislation. Equality California, July 26, 2015. http://www.eqca.org/ab-329-ca-healthy-youth-act/.

41   Burlingame, Phyllida, Goodman, Melissa, and Trujillo, David. "Sexual Health Education Implementation and the California Healthy Youth Act Letter to County Offices of Education." October 20, 2016. http://ccsesa.org/wp-content/ uploads/2016/11/CHYA-letter-to-County-Offices-of-Ed-2016-002.pdf.

42   "Common Core? 6th Graders Taught How to Use Strap-On Dildo." Interest Groups. TeaParty.org, April 3, 2018. https://www.teaparty.org/common-core-6th-graders-taught-use-strap-dildo-55644/.

43   "Parents Advocate League." Advocacy. ParentsAdvocateLeague.org, 2017 2014. http://parentsadvocateleague.org/#&panel1-2.

44   Haar, Charlene K., *The Politics of the PTA* (New Brunswick: Transaction Publishers, 2002).

45   Ibid., 79-80.

46   Ibid., 79.

47   Ibid., 80.

48   Dawn Urbanek. "April 26, 2010 Letter of Resignation from the PTA." Public Disclosure Capistrano Unified School District (blog), October 23, 2012. http://disclosurecusd.blogspot.com/2012/10/april-26-2010-letter-of-resignation.html.

49   Haar, 100.

50   Ibid., 88.

51   Ibid., 88.

52   Ibid., 87, 88.

53   "AB 329: CA Healthy Youth Act." Legislation. Equality California, July 26, 2015. http://www.eqca.org/ab-329-ca-healthy-youth-act/.

54   Haar, 82-83.

55   "Educated Teachers MN," June 27, 2018. http://www.educatedteachersmn.com/.

56   "U.S. Departments of Education and Justice Release School Discipline Guidance Package to Enhance School Climate and Improve School Discipline Policies/Practices." Archive. U.S. Department of Education, January 8, 2014. https://www.ed.gov/news/press-releases/us-departments-education-and-justice-release-school-discipline-guidance-package-.

57   Alejandra Matos. "Minneapolis Schools to Make Suspending Children of Color More Difficult." *Star Tribune*. November 9, 2014, eEdition edition, sec. Local. http://www.startribune.com/mpls-schools-to-make-suspending-children-of-color-more-difficult/281999171/.

58   Tad Vezner, and Mila Koumpilova. "St. Paul Teachers' Complaints with Mainstreaming, Disciplinary Policies Debated." *Twin Cities Pioneer Press*. November 3, 2015, Digital edition, sec. News. http://www.twincities.com/2014/05/19/st-paul-teachers-complaints-with-mainstreaming-disciplinary-policies-debated/.

59   Rubén Rosario. "Writing of St. Paul Teacher's Fear of Violence Strikes a Chord." *Twin Cities Pioneer Press*. February 11, 2016, Digital edition, sec. Opinion. https://www.twincities.com/2015/12/16/writing-of-st-paul-teachers-fear-of-violence-strikes-a-chord/.

60   Susan Du. "St. Paul Teacher Aaron Benner Claims Retaliation for Complaining About Discipline." *City Pages*. March 30, 2015, Digital edition, sec. News. http://www.citypages.com/news/st-paul-teacher-aaron-benner-claims-retaliation-for-complaining-about-discipline-6562084.

61   Ibid.

62   "Resolutions." Legislative. National Education Association, 2018. https://ra.nea.org/business-items/?type=resolution.

63   "Testimonials." Education. Courageous Conversation, 2017. https://courageousconversation.com/testimonials/.

64   Peter Berkowitz. "It's Radical Indoctrination Day at an Upscale Chicagoland School." *The Wall Street Journal*. February 17, 2017, Digital edition, sec. Commentary. https://www.wsj.com/articles/its-racial-indoctrination-day-at-an-upscale-chicagoland-school-1487375679.

65   "Because Real Change Takes Courage – Not Cliches." Free Speech. Parents of New Trier, 2017. http://www.parentsofnewtrier.org.

66   NEA General Counsel Bob Chanin Says Farewell, 2009. https://www.youtube.com/watch?v=bqn1rvv7Fis.

67   Ibid.

68   Haar, 88.

69   NEA Research. "Status of the American Public School Teacher 2005–2006." National Education Association, March 2010. http://files.eric.ed.gov/fulltext/ED521866.pdf.

70   "Who Are We: Northwest Professional Educators (NWPE) Provides Teacher Liability Insurance, Legal Services, and Caring Support without Paying for Controversial Political Agendas." Association. Northwest Professional Educators (NWPE), 2016. http://www.nwpe.org/.

71   "California Teachers Empowerment Network." Non-Profit. California Teachers Empowerment Network, 2014. http://www.ctenhome.org.

72   "Friedrichs v. CTA Press Release: Center for Individual Rights Files Suit on Behalf of Non-Union Teachers." The Center for Individual Rights (CIR), April 30, 2013. http://www.cir-usa.org/2013/04/files-suit-on-behalf-of-non-union-teachers/.

73   "Sabotage, Stalking, and Stealth Exemptions: Special State Laws for Labor Unions." Washington DC: Chamber of Commerce of the United States of America, August 9, 2012. https://www.uschamber.com/sites/default/files/documents/files/1208_StateLawReview_R2.pdf.

74   Matthew R. Durose, Alexia D. Cooper, Ph.D., and Howard N. Snyder, Ph.D. "Recidivism Of Prisoners Released In 30 States In 2005: Patterns From 2005 To 2010 - Update." Office of Justice Programs: Bureau of Justice Statistics, April 22, 2014. https://www.bjs.gov/index.cfm?ty=pbdetail&iid=4986.

75   Gwen Samuel. "Dropout Nation: When Teachers Feel Parents' Pain." News. Dropout Nation, September 9, 2015. http://dropoutnation.net/2015/09/09/when-teachers-feel-parents-pain.

76   Haar, 88.

77   Friedrichs v. California Teachers Association Oral Argument. Friedrichs v. California Teachers Association. Washington DC: C-Span, 2016. https://www.c-span.org/video/?401633-1/friedrichs-v-california-teachers-association-oral-argument.

78   "Manhattan Christian Academy." Institution. Manhattan Christian Academy, 2018. https://www.mcanyc.org/.

79   "The Gaudy and Joy Charitable Foundation Inc. Helps Students…" Fundraising. Gaudy and Joy Charitable Foundation, 2018. http://gaudyandjoy.org/.

80   Stephen Frank. "Sand: NEA's and Hillary's Bully Folly." *California Political Review*, November 1, 2016, sec. Commentary. http://www.capoliticalreview.com/capoliticalnewsandviews/sand-neas-and-hillarys-bully-folly/.

81   NEA Journal Staff. "Selections for Memorizing: Personal Growth Leaflet #284 Grade 4." Public Schools of Birmingham, Alabama, Chanute, Kansas, Cincinnati, Ohio, Washington DC, n.d. http://www.ctenhome.org/PDFdocs/4thGradeNEAJournal.pdf.

82   NEA General Counsel Bob Chanin Says Farewell, 2009. https://www.youtube.com/watch?v=bqn1rvv7Fis.

83   "Stop SeXXX Ed & Teachers Keep Your Local." Education. For Kids & Country, 2018. https://forkidsandcountry.org/.